OXFORD WORLD'S CLASSICS

DON CARLOS
AND
MARY STUART

FRIEDRICH SCHILLER was born in 1759 in Marbach in Württemberg. After the success of his first play, *The Robbers*, he abandoned his career as a regimental doctor and fled Württemberg, spending periods in Mannheim, Leipzig, Dresden, and Weimar and completing plays, poems, stories, and historical writings. In 1789 he settled in Jena, where he held a chair in history at the university. In 1790 he married Charlotte von Lengefeld (1766–1826). Four children were subsequently born.

After a severe illness in 1792 Schiller's life became outwardly uneventful. In 1794 he formed a friendship and close literary alliance with Johann Wolfgang von Goethe, out of which some of the central works of Weimar Classicism emerged. Though battling with failing health, in the last decade of his life he completed major works on aesthetics, his greatest poems, and a series of verse dramas. He died in 1805 at the age of 45.

Schiller is arguably Germany's greatest dramatist. In matters of form a tireless experimenter, he was a master of swift-moving action and of the thrilling set-piece encounter. His historical dramas—his finest plays—explore with compelling intensity the problem of moral choice and the nature of human freedom, both personal and political.

HILARY COLLIER SY-QUIA is enrolled at the University of California at Berkeley as a postgraduate student in the German Department.

PETER OSWALD is a playwright, whose plays and adaptations for the stage include *Valdorama* (1992), *Don Carlos* (1992), and *Don Juan* (1995).

LESLEY SHARPE is Reader in German Literature at the University of Exeter and has written extensively on Schiller and on eighteenth-century German literature. She is the author of *Friedrich Schiller: Drama, Thought and Politics* (Cambridge, 1991) and has recently completed a critical history of Schiller's aesthetics.

OXFORD WORLD'S CLASSICS

For over 100 years Oxford World's Classics have brought readers closer to the world's great literature. Now with over 700 titles—from the 4,000-year-old myths of Mesopotamia to the twentieth century's greatest novels—the series makes available lesser-known as well as celebrated writing.

The pocket-sized hardbacks of the early years contained introductions by Virginia Woolf, T. S. Eliot, Graham Greene, and other literary figures which enriched the experience of reading. Today the series is recognized for its fine scholarship and reliability in texts that span world literature, drama and poetry, religion, philosophy and politics. Each edition includes perceptive commentary and essential background information to meet the changing needs of readers.

OXFORD WORLD'S CLASSICS

FRIEDRICH SCHILLER

Don Carlos
and
Mary Stuart

Translated with Notes by
HILARY COLLIER SY-QUIA

Adapted in verse drama by
PETER OSWALD

With an Introduction by
LESLEY SHARPE

OXFORD
UNIVERSITY PRESS

OXFORD

UNIVERSITY PRESS

Great Clarendon Street, Oxford OX2 6DP

Oxford University Press is a department of the University of Oxford.
It furthers the University's objective of excellence in research, scholarship,
and education by publishing worldwide in

Oxford New York

Athens Auckland Bangkok Bogotá Buenos Aires Calcutta
Cape Town Chennai Dar es Salaam Delhi Florence Hong Kong Istanbul
Karachi Kuala Lumpur Madrid Melbourne Mexico City Mumbai
Nairobi Paris São Paulo Singapore Taipei Tokyo Toronto Warsaw

with associated companies in Berlin Ibadan

Oxford is a registered trade mark of Oxford University Press
in the UK and in certain other countries

Published in the United States
by Oxford University Press Inc., New York

Translation © Hilary Collier Sy-Quia and Peter Oswald 1996
Chronology, Explanatory Notes © Hilary Collier Sy-Quia 1996
Bibliography © Hilary Collier Sy-Quia and Lesley Sharpe 1996
Introduction © Lesley Sharpe 1996

British Library Cataloguing in Publication Data

Data available

Library of Congress Cataloging in Publication Data

Schiller, Friedrich, 1759–1805.
[Don Carlos. English]
Don Carlos and Mary Stuart / Friedrich Schiller ; translated with
notes by Hilary Collier Sy-Quia ; adapted in verse drama by Peter
Oswald ; with an introduction by Lesley Sharpe.
p. cm.
1. Carlos, Prince of Asturias, 1545–1568—Drama. 2. Mary, Queen
of Scots, 1542–1587—Drama. I. Sy-Quia, Hilary Collier.
II. Oswald, Peter. III. Schiller, Friedrich, 1759–1805. Maria
Stuart. English. IV. Title.
PT2473.D5S9 1996 832'.6—dc20 96-4317

ISBN 978-0-19-954074-7

2

Typeset by Graphicraft Typesetters Ltd, Hong Kong
Printed in Great Britain by
Clays Ltd, St Ives plc

CONTENTS

INTRODUCTION

At first sight *Don Carlos* and *Mary Stuart*, with *Wallenstein* Friedrich Schiller's greatest historical dramas, are striking in their similarity. Both are blank-verse plays, set against the background of religious strife in sixteenth-century Europe. Both explore the private emotions of the great and powerful as they confront the insoluble dilemmas of the political world. Both also display the hallmarks of Schiller's style and technique—swift-moving action, great set-piece encounters, impassioned rhetorical speeches, strongly contrasting characters, an unabashed theatricality. In both plays the historical setting is used not as a backdrop for a costume drama but to provide an opportunity to explore problems of Schiller's own age. The later eighteenth century was also a time of violent upheaval and ideological conflict, of the clash of tradition with experiment. His plays are concerned with freedom and tyranny, the relation of power and responsibility, of ends and means in political life and with the challenge facing those called to act upon the stage of history to preserve humanity and integrity.

On closer inspection the dissimilarities between the plays are striking and significant. *Mary Stuart* is a compact, lucidly organized, and highly stylized play with an action that moves swiftly and inexorably towards the tragic conclusion, in spite of the best efforts of most of the characters to avert it. Formally it stands within the European tradition of high tragedy and shows Schiller's concern to meet the challenge of the classical and neo-classical tradition. It is a play that, despite its clear departures from historical fact, is nevertheless based on a real political dilemma of the sixteenth century and firmly rooted in historical source study. *Don Carlos* is clearly a more youthful work and, for all its brilliant and moving moments, lacks this lucidity. It is based on a historical novel, while attested historical events provide only the background. It has a complex intrigue and confusing shifts of emphasis—is it mainly a dramatization of thwarted love, of kingly isolation, or of the idealist destroyed? The compositional shortcomings of the play reveal it as a work of transition, the final phase of Schiller's apprenticeship. After he completed the play in 1787 he wrote no more plays for over a decade, a silence indicative of the creative crisis the play had provoked in him. Only after lengthy deliberation on the nature of drama did he return to work as a playwright with his masterpiece, *Wallenstein*. *Mary Stuart* (1800) was the second play to be written after this long interval and thus is separated from *Don Carlos* by some thirteen years. In spite of its flaws *Don Carlos* is a rich and fascinating play for two reasons. First, it shows Schiller in the process of finding his own idiom as a dramatist. In it he moves away from the self-consciously radical tone and experimental style of his previous three dramas, all written in prose, towards deeper engagement with historical issues and the serenity and stylization characteristic of his later work. Secondly, along with Lessing's *Nathan the Wise* (1779) and Goethe's *Iphigenia on Tauris* (1787), it is one of the great literary expressions of the German Enlightenment (*Aufklärung*). All three works (all, incidentally, written in blank verse) carry the conviction that human beings, however cynical, weak, or foolish they may have been, however burdened by the guilt and wrongs of the past, can nevertheless find the courage to break free and choose a new way. In the case of *Don Carlos* that new way remains only a distant hope.

Johann Christoph Friedrich Schiller was born on 10 November 1759 in Marbach in Württemberg, the son of a low-ranking army officer. At the age of 14 he was spotted as a promising pupil and removed from his family in order that he might attend the military academy set up by the autocratic Duke of Württemberg, Karl Eugen, to train officers and servants of the state. There he specialized in law and later in medicine. While confined by the regimented and sequestered life at the academy Schiller's imagination was fired by the poetry of Klopstock, by Shakespeare, and by the new avant-garde writing of the 1770s known as the Sturm und Drang (Storm and Stress), the first phase of Romanticism in Germany. Goethe's first novel *The Sorrows of Young Werther* (1774) and his Shakespeare-inspired chronicle play *Götz von Berlichingen* (1772) are two of its best-known products. Schiller's first play, *The Robbers*, begun while he was still at the academy, came to the attention of the superintendent of the Mannheim National Theatre, Freiherr Wolfgang Heribert von Dalberg, where it was premièred in 1782. Schiller, by now a regimental doctor in Stuttgart, became instantly famous. An eye-witness account of the first night records the impact of this wildly melodramatic, yet powerful and gripping, play on its first audience:

The theatre was like a madhouse—rolling eyes, clenched fists, hoarse cries in the auditorium. Strangers fell sobbing into each other's arms, women on the point of fainting staggered towards the exit. There was a universal commotion as in chaos, out of the mists of which a new creation bursts forth.

Its impact in English translation was not lost on the young Coleridge, who on reading it in 1794 wrote to Robert Southey: 'My God! Southey! Who is this Schiller? This Convulser of the Heart?' and went on to write a sonnet 'To the Author of *The Robbers*'.

Forbidden by Karl Eugen to pursue his literary ambitions, Schiller was forced to choose between his country, family, and profession as a doctor on the one hand and the precarious existence of a writer on the other. He did a moonlight flit from Württemberg, in the hope of continuing his association with the Mannheim theatre. Dalberg was hesitant, however, and Schiller spent several months in seclusion (he was an army deserter) on the estate of a friend in Bauerbach, near Meiningen in Thuringia. It was in Bauerbach that the plan for *Don Carlos*, prompted by a suggestion from Dalberg, began to take shape. Schiller also toyed at that point with the Mary Stuart material but nothing came of it. Eventually, in August 1783, Dalberg offered him a one-year contract as playwright to the theatre with the task of delivering three plays, two of which were near completion, *The Conspiracy of Fiesco at Genoa* (1783) and *Intrigue and Love* (1784), Schiller's only excursion into domestic tragedy. The year at the Mannheim theatre did not go well. *Fiesco* was not a success and *Intrigue and Love*, though well received by the audience, was the occasion for internal rivalries in the company. It was clear that the one-year contract would not be renewed and Schiller turned to journalism to help keep himself afloat. At the invitation of admirers, one of whom, Christian Gottfried Körner, became his lifelong friend, he moved to Leipzig and Dresden, having published the first act of *Don Carlos* in his own journal, the *Rhenish Thalia*, before the whole play was complete. His difficulties in shaping the material were compounded thereafter because he began belatedly to immerse himself in historical study of the period, with consequent changes of emphasis in the handling of the material. Moreover, the plot was already set in motion and had to be brought to a conclusion. He published more extracts in the *Thalia* in 1786 and 1787. These break off early in the present Act III, before the audience scene between Philip and Posa. Schiller then completed a book version of the play, which was published in 1787. Cuts were made for subsequent versions, the final approved edition of 1805, on which the translation here is based, being now regarded as the standard text.

Schiller's starting-point for *Don Carlos* was not historical source study but a work of French fiction, the Abbé de Saint-Réal's *Dom Carlos. Nouvelle historique* (1672), which had been brought to Schiller's attention by Dalberg. The historical Carlos, Philip II's only son and heir, was weak and slightly deformed from birth. In his late teens he developed signs of mental instability and was later rumoured to be intending to flee Spain. This, coupled with increasing paranoia and eccentricity, led to his being virtually confined to his quarters, where he died in not wholly unmysterious circumstances at the age of 23. Saint-Réal builds his fiction on the unfounded rumour that Carlos and Elizabeth of Valois, Philip's third wife, who as children had been betrothed for a time, were secretly in love. Carlos's fall is the result of court intrigues, in particular on the part of the King's adviser Ruy Gomez and his wife Princess Eboli. The Marquis Posa, a secret friend of Carlos, carries letters between Carlos and Elizabeth and is assassinated as Philip's suspicions fall on him. Carlos, who intended to flee to the Netherlands for safety (the political dimension is not exploited), is handed over to the Inquisition. Elizabeth is poisoned on Philip's orders.

The complex genesis of *Don Carlos* has caused critics to diverge considerably in their assessment of the relative importance of love and politics in the plot. Some see a distinct shift from family drama (influenced by Diderot's theory of the *drame bourgeois*) to political play, as though the work fell into two halves. Others argue that the work remains throughout a family drama with the political elements imperfectly grafted on. Yet others strongly emphasize the clear continuities in theme and plot—as Schiller himself had done in his defence of the play in his *Letters on 'Don Carlos'* (1788)—arguing in some cases that the play changes less in theme than in dramatic technique, moving from a more expansive and static type of portraiture to a more dynamic interaction of plot and character. The first two approaches tend to understate the extent to which a political element was always present in Schiller's conception of the material. From the start he wanted to make more of this project than a romantic historical costume drama. His letters from the Bauerbach period suggest he intended to use the play to denounce religious bigotry and state persecution through his depiction of the Inquisition. From the first version of the play onwards, the unhappy royal family reflects the greater unhappiness of a state dominated by the Inquisition. But any argument supporting the unity of *Don Carlos* has to take account of the fact that Schiller himself in the *Letters on 'Don Carlos'* admits to a loss of interest in the figure of Carlos. His Bauerbach letters testify to his passionate identification with the unhappy prince and this is still clearly reflected in the early scenes of the play. However, wider reading in the course of composition gave Schiller a profounder grasp of historical context and made him probe the nature of tyranny and the problem of action within the political world. The result is that Carlos, who is essentially a passive character, is increasingly overshadowed by Philip and Posa. The romantic involvement between Carlos and Elizabeth, though still central to the play's complex intrigue, does lose prominence to the political theme. Though Schiller manages to bring all the threads together at the end, we are left with a sense of unevenness.

As in Schiller's earliest plan, it is the Catholic Church, embodied in the final scenes by the Cardinal Inquisitor, that is the driving force behind the repressive Spanish government. This allows him to make all the main characters—Carlos, Posa, Elizabeth, and Philip—ultimately its victims. For most of the play we identify Philip with this cruel and cynical system. Yet in spite of this, Philip is arguably the great triumph of characterization of the play and the figure who most holds the audience's attention. The other characters, Carlos and Posa, for example, we feel we can read clearly. Philip keeps us in suspense. When announcing the serialization of his play Schiller wrote: 'If this tragedy is to move people it must do so, as I see it, through the situation and character of King Philip.' In the *Thalia* scenes Philip still comes across as something of a stage villain. In the completed play, however, Schiller does succeed not only in showing us Philip's fears, his disappointments, and his isolation, but in making us feel them too. Proud of his self-sufficiency in Act Two, Philip rejects his son's attempt at reconciliation. Later he sees in Posa the kind of valorous, confident, urbane, yet passionate young man he would like as a son. In the audience scene (III. x), which parallels and contrasts with the audience between Philip and Carlos in Act Two, Posa can find the needs of the human being beneath the imperious exterior ('By God, | He reaches to my soul'). We should find any true change of heart on Philip's part dramatically unconvincing. Not only history but Schiller's recognition of the weight of the Church, Philip's habits of mind, and his cynicism dictate that he will not change. But Posa makes him feel for a brief moment as if he actually could remake the world with a stroke of his pen. We do not see Philip weep over Posa's betrayal but we feel the momentary pathos more keenly by witnessing the dismay and astonishment of his courtiers at the report of such an unambiguous display of emotion. Though we recoil in horror at his desire to destroy all that remains of Posa's vision, Philip himself is revealed to be the unhappy pawn of the Inquisition, chastised by the fanatical blind Cardinal Inquisitor for having forgotten for a moment that for kings human beings are simply numbers.

The most controversial figure in the play is the Marquis Posa, educator of the Prince and, briefly, confidant of the King. Posa's role was expanded in the course of the play's development. Though it is a structural flaw in the drama that Posa's increasing prominence pushes Carlos into the background, that prominence comes about by a turn of events that strikes us as being utterly plausible. Posa has held himself aloof from the court and thus seems to threaten none of the courtiers, who can therefore speak generously of him. His aloofness is a strategy to give him independence of action, and it is this impression of independence that attracts Philip. Here at last is a man who will give him the truth about Carlos and Elizabeth without trying to gain some advantage for himself. Instead Philip is given quite a different kind of truth by Posa, while the truth about Carlos and Elizabeth is exactly what Posa will never tell him. The fact that Posa can say so much to Philip before being silenced is an indication of the former's urbanity and diplomatic skill. The passionate personal appeal by Carlos to Philip in Act Two falls on deaf ears. Philip is impressed by the man who can do without him and who has the courage to put himself at risk to plead a cause that brings him no personal gain. Posa is judicious in his responses, waiting for Philip to prompt him into saying more, while Philip is refreshed as well as taken aback by his confidence and his honesty. Posa presents Philip to himself not as a wilful tyrant but as the victim himself of the system he has inherited. His subjects have surrendered their self-determination. They have made Philip a god. But where does a god find solace and human fellowship? Posa reveals Philip's position as that of the false god who enslaves rather than of the true God who gives freedom to nature to act according to its inherent laws. The play's persistent appeal to nature through its imagery of sowing, planting, blossoming, and withering is given full political expression in Posa's argument.

Posa is, of course, an anachronism. No sixteenth-century Spanish grandee could speak in such terms and Schiller was well aware of the fact. Woven into Posa's arguments are Schiller's knowledge of the political philosophy of his time. It is one of the vital debates of the Revolutionary age, Schiller's own age, which is being enacted. In it we detect the impact on German intellectuals of the American War of Independence and hear echoes of the German natural law tradition, of Rousseau's faith in natural sentiments, and of Montesquieu's famous characterization in *De l'esprit des lois* of the different types of government.[1] Posa stresses how Philip's rule is based on fear, for Montesquieu the specific characteristic of a despotism, and leads only to the peace of the graveyard. But Posa's vision cannot be reduced to a single political doctrine, nor is the discussion merely a rehearsal of political

[1] For detailed commentary on the political echoes in this scene see *Schillers Werke, Nationalausgabe*, vii/ii, ed. Paul Böckmann and Gerhard Kluge, and *Schiller. Sämtliche Werke, Berliner Ausgabe*, iii, ed. Hans-Günther Thalheim and Regine Otto, as well as Allan Blunden's article listed in the Select Bibliography.

argument. This scene is a turning-point of the play. Posa puts himself in extreme danger by revealing even this much of his mind to the King. He does so out of commitment to the cause of the Netherlands and in order by any means possible to slow the momentum of the intrigue against Carlos. Yet in winning the confidence of the King he is bound to disappoint him. Carlos, too, loses faith in his friend's loyalty, delivering himself a second time into the power of Eboli, whereupon Posa precipitates himself into the desperate attempt to throw suspicion on himself.

Posa would seem to be a wholly positive figure and spokesman for the playwright himself. This was certainly how he was viewed when the play first appeared and for one and a half centuries after. By the middle of the nineteenth century Schiller had become a cultural icon. The German liberals of the 1848 Revolution often borrowed quotations from *Don Carlos* in their speeches or saw their struggle as akin to that of Posa with Philip. The play has always had great resonance in situations of oppression. During the early years of the Third Reich in Germany audiences regularly applauded loud and long when Posa uttered his plea for freedom of thought, and such occurrences were taken by the regime as a form of protest. In 1946, when that regime had been overthrown, the play that seemed so to epitomize the noblest tradition of German thought was staged in no fewer than twenty-one theatres. Yet since the 1950s Schiller's plays have been universally recognized as more complex and ambiguous in their presentation of political change than may at first appear. Posa in particular has been seen as a manipulator, exploiting Carlos and abusing the King's confidence. He has been accused of insensitivity to Carlos's suffering and of indifference to the pain he causes the King. At the very least, it is claimed, he leaves devastation behind him after his death. Schiller has been seen as presenting in Posa the flawed idealist, who betrays actual human beings while proclaiming a love for humanity in the abstract. Posa certainly does play a very dangerous game and it is one of the triumphs of the play as a dramatic experience that we feel the bitterness of Philip's disappointment. Yet Posa is trying to save not just the Netherlands, arguably a distant and precarious goal, but also his friend, who is in the gravest danger, created in part through his own folly. Posa does the most he can to save him by sacrificing his own life. Schiller is not presenting the idealist as a flawed character; he is, however, exploring the gulf between political ends and means, a gulf that opens up for Posa in the audience scene.

Schiller looks at the history of the sixteenth century as a man of the Enlightenment. In the struggle for freedom of religion he sees the beginning of the struggle for a more tolerant and humane society. In *Don Carlos*, though the representatives of that new way of thinking are doomed, the movement of history is on their side. Philip himself is aware that his empire is waning, and Schiller brings forward the defeat of the Spanish Armada by twenty years in order to signal this incipient decline. Posa speaks with the assurance of one who knows the future, accusing Philip of trying to put his hand into the spokes of a wheel that must turn. His argument for liberal government on the grounds that nature is free within its own laws is reinforced by the natural imagery of the play. Posa himself says to Philip: 'You want your garden to flower eternally | But the seed you sow is death.' These images are further supported by an underlying implication that the Spanish court itself is based on an artificiality that is contrary to nature. The Queen may not see her daughter except at the appointed hour. She enjoys the more natural setting of Aranjuez, while the woman who epitomizes the corruption of the court, Eboli, longs to return to Madrid. The representative of cruelty and repression, the Cardinal Inquisitor, calls on Philip to suppress the voice of nature and deliver up his son. Though the representatives of a better future are destroyed, the implication is that the course of history will vindicate them. The tragedy is thus set within a framework of guarded hope.

Don Carlos provoked a creative crisis in Schiller. He believed his greatest achievements would be in the field of drama and yet *Don Carlos* was over-long and over-complicated, its theatrical viability also impaired. In 1787, having moved to Weimar, he first met his future ally, Johann Wolfgang Goethe, who already enjoyed a towering reputation as a writer. Goethe's neo-classical verse drama *Iphigenia on Tauris* had just appeared. Schiller's unfinished review of it reveals through his admiration of the work how urgently he wished to be able to write a drama that would have the same formal perfection. For the next ten years he devoted himself to historiography, aesthetics, and dramatic theory, returning to drama with *Wallenstein*, which was completed in 1799. Of these activities his work as a historiographer tends to be taken least seriously, though in fact it was an important stage in the clarification of his ideas. Given the comparative backwardness of German historiography at the time, his accounts, influenced stylistically by his reading of French and British historiographers such as Voltaire, Condorcet, Hume, and Gibbon, are both readable and stimulating, even if he relied on published sources. He made good use of the reading he had done in connection with *Don Carlos* to write the first part of a *History of the Revolt of the United Netherlands from Spanish Rule* (1788). Although the work was not completed it was sufficiently admired to secure its author a Chair of History at the University of Jena. Schiller's financial problems were far from over (there was little money attached to the post), but this appointment gave him a position within society and the opportunity to marry. His bride was Charlotte von Lengefeld and they were married on 22 February 1790 and subsequently had four children.

Schiller's historiographical writing shows his move away from Enlightenment optimism towards a more sober depiction of the struggle for domination in Europe. His second major work was his *History of the Thirty Years' War* (1791), a continuation therefore of his interest in the long period of religious strife in the sixteenth and seventeenth centuries. The confident introduction to the *History of the Revolt of the Netherlands* claims that the work will demonstrate how united effort in the good cause can win through. Yet in the process of writing he loses confidence in this analysis and comes to regard the people of the Netherlands and their leaders in a more critical light. This appreciation of the greater complexities of the period may help to account for Schiller's failure to finish the work. The *History of the Thirty Years' War* is an admirable work of synthesis, written without any expectation of finding a thread of progress. Though the two most fascinating figures of the war, the Swedish King Gustavus Adolphus and the Imperial General Wallenstein, are for a time made into hero and villain respectively, Schiller reverses his assessment of both, aware of the bias in his sources and the partiality of his own judgement.

After concentrating on historiography, Schiller turned to dramatic theory (discussed later in connection with *Mary Stuart*) and aesthetics. He had always had a lively interest in philosophy from the time of his medical studies. His friend Körner had long impressed upon him the importance of the work of Immanuel Kant. The occasion for detailed study arose in 1792 while he was recovering from a serious illness which nearly cost him his life and left him a permanent invalid until his death in 1805. He was concerned to develop an aesthetics that would make art central to what it is to be fully human. Taking up from Kant's *Critique of Judgement* the suggestion that the aesthetic provides a bridge between the phenomenal realm of nature and the noumenal realm of the ethical, Schiller developed a transcendental aesthetics in which the beautiful is the means of reuniting the sensuous and the spiritual in human beings and thus of re-creating their lost inner harmony. These deliberations were given added impetus by the shock delivered to German intellectuals by the course taken by the French Revolution. His comments on the initial phase of the Revolution are sparse, though in 1791 he was made an Honorary Citizen of France on the strength of *The Robbers*. By 1793, however, he was, like many of his compatriots, appalled by the bloodshed. His best-known work of aesthetics, *Letters on the Aesthetic Education of Man* (1794), is an attempt to analyse where enlightenment had failed and to propose that through art human beings find a way to reconcile reason and impulse. Far from being peripheral to a revolutionary age, art is the means by which we may progress towards a humane civil society. This treatise was followed by a major work of poetics, *On Naïve and Sentimental Poetry* (1795), in which Schiller addresses the question of different kinds of poetic consciousness and the inadequacy of traditional genre definitions to account for their literary products. These essays, both classic statements on the nature of modernity—the divided self and the fragmentation of society brought by the division of labour—have been immensely influential, and cultural commentators from Hegel to C. G. Jung, to Sir Herbert Read, and Herbert Marcuse have taken up their analyses.

On Naïve and Sentimental Poetry was shaped in part by Schiller's growing friendship with Goethe, which began in 1794 and continued to his death. Though for some years aloof, Goethe was eventually won over by Schiller's acute mind and by the recognition that they both treated art with the same high seriousness. They were also both committed to the creation of a literature that drew on the best traditions of European writing and, while incorporating elements of realism, moved towards the universal and symbolic. While Schiller never had Goethe's deep affinity with the art of the Ancients, he constantly used the myth of Greek perfection and wholeness as a starting-point for his elaboration of the modern writer's dilemma: how to bring into harmony the constraints of form and a subjective vision that constantly reached for the infinite. This striving for form and this belief in the universal applicability of notions of beauty separate Goethe and Schiller from the subjectivity of their younger Romantic contemporaries, writers such as August Wilhelm and Friedrich Schlegel, Ludwig Tieck and Novalis. Weimar Classicism—the work of Goethe and Schiller from the late 1780s through the decade of their collaboration—incorporates the legacy of the Enlightenment, that of the classical tradition, and elements of Romanticism. Though sometimes embattled by both their rationalist and Romantic critics, the two men drew out the best in each other's creativity. Schiller encouraged Goethe to take up work again on his *Faust*, an incomplete version of which had been published as *Faust: A Fragment* in 1790. He also proved an invaluable collaborator in the work of the Weimar theatre, of which Goethe was the Director, providing not only his own plays but adapting several others, including Goethe's *Egmont* and *Iphigenia*, Racine's *Phaedra*, and Shakespeare's *Macbeth*.

After *On Naïve and Sentimental Poetry* Schiller declared himself ready to shut up the philosophical shop and return to creative writing. He had already begun to write his series of great reflective poems. After the long break from drama his first project, *Wallenstein* (1799), took some three years to complete. There followed four more plays, *Mary Stuart* (1800), *The Maid of Orleans* (1801), *The Bride of Messina* (1803), and *William Tell* (1804), in rapid succession up to his death on 9 May 1805. His final, unfinished drama, *Demetrius*, was on his desk when he died. It was as though he had recaptured the power of rapid composition and was using it in his race to realize his potential and range as a dramatist before death overtook him. On reading in his letters about his physical struggle with ill health one senses that he kept himself going by sheer will power. Yet his creative writing is full of vigour and energy, a testimony to his extraordinary mental resilience and intellectual commitment. The later dramas, like the earlier ones, are very diverse. Schiller was constantly driven on to the next experiment, though always writing in verse and insisting on the essentially symbolic character of the plays. Increasingly he experimented with a more open form of drama and with the inclusion of operatic elements. In *Wallenstein* and *Mary Stuart*, however, he felt he needed to render account to the traditions of European high tragedy.

In the ten-year dramatic silence he had, in addition to putting down his thoughts on the theory of tragedy, translated Euripides, read Aristotle's *Poetics* and renewed his acquaintance with Shakespeare. In *Wallenstein*, though its genesis was as protracted as that of *Don Carlos*, the result is a perfectly lucid action, a vast panorama compressed into a plot that never loses momentum or clear direction. Yet he did not succeed in reducing his vast material to the scope of one five-act play but had to compromise by splitting it into three parts. In *Mary Stuart* he came closer to realizing his ambition to create a drama that rivalled the economy as well as the clarity of classical drama. The unities of time, place, and action are not slavishly adhered to but approached in spirit through the careful symmetry and compression of the plot. Mary is attended by a small retinue, chiefly her nurse Hannah. Elizabeth's court is presented with economy of means; Burleigh, Shrewsbury, and Leicester are those on whom she relies. Leicester and Mortimer provide the link between these two centres of action. Schiller spotted early on the dramatic possibilities in beginning the action after Mary's trial. To Goethe he wrote: '[The material] already has the important advantage that the action is concentrated in a dynamic moment and, balanced between hope and fear, must rush to its conclusion.' Hope is introduced in the form of Mortimer, Leicester, and the prospect of a meeting of the queens, but far from averting disaster these factors merely speed it up. The result is the sense of inevitability associated with great tragedy. A little later Schiller wrote, again to Goethe: 'Already in the process of writing I am beginning to be increasingly convinced of the truly *tragic* quality of my material. In particular this is because one can see the catastrophe immediately in the first scenes, and while the action of the play seems to be moving away from it, it is actually being brought nearer and nearer.'

Given Schiller's concern with dramatic form and his obvious departures from historical fact, one might be tempted to see the play as making as free with history as *Don Carlos* did. The queens are much younger than their historical counterparts. Schiller suggested that on stage Mary should appear about 25 and Elizabeth 30, whereas in fact Mary was 45 and Elizabeth 53 at the time of the execution. The meeting of the queens, the figure of Mortimer, the assassination attempt, and the romantic involvement of Mary and Leicester are all invented. Schiller chose to make his Mary guilty of complicity in the plot to murder Darnley but innocent of involvement in the Babington Plot— both matters of historical dispute—so that he could make her accept her death as an atonement for her earlier guilt. Yet many details of the historical situation are faithfully retained and given dramatic importance: the circumstances of Mary's trial; the details of her past life before her flight to England; the fact that she did not sign the Treaty of Edinburgh; Elizabeth's scapegoating of Davison after the execution. Schiller made a careful study of sources before beginning work, prominent among them being William Robertson's *History of Scotland*, which had been translated into German in 1762. Mary's final words in the play, for example, are given in several of these accounts. In spite of his freedom with history Schiller was impressed by the insoluble political dilemma posed by the Scottish Queen and his drama succeeds in conveying the intractability of the problem she posed, her continuing political importance to Catholic Europe as well as to English Catholics, and Elizabeth's struggle to maintain stability in turbulent times. By placing this insoluble problem at the heart of the drama and by constructing a closely integrated action, Schiller creates a world where decision and action swiftly draw their consequences after them. Yet those consequences are unpredictable and the only refuge from them is in duplicity or disguise. The framework of hope that relieved the tragedy of *Don Carlos* has disappeared and has been replaced by a much bleaker vision of the narrow scope for retaining integrity and humanity in the world of action.

Mary and Elizabeth seem at first sight to be conceived as polar opposites. Schiller frequently created pairs of contrasting figures, a favourite technique since his first play, *The Robbers*. Mary is accused, isolated, a queen without a throne or a country, condemned to suffer passively, the victim of a judicial murder. Elizabeth is powerful, outwardly confident, supported by loyal subjects and experienced counsellors, about to enter into a marriage that will forge a lasting alliance with France. Mary is Catholic and Elizabeth Protestant. Beyond this religious difference there is a gulf between them in their conception of their role and position. Mary belongs to a long tradition of monarchy as well as of religion. The Catholic Church, though not portrayed so negatively as it was in *Don Carlos*, is still clearly regarded as the power behind the throne in Catholic Europe and associated with tyranny, repression, and double-dealing. In her monologue Elizabeth recalls the arbitrary tyranny of her predecessor and half-sister Mary I. The French ambassador Aubespine is implicated in Mortimer's plot, even while negotiations for Elizabeth's French marriage are in progress. Mary's own record as a ruling monarch is morally shameful, but she considers herself no less a queen, for in her own eyes she is still God's anointed. Elizabeth finds herself in an experimental situation. Her legitimacy is in doubt. Her country needs stability and to consolidate her position she has to provide just and consistent government. Difficult though this way may be, it is presented as the better way, if only Elizabeth can live up to it. Though her life has contained reprehensible acts, her religion nevertheless provides Mary with a framework for moral evaluation and with the means of coming to terms with her unjust execution. Elizabeth tries to behave justly but less from a sense of moral conviction than from a sense of necessity. When she dismisses her counsellors in Act Four so that she can seek the counsel of a higher judge we know that this is simply a formula; in her monologue she takes counsel only with herself, and her calm tone in dismissing her counsellors is immediately followed when she is alone by rage and frustration. At the end of the play Mary would seem to have found freedom from the guilt that tormented her and she dies, mourned by her faithful retinue and in receipt of the sacrament administered by a priest of her own Church. Elizabeth by the end is alone, deceived by Mortimer and

Leicester, forsaken by Shrewsbury, and unwilling to acknowledge her debt to the banished Burleigh.

Yet Schiller's polar opposites reveal deeper similarities. By embedding his presentation of the two queens within a situation of irreconcilable political conflict, Schiller can explore through these similarities the complexities of the political world. Elizabeth strives for freedom, no less than Mary. For her, freedom is to be released from slavery to the will of the people, whose fickleness she despises. Her refuge is in ambiguous appearances as the only way to wriggle out of the consequences of her actions. Elizabeth's show of confidence and prudence in public is quickly revealed as covering fear and insecurity. And if Elizabeth is weaker than she at first appears Mary is stronger. Through the power of the Catholic monarchies of Europe she remains a key political figure, and though she is revealed as the pawn of the Catholic Church she can still strike at the very heart of Elizabeth's court. The assassination attempt in Act Four, as well as fuelling the post-quarrel crisis, shows that Mary is a threat to Elizabeth's life.

Most obviously, both Mary and Elizabeth are women exerting influence within a man's world, an aspect of the play that has received increasing attention in criticism and performances in recent years. The sexual rivalry between them is used by Schiller to increase the tension of their meeting and of the decision over the signing of the death warrant. But Schiller is not implying that women allow their feelings to dominate their decisions but rather shows how both women are trapped within traditional expectations. Mary's beauty has always made her the object of men's passionate desire. Her reputation has gone before her to England, and Paulet bemoans the day that brought this 'Helen' to trouble its peace. The Church exploits her beauty. It is a portrait of her that first captivates Mortimer, and the Cardinal of Lorraine soon capitalizes on that incipient passion to win him for Mary's cause. Mortimer wants not only to free her but to possess her, and he reminds her of her past amours. And Mary is complicit in this process. She has a reputation for receptivity to love and though she exclaims with indignation to Elizabeth that she is better than the world thinks her to be, she delivers herself up into the hands of two men who prove fatal to her.

Elizabeth has tried to break free of the traditional shackles of the expectations of a female. This is less a denial of her femininity than a wish to avoid being restricted by those expectations attached to her sex. She is aware of the great responsibility she carries for the stability of her country and has devoted herself to it. She resists marriage to the French Duke of Anjou, believing she has ruled 'like a man and a king' and that where a woman fulfils the highest tasks she should be allowed to be exempt from the duties of nature. The present of her ring to Bellièvre is not only an example of her vacillation, it also suggests her unwillingness to allow her very body to be invaded for state purposes, her biological function forced back on her in spite of her efforts to transcend it. But though imperious in manner and contemptuous of men's weaknesses, Elizabeth longs nevertheless for their approbation. Her vanity requires that she be thought desirable as a woman as well as dutiful as a monarch. We do not sympathize greatly with him, but Leicester bemoans the years he has spent as a slave to her whims, and while it is probably not the main reason why she agrees to meet Mary, the satisfaction of triumphing over her rival in the presence of Leicester plays a supporting role.

The meeting of the queens is at the centre of the action. Schiller was fully aware of the difficulties of handling such a scene but shows his skill in the way he lays bare the reasons why both parties desire it and why their hopes are bound to be frustrated. Mary knows that in spite of the support she enjoys both in England and abroad the way to freedom lies in persuading Elizabeth to grant it: 'neither guile nor violence can save me, | Only the will of Queen Elizabeth can set me free.' She aims to appeal directly to her as a kinswoman and move her to compassion. Burleigh vigorously opposes the meeting when Paulet brings Elizabeth Mary's letter, no doubt fearing that Elizabeth might weaken but also giving a prudent and logical reason:

> She is condemned to death! The axe is raised!
> To speak to someone under such a sentence
> Would compromise the standing of the monarch!
> The implication of the royal presence
> Is mercy—once the interview had happened
> The sentence would be inapplicable.

Mary may wish to move Elizabeth as though their dynastic quarrel could be settled by the exercise of humanity and compassion.

Burleigh, however, is alive to the ceremonial importance of such a meeting. Elizabeth cannot meet Mary unless it is to pardon her. By meeting her the world would be given a signal that pardon was not far off. This is also the reason why Leicester tries to gain Elizabeth's agreement to a meeting, as he says to Mortimer: 'It would bind her. | An execution after such a meeting, | As Burleigh says, would be against tradition.' Although flattery and her own curiosity play a part in her eventual consent to the meeting, it would be quite wrong to think that these are Elizabeth's primary motives. She has already, as she believes, won Mortimer's services to assassinate Mary. Now she can give the appearance to the world of considering mercy in the knowledge that Mary will be murdered before any hard decision will be required of her. Thus she will have disposed of Mary and rescued appearances. The meeting is thus foredoomed because Elizabeth does not come to it with any intention of pardoning Mary, whereas Mary assumes that the humiliation she has undergone in the course of the meeting must be the preliminary to the act of mercy she expects:

> Sister, finish now,
> Say what you came to say, for that you came
> Simply to mock me, I will not believe.
> Speak the word, tell me, 'Mary you are free'

But Elizabeth, spurred on by Leicester's ill-judged flattery earlier and by the added piquancy of his presence, goes too far in grinding her rival into the dust and Mary, also aware of her prospective lover's presence, retaliates. Once she has called Elizabeth a bastard to her face, challenging her right to the throne and activating all of Elizabeth's deepest insecurities, Elizabeth cannot maintain a pretence of wanting to pardon her.

It is in her monologue (IV. x), when Elizabeth signs the death warrant, that she adds the final words to the disastrous meeting. The people, whom she despises but on whose favour she depends, clamour for the death of Mary. But will they still applaud her after the deed is done? Her avoidance of the arbitrary exercise of power and her respect for the law now make it impossible to commit a manifest injustice. Her own example has tied her hands. Isolated from Europe and threatened by powerful enemies, betrayed by those closest to her, Elizabeth is overcome by rage and humiliation. 'Am I a bastard in your eyes?' She addresses Mary directly, taking up the quarrel where it broke off. Enraged and frustrated though she is, it is still the political threat that is uppermost in her mind: 'When there are no more Queens than I, the bed | Where I began will be an honoured one!'

Much critical controversy surrounds the treatment and significance of Mary's death. Mary comes to terms with being the victim of a judicial murder by regarding it as God's sign that she may atone for her complicity in Darnley's murder. The ability to accept her punishment allows her to triumph over the injustice and the humiliation of the execution. Thus the spectacle of her composure and dignity mediates to the audience a sympathetic experience of the indestructibility of the human spirit. To this experience of transcendence Schiller assigned the term 'sublime'. More than any other of his plays *Mary Stuart* has been interpreted as a demonstration of Schiller's theory of tragedy as he developed it during his philosophical phase in the early 1790s, in his essay *On Tragic Pity* (*Über das Pathetische*) in particular. The sublime was a phenomenon that fascinated numerous writers in the later decades of the eighteenth century. They recognized the existence of an aesthetic response of admiration and awe mixed with pain or terror, such as that occasioned by raging seas or deep ravines. It was a response distinct from the serenity and unalloyed delight associated with the beautiful. In his *Critique of Judgement* Kant interpreted the sublime in the light of his fundamental epistemological distinction between the phenomenal and the noumenal realms, the realm of nature and the realm of freedom. Human beings belong to the one by virtue of being physical creatures and to the other by virtue of being moral beings. When witnessing a scene of overwhelming natural power, human beings are at first terrified by their knowledge that nature can crush them but then exhilarated by the realization that within mankind is a moral dimension that transcends nature. Schiller saw the possibility of making this approach to the sublime fruitful in a theory of tragedy, which is an art form traditionally associated with the mixed response of pain and pleasure. In so doing he could demonstrate the interdependence of the moral and the aesthetic in the tragic response, without subordinating the aesthetic to the moral. The sublime response is mediated to the audience by the spectacle of the suffering of the tragic figure and his or her inner freedom, shown in resistance to being defeated by that suffering. Resistance could be active, as when someone freely chooses to die to uphold the right, or passive, when the suffering is stoically accepted. Though Schiller's essays on tragedy are couched in the language of Kantian philosophy, he can be seen as finding a new idiom in which to make intelligible to his contemporaries Aristotle's notion of catharsis. The play does not teach us a moral lesson but rather mediates an experience that reminds us that we are autonomous moral beings.

Mary Stuart has often been interpreted as if it were an exact demonstration of that theory. The problem with seeing any work of art as a demonstration of a theory is that with truly great art the theory never seems equal to the complexity of the work. Great emphasis on Mary's final moral freedom tends to reduce the scope of the work almost irretrievably. Most of the outer action of the play, particularly the scenes at Elizabeth's court, becomes secondary to this spiritual victory. The rich pattern of comparisons and contrasts between the two worlds of the play is lost, Elizabeth becomes the villain, and the world of politics stands condemned as morally tainted. Yet it is clear that even Mary's death has its own ambiguity. She knows it is her final appearance on the public stage and she can be seen as being determined to use it for maximum impact. Even her avowed innocence in the confession scene of plotting against Elizabeth can be put in doubt when one thinks of her association with Mortimer. She may not have wanted her rival to be assassinated but she has put herself in the hands of those who vow to free her by whatever means. On the other hand, she is about to die and she undoubtedly arouses pity and admiration for her ability to invest her death with the meaning that gives her the strength to face it. The play as moral triumph and the play as political tragedy need not be mutually exclusive. Schiller was as concerned with the art of living as with the art of dying, and it is not to detract from his portrayal of the possibility of transcendence to recognize his fascination with the ambiguities of the political world. It allows us to reserve a little sympathy for Elizabeth as she stands alone at the end, knowing she has failed the test of her humanity.

NOTE ON THE TRANSLATION

The German texts used in these translations are those published
by Philip Reclam Jun. in Stuttgart. *Don Carlos* was published in
its first complete form by Göschen in Leipzig in 1787; *Maria
Stuart* was published in 1801 by Cotta in Tübingen.

For this edition *Don Carlos* and *Mary Stuart* were translated
into prose by Hilary Collier Sy-Quia and then put back into
blank verse by Peter Oswald. The opening lines of *Don Carlos*
give a clear example of this two-step process at work:

> Die schönen Tage in Aranjuez
> Sind nun zu Ende. Eure Königliche Hoheit
> Verlassen es nicht heiterer. Wir sind
> Vergebens hier gewesen. Brechen Sie
> Dies rätselhafte Schweigen. Öffnen Sie
> Ihr Herz dem Vaterherzen, Prinz. Zu teuer
> Kann der Monarch die Ruhe seines Sohns—
> Des einzigen Sohns—zu teuer nie erkaufen.

The pleasant days in Aranjuez are now over. Your Majesty is not leaving
it any happier. We have been here in vain. Break this mysterious [lit
riddle-like] silence. Open your heart to your father's heart, Prince. The
monarch can never buy the contentment of his son—his only son—too
dearly.

> The pleasant days in Aranjuez are over.
> Your Royal Majesty will leave this place
> No happier than when he came. Our stay
> Has been a waste of time, but why? Explain
> The riddle of your silence to us, Prince,
> Lay your heart open to your father's heart.
> To buy contentment in his only son
> There is no price the monarch would not pay.

After writing his first three plays in prose, Schiller, who greatly
admired Shakespeare, adopted blank verse as his medium for *Don
Carlos* and continued using verse for all his subsequent plays.
The versification of *Don Carlos* follows the literal translation very
closely, whereas the versification of *Mary Stuart* is a little freer, in

an attempt to re-create the poetry of the original as the highest priority.

Plays on words are the greatest challenge for any translation and, by placing more importance on the sense than on the words, Peter Oswald was able to reproduce the elegant turns of phrase used in the original, as in one of Mortimer's lines in Act One, Scene VI, without losing loyalty to Schiller's text:

> Ich weiß nunmehr, daß Euer gutes Recht
> An England Euer ganzes Unrecht ist

I know now that your good right to England is also your entire misfortune [lit. injustice done to you]

> You suffer wrong because your right is known

Another particularly successful example is in Act Three, Scene IV:

> Es kostet nichts, die *allgemeine* Schönheit
> Zu sein, als die *gemeine* sein für alle!

In the English versification this becomes:

> Beauty, to purchase common approbation,
> Needs only to be common property.

We hope to satisfy the purists in favour of a literal translation with our version of *Don Carlos*, and to content the advocates of reproducing the 'feel' of a play as the first prerogative with *Mary Stuart*, but not to horrify supporters of either side of the translators' debate with either play.

The translation of *Don Carlos* was commissioned by a theatre company and performed, in a cut version, at the Lyric Studio, Hammersmith, in 1992.

SELECT BIBLIOGRAPHY

Background to Schiller's work

Borchmeyer, D., *Die Weimarer Klassik. Eine Einführung*, 2 vols. (Königstein im Taunus, 1980).

Bruford, W. H., *Germany in the Eighteenth Century: The Social Background to the Literary Revival* (Cambridge, 1935).

Bruford, W. H., *Culture and Society in Classical Weimar* (Cambridge, 1962).

Lamport, F. J., *German Classical Drama: Theatre, Humanity and Nation 1750–1870* (Cambridge, 1990).

Reed, T. J., *The Classical Centre: Goethe and Weimar 1775–1832* (London, 1980).

General critical and biographical studies

Buchwald, R., *Schiller*, 2 vols. (repr. Wiesbaden, 1954).

Garland, H. B., *Schiller the Dramatic Writer* (Oxford, 1969).

Graham, I. A., *Friedrich Schiller's Drama: Talent and Integrity* (London, 1974).

Lahnstein, P., *Schillers Leben* (Munich, 1981).

Mainland, W. F., *Schiller and the Changing Past* (London, 1957).

Reed, T. J., *Schiller* (Oxford, 1991).

Sharpe, L., *Friedrich Schiller: Drama, Thought and Politics* (Cambridge, 1991).

Stahl, E. L., *Friedrich Schiller's Drama, Theory and Practice* (Oxford, 1954).

Wiese, B. von, *Schiller* (Stuttgart, 1959).

Witte, W., *Schiller* (Oxford, 1949).

Studies of Don Carlos

Blunden, A. G., 'Nature and Politics in Schiller's *Don Carlos*', *Deutsche Vierteljahrsschrift*, 52 (1978), 241–56.

Böckmann, P., *Schillers Don Karlos. Edition der ursprünglichen Fassung und entstehungsgeschichtlicher Kommentar* (Stuttgart, 1974).

Bohnen, K., 'Politik im Drama. Anmerkungen zu Schillers *Don Carlos*', *Jahrbuch der Deutschen Schillergesellschaft*, 24 (1980), 15–31.

Crawford, R. L., 'Don Carlos and Marquis Posa: The Eternal Friendship', *Germanic Review*, 58 (1983), 97–105.

Ebstein, F., 'In Defense of Marquis Posa', *Germanic Review*, 36 (1961), 205–20.

Gronicka, A. von, 'Friedrich Schiller's Marquis Posa', *Germanic Review*, 26 (1951), 196–214.

Harrison, R. B., '"Gott ist über mir": Ruler and Reformer in the Twofold Symmetry of Schiller's *Don Carlos*', *Modern Language Review*, 76 (1981), 598–611.

Malsch, W., 'Moral und Politik in Schillers *Don Carlos*', in W. Wittkowski (ed.), *Verantwortung und Utopie. Zur Literatur der Goethezeit. Ein Symposium* (Tübingen, 1988), 207–37.

Orton, G., *Schiller: 'Don Carlos'* (London, 1967).

Studies of Mary Stuart

Beck, A., '*Maria Stuart*', in Benno von Wiese (ed.), *Das Deutsche Drama vom Barock bis zur Gegenwart*, 2 vols. (Düsseldorf, 1958), i. 305–21.

Berman, J., 'Schiller's Mortimer and the Gods of Italy', *Oxford German Studies*, 8 (1973–4), 47–59.

David, C., 'Le Personnage de la reine Elisabeth dans la *Maria Stuart* de Schiller', *Deutsche Beiträge zur geistigen Überlieferung*, 4 (1961), 9–22.

Harrison, R. B., 'Ideal Perfection and the Human Condition: Morality and Necessity in Schiller's *Maria Stuart*', *Oxford German Studies*, 20/21 (1991/2), 46–88.

Lamport, F. J., 'Krise und Legitimitätsanspruch. *Maria Stuart* als Geschichtstragödie', *Zeitschrift für deutsche Philologie*, 109 (1990), Sonderheft: Schiller: Aspekte neuerer Forschung, 134–44.

Sammons, J., 'Mortimer's Conversion and Schiller's Allegiances', *Journal of English and Germanic Philology*, 72 (1973), 155–66.

Sautermeister, G., '*Maria Stuart*', in W. Hinderer, *Schillers Dramen. Neue Interpretationen* (Stuttgart, 1979), 174–216.

Swales, E., *Schiller. 'Maria Stuart'* (London, 1988).

A CHRONOLOGY OF DATES AND EVENTS DURING SCHILLER'S LIFE

Year	Contemporary literary and political events	Events in Schiller's life	Plays	Essays and poems
1759	G. E. Lessing, M. Mendelssohn, F. Nicolai, E. von Kleist, *Briefe die neueste Literatur betreffend* (24 volumes to 1765)	Schiller is born in Marbach on 10 November		
1762	J. J. Rousseau, *Le Contrat social*			
1763	Voltaire, *Traité sur la Tolérance*			
1767	G. E. Lessing, *Minna von Barnhelm*; *Hamburgische Dramaturgie*			
1771–8	Sturm und Drang literary movement			
1772	G. E. Lessing, *Emilia Galotti*; J. W. Goethe, *Götz von Berlichingen*; J. G. Herder, *Von deutscher Art und Kunst*			
1773–80		Schiller attends the military academy (later called the		

Year	Contemporary literary and political events	Events in Schiller's life	Plays	Essays and poems
		Karlsschule) established by the Duke of Württemberg, Karl Eugen		
1773	J. W. Goethe starts work on *Faust* (Part I pub. 1808, Part II pub. 1832)			
1774	J. W. Goethe, *Die Leiden des jungen Werthers*			
1775	J. W. Goethe moves to Weimar	Schiller is transferred to the new medical school within the academy		
1776	American Declaration of Independence; Adam Smith, *An Enquiry into the Nature and Causes of the Wealth of Nations*	Begins to read Shakespeare		
1777			First scenes of *Die Räuber* written clandestinely, whilst still at the Karlsschule	
1779	G. E. Lessing, *Nathan der Weise*			
1780		Schiller graduates from the Karlsschule and is posted as regimental surgeon to the		

1781	I. Kant, *Kritik der reinen Vernunft*; Kaiser Joseph II initiates reforms, such as the abolition of serfdom	grenadiers in Augé, near Stuttgart	Schiller publishes *Die Räuber* at his own expense
1782	W. A. Mozart, *Die Entführung aus dem Serail*	Schiller flees the jurisdiction of the Duke of Württemberg with his friend Andreas Streicher. They stop briefly in Mannheim and Frankfurt, before staying in Oggersheim in secrecy	
1782–3		Henriette von Wolzogen invites Schiller to live in her country house in Bauerbach (Thüringen)	*Kabale und Liebe* finished
1783	J. G. Herder, *Ideen zur Philosophie der Geschichte der Menschheit*	Unhappy infatuation with Charlotte von Wolzogen, his host's daughter; leaves abruptly for Mannheim	*Fiesko*; work on *Don Carlos* started
1784		Falls in love with Charlotte von Kalb	
1785–7	W. A. Mozart, *Figaros Hochzeit, Don Giovanni, Eine kleine Nachtmusik*; J. W. Goethe, *Iphigenie auf Tauris*	Schiller is C. G. Körner's guest in Leipzig and Dresden: lifelong friendship begins	*1787 Don Carlos* completed and published by Göschen in Leipzig; *An die Freude*; Schiller launches his own magazine, *Rheinische Thalia*,

Year	Contemporary literary and political events	Events in Schiller's life	Plays	Essays and poems
				continued as *Thalia* and *Neue Thalia* until 1793
1787–8	J. W. Goethe, *Egmont*; I. Kant, *Kritik der praktischen Vernunft*	Schiller spends time in Weimar. In nearby Rudolstadt he makes first acquaintance with the von Lengefeld family; first meeting with Goethe		*Geschichte des Abfalls der vereinigten Niederlande von der spanischen Regierung* published; *Die Götter Griechenlands* published; *Briefe über Don Carlos* published
1789	French Revolution begins	Moves to Jena to assume Professorship in History; first acquaintance with Wilhelm von Humboldt		Famous opening address at University of Jena, *Was heißt und zu welchem Ende studiert man Universalgeschichte?*
1790	J. W. Goethe, *Torquato Tasso*; *Faust, ein Fragment*; I. Kant, *Kritik der Urteilskraft*	Schiller is made a Court Councillor; marries Charlotte von Lengefeld		First part of *Die Geschichte des Dreißigjährigen Krieges* appears

1791	W. A. Mozart, *Die Zauberflöte*; D. A. F., Marquis de Sade, *Justine*	Falls seriously ill: Schiller's health to plague him for the rest of his life. His financial worries are greatly eased by a three-year stipend from the Danish crown prince, Friedrich Christian, at the recommendation of poet Jens Baggesen	*Über den Grund des Vergnügens an tragischen Gegenständen; Über die tragische Kunst*
1792	French war against Austria; storming of the Tuileries	Continues his study of Kant's philosophy; the French National Assembly makes him an honorary French citizen	
1793	Execution of Louis XVI, rule of the Jacobins; second division of Poland; J. G. Herder, *Briefe zur Beförderung der Humanität*; J. G. Fichte, *Zurückforderung der Denkfreiheit*	Karl, first of four children, born	
	Danton and Robespierre are executed		
1794	Makes first contacts with publisher Johann Friedrich Cotta; friendship with Goethe initiated; friendship with Wilhelm von Humboldt		*Über Anmut und Würde; Über das Erhabene; Über die ästhetische Erziehung des Menschen; Ästhetische*

Year	Contemporary literary and political events	Events in Schiller's life	Plays	Essays and poems
				Briefe mainly written; a new literary journal, *Die Horen*, to be edited by Schiller and published by Cotta (1st issue 1795) *Über naive und sentimentalische Dichtung*
1795	J. W. Goethe, *Wilhelm Meisters Lehrjahre*; I. Kant, *Zum ewigen Frieden*; J. Haydn, London symphonies; rule of the Directory in France; peace treaty between Prussia and France; third division of Poland			
1796	Catherine II of Russia dies		Work on *Wallenstein*	Goethe and Schiller jointly publish satirical poems, *Xenien*
1797	J. W. Goethe, *Hermann und Dorothea*; F. W. J. Schelling, *Ideen zu einer Philosophie der Natur*; F. Hölderlin, *Hyperion*; I. Kant, *Die Metaphysik der Sitten*		*Wallenstein* rewritten in blank verse	Year of the ballads: *Der Taucher, Der Handschuh, Die Kraniche des Ibykus*

1798	Novalis, *Blütenstaub* appeared in *Das Athenäum*			
1799	Fall of the Directory, Napoleon Bonaparte becomes first Consul; ban on trade unions in England; Novalis, *Die Christenheit oder Europa*; F. Hölderlin, *Gedichte*; F. Schlegel, *Lucinde*	Schiller family moves to Weimar, where Schiller stays until his death	*Wallenstein* completed; work begins on *Maria Stuart*	*Das Lied von der Glocke*
1800	United Kingdom of Great Britain and Ireland founded; Jean Paul, *Titan*; Novalis, *Hymnen an die Nacht*		Completes *Maria Stuart*; adapts German translation of Shakespeare's *Macbeth* for the Weimar stage; begins work on *Die Jungfrau von Orleans*	
1801			*Die Jungfrau von Orleans* finished; adapts Gozzi's *Turandot* for the stage	
1802	Novalis, *Heinrich von Ofterdingen*; *Geistliche Lieder und Schriften*	Schiller is admitted to the nobility	Work on plan of *Wilhelm Tell*; work on *Die Braut von Messina*	

Year	Contemporary literary and political events	Events in Schiller's life	Plays	Essays and poems
1803	C. Brentano, *Die lustigen Musikanten*; J. W. Goethe, *Das Leben des Benvenuto Cellini*; H. von Kleist, *Die Familie Schroffenstein*; death of Herder, death of Klopstock		*Die Braut von Messina* completed	
1804	Bonaparte is crowned Napoleon I, emperor of France, blessed by the Pope; L. van Beethoven, Third Symphony; Jean Paul, *Vorschule der Ästhetik*	Travels to Berlin and contemplates a move	*Wilhelm Tell* completed; starts working on *Demetrius* material	
1805		9 May: Schiller's death	Adapts Racine's *Phaedra* for Weimar stage; continues work on *Demetrius*	
1806	Dissolution of the Holy Roman Empire; Napoleon assembles the German territories he has conquered since 1792 in a German Confederation			

THE HISTORICAL RELATIONSHIP BETWEEN MARY STUART AND DON CARLOS

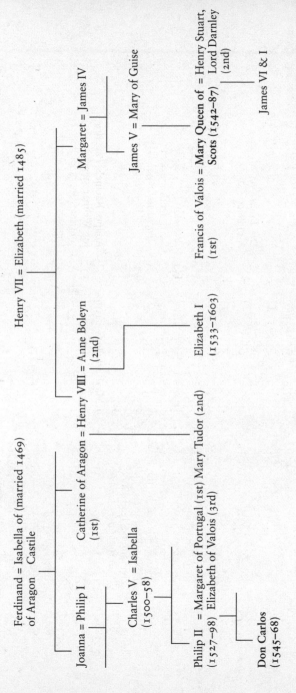

Ferdinand = Isabella of (married 1469)
of Aragon   Castile

Henry VII = Elizabeth (married 1485)

Joanna = Philip I

Catherine of Aragon = Henry VIII = Anne Boleyn
(1st)   (2nd)

Margaret = James IV

Charles V = Isabella
(1500–58)

Elizabeth I
(1533–1603)

James V = Mary of Guise

Philip II = Margaret of Portugal (1st) Mary Tudor (2nd)
(1527–98) Elizabeth of Valois (3rd)

Francis of Valois = Mary Queen of = Henry Stuart,
(1st)   Scots (1542–87)   Lord Darnley
                                        (2nd)

Don Carlos
(1545–68)

James VI & I

Acknowledgements to David Collier.

DON CARLOS

DRAMATIS PERSONAE

Philip II, King of Spain
Elizabeth of Valois, his wife
Don Carlos, the crown prince
Alexander Farnese, Prince of Parma, the King's nephew
Infanta Clara Eugenia, a 3-year-old child
Duchess Olivarez, head lady-in-waiting
Marquise of Mondecar ⎫
Princess Eboli   ⎬ ladies-in-waiting
Countess Fuentes   ⎭
Marquis of Posa, a Knight of Malta ⎫
Duke of Alba |
Count of Lerma, Colonel of the Guards ⎬ Grandees of Spain
Duke of Feria, Knight of the Fleece |
Duke of Medina Sidonia, Admiral |
Don Raimond of Taxis, Master of the Post ⎭
Domingo, Father Confessor to the King
The Grand Inquisitor of the kingdom
The Prior of a Carthusian monastery
A Page of the Queen
Don Ludwig Mercado, the Queen's physician

Several ladies and grandees, pages, officers, the guards, and
various silent figures

ACT ONE

SCENE I

[*The royal garden in Aranjuez.**]

[CARLOS *and* DOMINGO.*]

DOMINGO. The pleasant days in Aranjuez are over.
  Your Royal Majesty will leave this place
  No happier than when he came. Our stay
  Has been a waste of time, but why? Explain
  The riddle of your silence to us, Prince,
  Lay your heart open to your father's heart.
  To buy contentment in his only son
  There is no price the monarch would not pay.
          [CARLOS *casts his eyes to the floor and is silent*
  Could there be any last remaining wish
  That heaven has failed to grant its best-loved son?   10
  I stood there when within Toledo's walls
  Carlos received the homage of his lords,*
  Who vied to be the first to kiss his hand;
  When with one gesture of subservience
  Six kingdoms knelt together at his feet;*
  I saw the proud blood rising to his face,
  I saw him swell with noble resolutions,
  I saw his eyes, so glad they almost cried,
  Take in the whole assembly, drunk with joy.
  And Prince, those eyes confessed: I am fulfilled.   20
          [CARLOS *turns away*
  The sad religion of your silence, which
  For eight months now has been your only discourse,
  Baffles the court and terrifies the kingdom.
  It keeps his Majesty awake at night
  And costs your mother many tears—*

CARLOS [*turns around quickly*].   My Mother?
  Oh heaven grant me that I might one day
  Forget that he did that, made her my mother!

DOMINGO. Prince?

CARLOS [*collects himself and runs his hand over his forehead*].
                    I am unlucky with my mothers, Sir.
  When my eyes opened on the world of light
  I killed my mother. That was my first act.*   30

DOMINGO. My noble prince, can it be possible
  That you should suffer self-reproach for that?

CARLOS. And my new Mother—has she not already
  Cost me my father's love, such as it was?
  My only merit in my father's eyes
  Was that I was his only child. And now*
  A sister blots me out. Oh who can see
  What sleeps in time, behind the face of things?

DOMINGO. You joke with me, my Prince, can you alone
  Despise this Queen, whom all of Spain adores?   40
  Or can you only love her when you see her?
  Hate her, the finest lady on the earth,
  A Queen, a woman who was once your bride?
  I cannot think it, let me never hear it,
  Carlos is not so strange a contradiction.
  Be careful Prince, you must not let her know,
  She would be sad to think her son dislikes her.

CARLOS. You think so?

DOMINGO.   If your Highness can remember
  The tournament of late at Saragossa,*
  The splinter from a lance that grazed the King—   50
  The Queen was sitting on the middle rostrum,
  And watching with the ladies of the palace—
  There was a sudden shout, 'The King is bleeding!'
  People ran madly here and there, a murmur
  Of chaos reached faintly to the Queen, who cried,
  'The Prince?' and would have, would have flung herself
  Over the very topmost balustrade,
  But someone shouts back, 'No the King himself!'

'Fetch doctors then,' she cries, and breathes again. [*After a
    silence*]
What are you thinking of?

CARLOS.   I am amazed.   60
Who would have thought the King's august confessor
Could tell such entertaining little stories? [*Serious and
    sinister*]
But I have heard that those who see and tell
Have wrought more evil in the world than knives
And poisons in the hands of murderers.
You could have spared your breath the effort, sir—
Go seek the King, though, if you would be thanked.

DOMINGO. This caution suits you well, my Prince. The wise
    man
Does not trust all men—but one must distinguish:
Many are hypocrites, but some are friends: 70
I wish you well.

CARLOS.   Be careful, if my father
Learns of it, you will never be cardinal.

DOMINGO [*stops short*]. What?

CARLOS.   Oh the purple has been promised you,*
The first that Spain bestows.

DOMINGO.   My Prince, you play.

CARLOS. No! God forbid that I should laugh at you,
The man of terror with the power of heaven
To damn or save the king.

DOMINGO.   My royal Prince,
I would not be so rash as to adventure
To trespass in your sorrow's secret place.
But I do beg your Highness to remember,   80
The stricken conscience has a sanctuary,
The Church, to which no monarch has a key,
Where crimes can lie forever undisclosed,
Under the safeguard of the sacrament.
You know my meaning, I have said enough.

CARLOS. No! I will never be the man to bring
  Such a temptation to the ministry!

DOMINGO. Prince—this mistrust—you fail to recognize
  Your most devoted servant.

CARLOS.   So I do,
  So you had better drop me as a friend.   90
  All the world knows you are a Holy man,
  But frankly, though your loyalties are strong,
  They are too many for the likes of me.
  The road that leads you to St Peter's chair,*
  Good father, is the widest in the world,
  But too much truth might slow you down. The King,
  Who sent you here, must be content with that.

DOMINGO. Who sent me here?

CARLOS.   So say I. Oh I know,
  I know too well that I have been betrayed,
  That in this court a hundred eyes are hired*   100
  To guard me round, that his most wretched slave
  Could buy King Philip's only son from him,
  That any syllable I utter pays
  Better than any deed of excellence,
  The man who brings it to the king—I know—
  Oh quiet now, before I break my heart,
  I have already said too much, I know.

DOMINGO. The King intends to reach Madrid tonight.*
  The court is gathering already. Have I
  The honour, noble Prince—

CARLOS.   Well then, I'll follow.   110
                    [Exit DOMINGO. After a pause
  I pity you, King Philip, pity me,
  We both have need of it. I see your soul,
  Bitten already by the snake, suspicion,
  Swollen and livid where the poison entered.
  Your fateful questioning will drive you on
  Towards disclosures reason would not seek,
  And you will rage at that uncovering.

SCENE II

[CARLOS *and the* MARQUIS OF POSA.]

CARLOS. What? Can it be? It is, God, God, Roderigo!

MARQUIS. Carlos!

CARLOS.   I must be dreaming! Is it you?
  Can this be really you—tell me! It is!   120
  I hold you to my soul; I feel your own
  Beating against it, indestructible!
  Oh all is well again, and this embrace
  Heals my sick heart. I lie against the neck
  Of my dear friend Roderigo—

MARQUIS.   What, your heart?
  That needed to be made all well again?
  This frightens me—

CARLOS.   And you, what brings you here
  From Brussels? I was not expecting you!*
  Who is to thank for this astonishment?
  Forgive me my excitement, yes, I know,   130
  My questioning is almost blasphemy—
  For it was You, who gave us everything,
  You saw I lacked the company of angels,
  And sent me one, and still I ask who sent him!

MARQUIS. My dearest Prince, forgive me, but this storm
  Of ecstasy is not what I foresaw.
  Don Philip's son has changed, and I am worried.
  Your cheeks are pale, but touched with red like flames,
  They should not be like that—your lips are trembling
  As if with fever—what oppresses you?   140
  Is this the lionheart a race of heroes
  Sent me to find, to lighten their oppression?
  I do not stand before you as a friend,
  As Roderigo, your boyhood playfellow,
  But as a representative of man;
  Mankind embraces you—do not hear me,
  But listen to the provinces of Flanders,*

They weep upon your neck. And solemnly
They greet you and beseech salvation from you.
When Alba, the fanatic, the tormentor,*   150
Shall prosecute the law of Spain in Brussels,
Your dearest land is lost. That land of nobles
Rests its last hope on the heroic grandson
Of Charles the Emperor. But she will fall*
If this great heart beats for mankind no more.

CARLOS. Then she will fall.

MARQUIS.   What's that? What must I hear?

CARLOS. You speak of long ago and vanished times.
  I was a dream of Carlos just like yours
  In those days—if a man should speak of freedom
  My blood was fire—but now the dream is buried.   160
  What you see here is not that other Carlos,
  Who said farewell and left you in Alcala,
  Who drowned his spirit in the wine of dreams
  To find another Spanish Golden Age.
  My dreams were childish, though they were of heaven.
  But they have ended.

MARQUIS.   Dreams, Prince? Only dreams?

CARLOS. My only friend, oh let my heart be eased
  At last by weeping of these scalding tears,
  For I have no one, no one in the world,
  No one in all the vastness of the sphere;   170
  As far as ships can bear the flag of Spain,
  Is everywhere my father's sceptre rules,
  And there is nowhere on the earth but this
  For me to rest the burden of my tears.
  By all our hopes of heaven, my Roderigo,
  Do not reject me from this resting place.
            [*The* MARQUIS *bows over him moved and*
                  speechless
  I am an orphan you have found, imagine,
  And seated as a game upon the throne.
  And I have never known what father means—

I am a King's son—oh if it were true,   180
As my heart tells me that it must be so,
That you are chosen from the mass of man
To understand me, that the hand of nature
Made Carlos and Roderigo like one person—
And if in the beginning our two souls
When played together made a single sound,
If one tear wrung from me to ease my pain
Is dearer to you than my father's favour—

MARQUIS. Oh dearer than the whole world.

CARLOS.   I have fallen
So deep, and am become so poor in spirit,   190
That I must ask you to remember vows
And obligations made when we were children.
When we were in our sailor suits we made them,*
When you and I had grown so brotherly
From growing up together, two wild boys,
That there was nothing that could hurt me more
Than to be out of favour in your eyes.
I finally courageously decided
To love you wholly since I could not be you;
Then I would pester you with loyalty,   200
And with a thousand brotherly caresses;
You, proud heart, gave them coldly back. And often—
And this you never noticed—heavy tears
Stood hotly in my eyes when you passed by
And paid attention to inferiors.
Why only them, I used to cry in sorrow,
Am I not also and most truly worthy?
But you would kneel before me seriously
And coldly say, one acts like this with princes.

MARQUIS. Oh quiet, prince, forget these childish stories,   210
They make me blush for shame.

CARLOS.   I had not won you.
You could despise me, tear my heart to pieces,
But never banish it. Three times your Lord

Left you, repulsed, and three times he returned,
Begged for your love, and pressed his love on you,
But chance gave Carlos what he could not take.
My Aunt, the Queen of Bohemia, passing by*
Where we were playing, happened to receive
A shuttlecock you hit, full in the face.
Feeling quite certain that it had been aimed,   220
She ran, in floods of tears, to tell the King;
And all the palace youth were called at once
Before his face, to name the guilty one.
He thundered that he would avenge the deed,
Even upon his own son, terribly.
And then I saw you shaking in the background,
And at that very instant, I stepped forward,
I did not hesitate, I threw myself
At the King's feet, and cried, I did the deed,
I only—be avenged upon your son.   230

MARQUIS. Oh Lord, these memories, my Prince!

CARLOS.   He was.
Before the very servants of the court,
Who stood in sorrow in a circle round me,
Your Karl was punished as a slave is punished.
I looked at you and did not cry. My teeth
Were forced to grind together by the pain.
I did not cry. My royal blood flowed out
Most shamefully beneath relentless strokes—
I looked at you and did not cry. And after,
You wept indeed and fell before my feet—   240
Yes, yes, you cried, my pride is overcome,
And I will pay you back when you are King.

MARQUIS [gives him his hand]. I want to, Karl; I here renew
    my vow,
Made as a child, now that I am a man.
I want to pay. Perhaps my hour has come.

CARLOS. Now, now, do not delay, the hour is here,
The time has come for you to pay in full—

I need love now. The secret in me burns,
It is a horror destined to be known.
I want the verdict of my death to be   250
Your sudden pallor when I tell you this—
Listen, and turn to stone, but make no answer—
I love, desire my Mother.

MARQUIS.   Oh my God!

CARLOS. Oh please, you show too much consideration,
Speak out and say that in the world's great sphere
No misery can stand by mine—say it!
I know already all that can be said.
The customs of the world, and nature's order,
And Rome's decrees combine to damn my feelings.*
It is a trespass and a dreadful one   260
Upon my father's rights. I feel all this
And still I love. The path I tread will lead me
Either to madness or to execution,
My love is evil, puts my life in danger,
Lives without hope and in the face of death—
All this I see and know, and yet I love.

MARQUIS. Does the Queen know this?

CARLOS.   How could I tell her?
She is King Philip's wife, and this is Spain.
Under his jealousy, whose strength extends
Long ties of etiquette and protocol,   270
How could I hope to visit her unseen?
For eight months I have lived in fear of hell,
Since my recall from university—
My curse has been to see her every day,
And to preserve the silence of the grave;
Roderigo, eight months in the eyes of hell,
Whose fires are in me—and a thousand times
The horror of the truth was on my lips,
But always crept back trembling to my heart,
O my dear friend, to be alone with her,   280
Just for a moment—

MARQUIS.   Ah! Your father, prince.

CARLOS. What, is it him you think I fear, vile man?
    Speak to me of the Furies in my head,*
    Do not add father to the words they shout.

MARQUIS. Do you despise your father?

CARLOS.   I do not,
    Nor do I hate him, but I fear his name,
    It makes me shake like a convicted thief.
    Am I to blame if love's young life in me
    Was broken by a savage upbringing?
    I saw him first when I was six years old,   290
    When lo, the man of fear they called my father
    Appeared. It was a morning, he had risen,
    And forthwith signed four sentences of death.
    From that day on I only glimpsed this figure
    When I was sent to suffer for some crime.
    Oh God, a wave of bitterness is rising
    Inside me. Let us speak no more of this.

MARQUIS. No, prince, far better for your grief to speak,
    Speaking can solve the struggles of our hearts . . .

CARLOS. Oh I have often struggled, often woken,   300
    At midnight, when my guards were sleeping, crying—
    In floods of tears—and knelt before the picture
    Of the Most Blessed Virgin, praying, begging
    To be a child again. I was not answered.
    Ah but Roderigo, you unweave the spell
    Of my long silence—you unlock my sadness.
    Why, out of all the fathers in the world
    Was I bequeathed precisely this one? Why
    Of all the sons was he condemned to me?
    Nature cannot discover in her sphere   310
    Two opposites more absolutely fixed.
    How can she tie the two ends of the string
    Of human kind, in such a sacred bond?
    Terrible fate! Why must it be like this?
    Why must two men, who never wish to meet,

Be cast together by the same desire?
Roderigo, here you see two constellations,
Fatal to one another, that will touch,
Once, in the course of time's entirety,
Shatter each other and then part for ever.   320

MARQUIS. That moment will be terrible.

CARLOS.   It will.
Horrible figures, furies, follow me,
My spirit doubts, it broods on dreadful schemes,
And then in terror, thrusts the thought away;
My thinking, wrong at every twist and turn,
Wanders through labyrinths of sophistry,
Until it stops up short at hell's stretched mouth.
Oh Roderigo—what if I should forget,
No longer see him as a father—oh—
Your deathly colour shows you understand—   330
If I should ever cease to call him father,
How would I serve him as a King?

MARQUIS.   My Carlos,
May I beg one request of you? Please promise,
Whatever you decide you have to do,
Not to do anything without your friend.

CARLOS. I put myself completely in your power.
Anything that your love demands of me,
That I surrender.

MARQUIS.   What is said is true,
The monarch is returning to the city.
The time is short. If you would see the Queen,   340
The meeting must be in Aranjuez.
The peace, the unoppressive atmosphere
Are in our favour.

CARLOS.   That was my hope too,
It was in vain however!

MARQUIS.   Not entirely.
I will present myself to her at once.

If she is as she was at Henry's court,*
If Spain has not entirely altered her,
She will be glad to see me. If I read
Of any hope for Carlos in her eyes,
And if she seems to warm towards this meeting,   350
And if her women can be sent away—

CARLOS. Most of them smile upon me—Mondecar
Especially, my page boy is her son.

MARQUIS. Good. Be nearby, and when I give the signal,
You must be ready to appear at once.

CARLOS. I will—I will be—you must hurry now.

MARQUIS. I must, my Prince, this will not bear delay.
Until we meet again!

[*Exeunt different ways*

SCENE III

[*The court of the* QUEEN *in Aranjuez.*]
[*The* DUCHESS OF OLIVAREZ, *the* PRINCESS OF EBOLI,
and the MARQUISE OF MONDECAR.]

QUEEN [*to the* MARQUISE]. Let me have you beside me,
    Mondecar;*
The Princess strives to hide her mood in vain,   360
Her happiness has tortured me all day:
She loves to leave the countryside.

EBOLI.   My Queen,
That I will see Madrid again with joy
I do confess.

MONDECAR.   But not your Majesty?
Are you so sad to leave Aranjuez?

QUEEN. It makes me sad to leave this beauty, yes.
This is the place I love, and which I chose
So long ago, it seems my own small world.
My love of nature always finds me here,

And runs to greet me like a childhood friend.   370
Some breeze has found its way from France to here,
Reminding me of games I used to play—
Do not be cross with me. Our fatherland
Will keep our hearts, no matter where we are.

EBOLI. It is so lonely though, so dreary here,
One feels so stuck, as in a lovely tomb.

QUEEN. For me Madrid is death. But what about
The Duchess, what do you say?

OLIVAREZ.   My opinion*
Is that the custom is, spend one month here,
Then undergo another in the Pardo,*   380
Then spend the winter in the residence.
This has been so since there were Kings in Spain.

QUEEN. Yes, Duchess, and of course I must agree.
To argue things with you is to be wrong.

MONDECAR. Madrid will be so full of life soon though!
There is a bullfight in the Plaza Mayor,*
It is preparing now, and we are promised
Autos da Fe.*

QUEEN.   Promised? Sweet Mondecar,
Are you so harsh?

MONDECAR.   But they are heretics.

QUEEN. I hope my Eboli feels differently.   390

EBOLI. I earnestly implore your Majesty,
Think me as true to Christ as the Marquise.

QUEEN. I am forgetting where I am. Come, friends,
Let us speak on about the countryside.
The month is over, and it has passed by
With unforgiving swiftness, to my mind.
I could have sworn it promised happiness,
This little stay, I swore I would be happy,
But I have not found what I hoped to find.
Are all hopes like this? Mine have failed so badly   400
That I cannot remember what they were.

OLIVAREZ. You have not told us, Princess Eboli,
Of Gomez yet. May he still live in hope?*
Will we perhaps soon greet you as his bride?

QUEEN. Ah, Duchess, thank you for reminding me—[*to* EBOLI]
A man has begged me to support his claim;
How can I though? Could anyone be worthy
To be rewarded with my Eboli?

OLIVAREZ. Your Majesty, he is the worthiest,
A man to whom the favour of your Highness   410
Is not unknown.

QUEEN.   What I would bless him with
If his suit sped, would be the bliss of heaven.
But we would know first if the man can love,
And if he can be loved, and Eboli,
This I must ask you.

EBOLI [*stands silent and confused, her eyes cast down: finally
    she falls at the* QUEEN'*s feet*].
                        Oh have mercy on me,
Bountiful Queen. And do not let me—God—
Do not permit me to be sacrificed!

QUEEN. I need to hear no more. Stand up, sweet lady.
You were not made to be a sacrifice.
I do not doubt the weight of what you say.   420
How long ago did you refuse the Duke?

EBOLI. Your Highness, it was many months ago.
The Prince was still at University—

QUEEN [*stops and looks searchingly at* EBOLI].
And are the reasons of your own divining?

EBOLI [*with force*]. Your Highness, it can never be allowed,
Never, for many, many reasons, never.

QUEEN [*very gravely*]. One is enough. The man is not your
    love.
No need to add to that. No more of this. [*To the other
    ladies*]

I have not seen my daughter yet today.*
Bring her to me, Marquise.

OLIVAREZ.   It is too early,   430
Your Majesty.

QUEEN.   That news is sad to hear.
Not yet the time for me to be a mother.
Do please inform me when the hour arrives.
         [*A page arrives and speaks quietly to the head
         lady-in-waiting, who then turns to the* QUEEN

OLIVAREZ. The Marquis of Posa is here, your Majesty.

QUEEN. Posa?

OLIVAREZ.   He has been in the Netherlands
And France, and asks the grace to be permitted
To give you letters that the Regent's mother*
Sends by his hand.

QUEEN.   And is this customary?

OLIVAREZ. This special circumstance is not defined,
In my experience of protocol—   440
There are some letters from a foreign court,
To be presented to the Queen of Spain,
And she receives them in her orchard from
A nobleman whose home is in Castile—

QUEEN. So if I risk it let the blame be mine!

OLIVAREZ. But will you please permit me to withdraw,
While this is taking place, your Majesty?

QUEEN. Duchess, do as you wish.

SCENE IV

         [*The* QUEEN, PRINCESS EBOLI, *the* MARQUISE OF
         MONDECAR, *and* MARQUIS OF POSA.]

QUEEN.   Chevalier,
I bid you welcome to the air of Spain.

MARQUIS. That never justified my love of it   450
  More perfectly than it does now.

QUEEN [*to the ladies*].   The Marquis
  Of Posa, in the tournament at Reims,*
  Broke lances with my father, and three times
  Carried my colours to a victory;
  It was through him that I began to learn
  That it is something to be Queen of Spain.
                 [*Turning to the* MARQUIS
  I do not think you dreamt, Chevalier,
  When we last saw each other, in the Louvre,
  That I would entertain you in Castile.

MARQUIS. Queen, it was far from my imagination,   460
  That France would ever let us take from her
  The only thing of hers we coveted.

QUEEN. The only thing! Proud Spaniard! And you dare
  To say this to a daughter of the Valois!

MARQUIS. I can admit it now, your Majesty,
  Because we have you.

QUEEN.   I have heard your journey
  Brought you through France. What have you got for me
  From my dear brothers and most honoured mother?

MARQUIS [*hands over the letters*]. I found the Queen your
    mother very ill,
  And far from all the pleasures of the world,   470
  Except the knowledge of her daughter's bliss
  Upon the throne of Spain.

QUEEN.   How could I be
  Anything less than happy, with the thought
  Of such love? And the lovely memory
  Of . . . You have studied in your wide-flung travels
  Many courts, many customs, many countries,
  But finally, I hear, you have decided
  To try the climate of your fatherland.
  A greater ruler in his own four walls

Than is King Philip on the throne of Spain!   480
A citizen! And a philosopher!
I doubt Madrid will stimulate you much—
One is so very—placid in Madrid.

MARQUIS. A peace so rare that in the rest of Europe
No sum can buy a single minute of it.

QUEEN. I know this, though the business of the world
Is nothing but a memory to me. [to EBOLI]
Is that a hyacinth? I think it is—
Will you not bring it to me, Eboli?
   [The PRINCESS goes over to the place. QUEEN
    more quietly to MARQUIS
Chevalier, unless I am mistaken,   490
Your coming here has changed the court already,
Increased by one the number of the happy.

MARQUIS. I found a sad one, whom in all the world
One thing alone, and not myself, can gladden—
   [The PRINCESS returns with the flower

EBOLI. Since the brave Knight has seen so many countries,
There must be many fabulous encounters
That he can tell us of.

MARQUIS.   A host, for certain.
Adventure is the duty of a knight,
As is well known, though his most holy vow
Is to defend all women.

MONDECAR.   Yes, from giants!   500
Although there are no giants now, I fear.

MARQUIS. No, they still crush the weak, in every country.

QUEEN. The Chevalier is correct. Giants are rife,
Unhappily the Knights have all died out.

MARQUIS. As I returned from Naples recently
I was the witness of a moving story
The sacred gift of friendship makes me part of.
If I was sure the telling of the tale
Would not fatigue and vex your Majesty—

QUEEN. Marquis, the choice is not my own. To cure   510
  The Princess of her curiosity
  Is far beyond my wishes or my power.
  But tell—I am a friend of stories too.*

MARQUIS. Two noble houses in Mirandola,*
  Tired of the enmity and jealousy
  That centuries of Guelfs and Ghibellines*
  Had carried on, decided to combine,
  Through the frail bond of consanguinity,
  In everlasting friendliness. Fernando,
  Son of the sister of the great Pietro,   520
  And good Matilda, daughter of Colonna,
  Were chosen to contract their families
  In graceful union. Never in the world
  Had nature made two hearts more beautiful,
  The world said, so designed for one another.
  And all agreed the choice could not be bettered.
  Now up to now, in Padua, Fernando,
  Tied to his studies, had adored his bride,
  So worthy worship, only in a picture.
  And how he trembled when he found it true,   530
  What his imagination had not dared,
  There in the picture! Now he only waits
  For time to let the blissful moment come
  When he will stammer at Matilda's feet
  The first free declaration of his love.
                    [*The* QUEEN *becomes more attentive. The*
                    MARQUIS *continues after a short pause*
                    to tell the tale, mainly addressing
                    himself to PRINCESS EBOLI, *as far as*
                    the QUEEN's *presence will allow it*
  But meanwhile, old Pietro's wife has died
  Leaving him free—Matilda's fame has reached him,
  Through all the rumours that delight in her,
  And lit the fire of youth in him again;
  He comes to her, he sees her and he loves,   540
  Fernando's rights are strangled by the impulse:

The Uncle woos and takes the nephew's bride,
And makes his theft official on the altar.

QUEEN. What does Fernando then decide?

MARQUIS.   He flies,
In ignorance of this depravity,
On wings of passion to Mirandola,
Drunk with his love; his swift steed reaches it
By starlight, and he stands before the gates,
Where, from the vast illuminated palace,
The sound of drums and drunken dancing thunders.   550
He climbs the steps in great bewilderment
And stands unrecognized amid the noise
Of the great wedding hall where in the midst
Of crowds of reeling guests Pietro sits.
There is an angel sitting next to him,
Fernando knows her but he never saw her,
Even in dreams, shine with such brilliance.
A single moment shows him what was his
And what is lost to him eternally.

EBOLI. Oh, Poor Fernando!

QUEEN.   What can happen now?   560
Surely it is the end, Chevalier?

MARQUIS. Not quite.

QUEEN.   You said Fernando was your friend,
I think?

MARQUIS. He is the dearest that I have.

EBOLI. Chevalier, continue with the story.

MARQUIS. It is so sad—the memory is painful—
Excuse me of the ending—[silence]

QUEEN [turns to EBOLI].   Surely now
I am permitted to embrace my daughter
Finally. Princess, would you bring her to me?
        [Exit EBOLI. The MARQUIS signals to a page, who
        appears in the background and disappears

immediately. The QUEEN *opens the letter the*
MARQUIS *has given her and seems to be*
surprised. In the meantime the MARQUIS *is*
speaking secretly and urgently to MONDECAR.
The QUEEN *has read the letters and turns to the*
MARQUIS *with a searching expression*
You have not told us what Matilda thinks.
Perhaps she is entirely unaware   570
Of how Fernando pines.

MARQUIS.   Matilda's heart
Has not been fathomed yet by anyone—
But great souls break in silence.

QUEEN. You stare around. What has distracted you?

MARQUIS. Only a shudder of the happiness
    That someone—whom I must not name—would have,
If he was here with you instead of me.

QUEEN. Who is to blame that he is not? Who bars him?

MARQUIS [*forcefully interrupting*]. May I interpret that the
    way I wish?
If he appeared now, could he be forgiven?   580

QUEEN [*startled*]. Now, Marquis?

MARQUIS.   Could he hope?

QUEEN.   You frighten me—
    He would not come here.

MARQUIS.   He is here already.

SCENE V

[MARQUIS *and* MONDECAR *recede into the*
background. QUEEN, DON CARLOS.]

CARLOS [*having thrown himself down before the* QUEEN].
    It comes at last, the moment. And now Karl
Touches this dear hand.

QUEEN.   This is lunacy,
  And criminal—stand up—my retinue!—

CARLOS. I will not rise. I will kneel here for ever.
  I want to stay here in this place bewitched,
  Transfixed—I never want to move again.

QUEEN. Madman! My mildness has encouraged you—
  It is the Queen you speak to so directly—   590
  Your mother—do you know that? Do you know
  That I, that of this outrage, this attack,
  The king—

CARLOS.   The king must know and I must die.
  I will be swept from here to execution.
  But death is not too high a price to pay
  For having briefly been in heaven alive.

QUEEN. And what will my fate be?

CARLOS.   God, God, I leave you;
  I want to leave you now, how can I not
  When this is how you ask me to? Oh, mother,
  It is like death, the game you play with me—   600
  The one sign, or a half-look, the one sound
  Orders me both to shatter and to be.
  What would you have me do? There can be nothing
  Under the sun, I would not gladly cast
  Into hell's furnace, if you ask me to.

QUEEN. Then run away from here.

CARLOS.   Oh God!

QUEEN.   No more!
  In terror I beseech you, leave me, Karl!
  Before my ladies and my other keepers,
  Can bear the dire news to your father's ears
  That you and I were found alone together.*   610

CARLOS. I only wait for life or death to take me.
  I have not rested all my hopes on this,
  A moment at the last alone with you,
  Given to me by you, to turn away,

In terror of the dragons at the gates.
No, Queen! The earth could rove around its poles
A hundred or a hundred thousand times
Before this blest chance could be mine again.

QUEEN. It would be better if it never came.
Oh wretched man, what do you want from me?   620

CARLOS. Oh Queen, that I have struggled with myself,
Harder than any mortal can imagine,
God be my witness. Queen, I was defeated!
I broke, and all my heroism left me.

QUEEN. Oh, for my peace of mind, please, speak no more.

CARLOS. You were my own. The whole world saw you were;
Vouchsafed to me by two unrivalled powers,
Considered mine by nature and by heaven,
And Philip, Philip came and took you from me.

QUEEN. He is your father.

CARLOS.   Husband of my love.   630

QUEEN. The greatest empire in the world is his,
Which he will give to you.

CARLOS.   And give me you
To be my mother.

QUEEN.   You have lost your mind.

CARLOS. And does he prize you? Can he understand
What he possesses? Is your heart his treasure?
If he was happy I would not be bitter,
I would forget the bliss I could have had,
But he is not. And that I cannot bear.
He is not now, nor will he ever be.
You gave away my heaven to the king,   640
And watched it fade to nothing in his arms.

QUEEN. Repulsive thought!

CARLOS.   Oh I know very well
Who was the author of this marriage death.

I know how Philip keeps the things he loves.
And what is your position in this empire?
Are you his regent, Queen? I do not think so.
Could Albas do their will if you were regent?
Could Flanders be destroyed for its religion?
Impossible, when you are Philip's wife!
Your husband's wishes should be yours, yours his.   650
And when from time to time his lust may drive him
To pester you for intimacy, does he
Plead with his age or order with his sceptre?

QUEEN. Who told you that my life is horrible?

CARLOS. My burning heart, that tells me that with me
  You would be enviable.

QUEEN.   Insolence!
  What if my own heart says the opposite?
  What if your father's language of expressions,
  His silent and respectful tenderness,
  Moves me more deeply than this eloquence   660
  And this audacity! If the attentions—
  If an old man's consideration—*

CARLOS.   Well then—
  If that is so, it is another matter.
  I did not know you loved the King. Forgive me.

QUEEN. To honour him is my delight and wish.

CARLOS. And have you ever loved?

QUEEN.   Ungentle question!

CARLOS. But have you ever loved?

QUEEN.   I love no more.

CARLOS. Because your heart and oath forbid you to?

QUEEN. Leave me now, Prince, and do not come to me
  For further conversations of this kind.   670

CARLOS. Because your oath and heart forbid you to?

QUEEN. Because my duty—oh, you wretched man,
   Why this distressful questioning of fortune,
   Whose bitter pathway we can only follow?

CARLOS. Must? Must we follow?

QUEEN.   What? What do you mean
   By this commanding tone?

CARLOS.   Only this much:
   That Carlos is inclined to disobey
   When what must be is not what he desires.
   That Carlos is unwilling to submit
   To misery, the greatest in the empire,   680
   When, if he broke its laws, he could be happy.

QUEEN. What? Do I understand you? You still hope?
   You dare to hope when all is lost already?

CARLOS. Only the dead, I think, lose hope for ever.

QUEEN. And me, your mother, you still hope for me?
         [*She looks at him penetratingly for a long time,
             then says with dignity and gravity*
   Why not? Oh why not? After his accession
   The newly risen ruler can do more,
   Can throw the edicts of the lately dead
   Into the fire, and haul his picture down,
   Can even—what can stop him? Drag his corpse   690
   Forth from its sleep in the Escorial,*
   And scatter the cursed dust to the four winds
   In the light of day; and lastly, to be done
   With honour once for all—

CARLOS.   No, do not finish!

QUEEN. Can join himself in marriage to his mother.

CARLOS. The son is damned!
                [*He stands for a moment motionless and
                    speechless*
                      Oh, it is over, over.

Yes, I can see now clearly, perfectly
What I should never, ever have been shown.
You are not here, you are far off for ever,
This is the future, you are lost to me,   700
And hell would be the price for having you.
I cannot bear this, oh my nerves are breaking!

QUEEN. Oh Karl, I feel what rages through you now,
The nameless agony—the pain is endless
Because the love is endless, but the fame
For overcoming this is also endless.
Win that, young hero—for the prize is worthy
Of such a mighty and exalted fighter,
The youth whose heart is swollen with the virtue
Of such a famous royal ancestry!   710
Summon your courage, noble prince. The grandson
Of great King Charles begins the fight again
When lesser men's descendants cease for fear!

CARLOS. Too late! Oh God!

QUEEN.   Too late to be a man?
Karl, your resistance will destroy our hearts,
But that will make our grace so much the greater!
You will be set by this hard-fought restraint
Above the easy millions of your brothers.
Fate took this chance from them to give to you,
You are her chosen son, and millions question,   720
How in his mother's womb did Carlos win
The sanctity that overshadows us?
Go, and recover heaven's good opinion,
And seize the right to be mankind's example,
By giving God the greater sacrifice.

CARLOS. Yes, though I am too weak to let you go,
I have a giant's strength to fight for you.

QUEEN. Carlos, you have to understand that pride,
Bitterness and defiance drove your will
So powerfully towards your mother. The heart   730
You sacrifice so wastefully to me,
The love, belongs to all your future kingdoms.

Look, you are living in the luxury
Of all the goods entrusted by your wards;
Love is a public office you corrupt
By concentrating on your mother—take it,
Take it and give it to your future kingdoms,
Shake off the agony of conscience, seize
The rapture of a God. Elizabeth
Was your first love, but Spain will be your second.   740
And with what swiftness and humility,
Good Karl, shall I accept the better mistress!

CARLOS. You are as great as heaven and creation.
  Everything you have asked of me shall be! [*stands*]
  I stand within the strength of God Almighty,
  And swear, to you and to eternity—
  Oh heaven, no, not to forget for ever,
  But to be silent always, like the sun.

QUEEN. How can I ask of Karl the sacrifice
  That I myself have no desire to give?   750

MARQUIS [*hurries out of the avenue*]. The King!

QUEEN.   God!

MARQUIS.   Go, get far away from here.

QUEEN. Prince, his suspicions are a constant storm.
  If he sees you—

CARLOS.   I stay!

QUEEN.   Then who will fall?

CARLOS [*pulls* MARQUIS *by the arm*]. Come then, my friend.
                    [*He goes and then returns*
                    But must I leave with nothing?

QUEEN. Go with your Mother's friendship.

CARLOS.   Friendship? Mother?

QUEEN. And this sad pleading from the Netherlands.
                  [*She gives him some letters.* CARLOS *and*
                  MARQUIS *exeunt.* QUEEN *looks round*

*uneasily for her ladies-in-waiting, who
are nowhere to be seen. As she would
retreat into the background, the* KING
appears

SCENE VI

[KING, QUEEN, DUKE OF ALBA, COUNT LERMA,
DOMINGO, *some ladies and grandees, who remain in
the background.*]

KING [*looks around with an estranged expression and is
    silent for a while*].
What's this? You here? But so alone, Madame!
Is not one lady in your company?
I find this very strange. Where are your ladies?

QUEEN. My worthy husband—

KING.   Why is she alone? [*To the others*]
This oversight is unforgivable.   761
The explanation will be most precise.
Whose office is the service of the Queen?
Whose turn is it to tend to her today?

QUEEN. I am the guilty one. Do not be angry,
My husband—it was at my own request
The Lady Eboli abandoned me.

KING. Your own request?

QUEEN.   To call the chambermaid,
Because I wanted the Infanta here.

KING. For that you must dismiss your retinue?   770
This only serves to let the first one go,
What of the second lady?

MONDECAR [*who has in the meantime returned and mingled
    with the other ladies, now steps forward*].
                    Majesty,
I think the fault is mine.

KING.   Since that is so,
I give you ten years space to meditate
Upon the fact, in exile from Madrid.

> [*The* MARQUISE *steps back, crying. There is
> silence. All those standing round look at
> the* QUEEN *in consternation*

QUEEN. Marquise, why are you crying? Noble husband,
If I am guilty, then the crown of empire,
Which I have never touched, should all the more,
And at the very least, guard me from blushes.
Or does this kingdom usually compel   780
Daughters of Kings to stand in courts of law?
In Spain are women only safe in prison?
Is unseen virtue inadmissible?
And now forgive me, it is not my way
To honour those who served me happily
By sending them away in tears. My friend!

> [*She takes off her belt and gives it to the*
> MARQUISE

The King is angry with you, but not I,
So take this token of my grace with you.
Remember that when you remember this.
Escape the empire—you have sinned in Spain,   790
In France we wipe away such tears as these
With joy—oh must I always be reminded?

> [*She leans her head against the chief lady-in-
> waiting*

It was not like this when I was in France.

KING [*somewhat agitatedly*]. How can this accusation trouble
   you
When it arises from my love for you?
The words my tenderest concern for you
Brings to my lips should not sound harsh to you!

> [*He turns to the grandees*

The vassals of my throne are standing here!
These eyes, they know, are never closed in sleep
Unless by evening I am satisfied   800
That I have understood what moves the hearts

Of all my people—and my lands reach far—
And should I be more anxious for my throne
Than for my heart and she who rules me there?
My sword can answer if I doubt my people—
And you, Duke Alba—but my wife's true feelings
These eyes alone can vouch for.

QUEEN.   If I have
Offended you, my husband—

KING.   I am called
The richest man in the believing world.
In my domain the sun does not go down.*   810
But all this once belonged to someone else,
And many will possess it after me:
But this is mine. Good fortune made me King,
But Philip gave himself Elizabeth,
And in her only can he suffer loss.*

QUEEN. Are you afraid, my Lord?

KING.   Of these grey hairs?
If I should ever feel the hand of fear,
I'd sever the whole arm. Where is my son?
I count the great ones of my court and note
The greatest one is absent—the infante.   820
Where is Don Carlos? [*No one answers*] Young Don Karl
   begins
To have a dreadful aspect in my mind.
Since his return from university
He goes around the places where I am;
His blood is hot, why are his eyes so cold?
And his demeanour, sadness so well done.
I recommend great watchfulness.

ALBA.   Of course.
While flesh and blood are living in this armour,
Philip may lay himself to sleep in safety.
The Duke of Alba stands before the throne   830
As angels stand before the gates of heaven.

LERMA. If I may dare in all humility*
To contradict the wisest of all kings—

I owe his highness too much reverence
To let myself condemn his son so harshly.
I fear Don Carlos for his headstrong moods,
And yet I know his heart is pure.

KING.   Count Lerma,
The father could be flattered by these words,
The king, however, leans upon the Duke.
No more of this. [*He turns to his followers*] Now, to
    Madrid with speed,   840
My royal duty calls me. Heresy
Is spreading through my peoples like a plague,
And storms are brewing in the Netherlands.
Dreadful examples shall persuade the faithless—
The time for action has arrived—the oath
That all the kings of Christendom must swear
Shall be renewed tomorrow, and then blood*
Will justly flow beyond all precedent.
Which I invite, convoke, this court to witness.

                                    [*Exeunt*

SCENE VII

[DON CARLOS, *with letters in his hand, and* MARQUIS
VON POSA *enter from opposite sides.*]

CARLOS. I have decided. Flanders shall be saved.   850
It is enough for me that she desires it.

MARQUIS. Then there is not a moment to be lost;
The Cabinet has named the Governor—
It is Duke Alba.

CARLOS.   But it shall not be.
I will demand an audience tomorrow,
And ask my father for the post myself.
I never asked for anything before,
I have not dared; this he cannot refuse.
He hates to have me near him in Madrid,
He will be glad to send me far away!   860

Further, I must confess to you, Roderigo,
I hope for more—perhaps I will succeed,
By facing him, and making him face me,
In winning back the grace I had before.
For he has never heard the voice of nature—
And I must try to make it speak through me,
And we will see what Carlos can achieve!

MARQUIS. Now I hear Carlos, now he is himself!

SCENE VIII

[COUNT LERMA, CARLOS, VON POSA.]

LERMA. Just now the monarch left Aranjuez.
I have the order—

CARLOS.   Very well, Count Lerma,   870
I will catch up with him.

MARQUIS [*makes to leave, with some ceremony*].
                        That is, I take it,
All that your Highness needs from me at present?

CARLOS. Indeed, Chevalier. May heaven bless you
With a safe journey. I will ask you more,
When we next meet, about the Netherlands.
                        [*To* LERMA *who still waits*
I will be with you.

SCENE IX

[CARLOS, MARQUIS.]

CARLOS.   Did I play my part?
You played yours well. But we must only act
When we are with another. We are brothers.
The pantomime of rank shall be forbidden
From this day on, when we are on our own.   880
Imagine we are at a masquerade,

And you have chosen for no earthly reason
To be a slave, and I to be a king.
As long as we are in the carnival
Our lie must stand, and we must honour it
Like courtly clowns with comic earnestness,
To keep the sweet illusion unimpaired—
But I can smile at you through my disguise,
And you can nudge me when you pass me by.

MARQUIS. This dream is sweet, but will it last for ever?   890
And is my Karl so true as to defy
The mad attractions of omnipotence?
The hardest test of all is yet to come—
I have to warn you—when this heroism
Will surely founder in a greater challenge.
Don Philip dies. The highest earthly power
Falls to his son—a bottomless abyss
Opens between him and the race of men;
One day you are yourself, the next a god,
Free of all weaknesses—eternity   900
Fills you with silent duty—humankind,
Today a venerable word to you,
Falls to its knees and creeps around your shrine;
Your agony destroys your sympathy,
Lust of the flesh extinguishes your virtue;
Peru sends gold to please your mindlessness,
The court hires demons to supply your sins—
You fall asleep, outwitted by your slaves,
In a drunk heaven woven by their hands—
Your godhead is as lasting as your dream,   910
And woe betide the madman who awakes you!
And what can weak Roderigo do? His friendship
Is brave and true—your brainsick Majesty
Cannot abide the brightness of its ray—
You would not bear your citizen's defiance,
I could not bear the pride of Majesty.

CARLOS. This picture of a king is horrible,
But true, Roderigo. But it was their lust
That opened former kings to wickedness.

I am a youth of twenty-three and pure,   920
I have preserved what thousands threw away,
Abandoning themselves to shamelessness—
The spirit's better part, the strength of manhood.
And that will be my character as ruler.
And what could drag you from my heart, my friend,
When women cannot do it?

MARQUIS.   I will do it.
How will I love you as I truly should
When I will have to fear you?

CARLOS.   Never fear me.
What can I give to you? Do you have passions
The throne might help you slake? Does gold excite you?
You are a richer subject in yourself   931
Than I will ever be as king—not even
Honour can tempt you; when you were a youth
You drained that barrel dry, you shattered it.
Which of us is the debtor of the other,
And which the creditor? You do not answer?
You tremble—is temptation in your veins,
Have you forgotten who you are?

MARQUIS.   Well then,
My doubts were wrong. Here, take my hand—

CARLOS.   For ever?

MARQUIS. For ever, and with the courage of that word.   940

CARLOS. Will it be given to me as the King
As warmly as it is to the Infante?

MARQUIS. I swear it.

CARLOS.   And when flattery surrounds
My unguarded heart, and when these eyes forget
To cry the tears they would have cried before,
And when these ears are closed against all cries,
Will you, a fearless watchman of my virtue,
Seize me with all your strength and call my soul
By its true name, to show me what I am?

MARQUIS. Yes.

CARLOS.   And once more I ask you—be my brother!
  This brotherly address was never mine,   951
  And I have always envied men like you
  The privilege of ease, of intimacy;
  The sweet conception of equality
  Tempts and torments me—do not interrupt,
  I guess precisely what you wish to say,
  This gift is very trivial to you,
  But for a King's son it is much to ask.

MARQUIS. Your brother!

CARLOS.   There is nothing now to fear.
  To the King! You are my second, lead me out   960
  To single combat with my century.

                                       [*Exeunt*

ACT TWO

SCENE I

[KING PHILIP *beneath a throne canopy.* DUKE OF
ALBA, *wearing a helmet, standing some distance away
from the* KING. DON CARLOS.]

CARLOS. The realm has precedence. And I will gladly
  Give place before the minister. He speaks
  For Spain—I am the young son of the house.
                              [*He steps back with a bow*

KING. The Duke will stay while the Infante speaks.

CARLOS [*turning to* ALBA]. Then I must ask your generosity
  To make a present of my father to me;
  You know a child has many heartfelt things,
  Unsuitable for other ears to hear,
  To tell his father, Duke. He will be free.
  The King will not be stolen from your heart,—   10
  I only want my father for an hour.

KING. This is my friend.

CARLOS.   And may I not suspect
  The Duke of friendship with myself as well?

KING. When have you ever earned it? I dislike
  Those sons who win their fathers' friends from them.

CARLOS. How can the Duke of Alba's honour bear
  To be a witness to this spectacle?
  By God I would not damn myself to stand,
  Unasked, between a father and his son,
  To play the part of the importunate,   20
  Listening shamelessly, expressionless,
  If I could get a diadem for it.

KING [*leaves his seat with an angry look at the* PRINCE].
  Duke, you may leave. Wait in the cabinet,
  Until I call you.

SCENE II

[*The* KING, DON CARLOS.]

CARLOS [*as soon as the* DUKE *has left the room,* CARLOS *goes*
towards the KING *and falls on his knees in front of him*
in an expression of the greatest emotion].
                              Now you are my father,
Now once again—and for this honour thank you!
Give me your hand, my father—oh sweet day,
Your child has been denied the happiness
Of kisses such as these for far too long.
What did I do, my father, may I know?
Why has your heart for so long kept me out?   30

KING. Infante, your deceit is unconvincing;
It is distasteful to me, spare me it.

CARLOS. I hear the voices of your courtiers there,
And it is not true, God! all is not true
That priests may say, my father, or their creatures—
I am not evil, youth is my mistake,
And indiscretion all my wickedness;
I am not evil, truly not; although
Stormwaves of trouble often rush through me,
My heart is good.

KING.   I know your heart is pure,   40
Pure in your prayers.

CARLOS.   The time is now or never.
We are alone. The anxious barrier
Of etiquette must vanish from between us—
This is the moment—I can feel the light
Of hope arising in me, and the sweetness
Of what could be floods through my heart like summer;
Heaven looks on, ranks of rejoicing angels
Bend their heads down—the Holy Trinity
Is awestruck by the spectacle—my father!
Reconciliation!

                              [*He falls at his feet*

KING.   Stand up! Leave!   50

CARLOS. Reconciliation!

KING [*tries to pull himself free*].
                         This charade
  I find a little much—

CARLOS.   A little much
  That your son loves you?

KING.   Now at last the tears.
  Disgraceful sight! Leave me! Get out of here!

CARLOS. Now or never! Reconciliation,
  Father!

KING.   Get out of here! Return to me
  In deep disgrace, defeated in my wars,
  And I shall spread my arms to take you in,
  But as you are I spurn you. Cowardice
  Alone desires this shameful baptism—   60
  He who shall never blush for failed endeavours
  Shall blush for having never tried, forever!

CARLOS. Through what dire oversight has this strange creature
  Wandered into the world? Tears are the sign
  By which we know that we are human, always.
  The man who never weeps is not of woman.
  Oh force the eyes that never wept to cry,
  Or else too late they must make up for it,
  And that will be a terrifying hour.

KING. And do you think the beauty of your words   70
  Can ease the burden of my doubts?

CARLOS.   Your doubts?
  These are the clouds I mean to chase away,
  And I will hang upon my father's heart
  And tear with all my might until the case
  Of rock-hard doubt around it breaks in pieces.
  Where are the men who banished me from there,
  From your goodwill? What did the wise monk bid
  The father for the son? What compensation

Will Alba pay you for a childless life
Lived for no reason? Is it love you want?   80
I am a fresher and more healthful spring
Than those decrepit and unflowing ones
That Philip's gold alone inspires—

KING.   Enough!
Show them respect. The men you dare to scorn
Are the well-trusted servants of my will,
And you will honour them.

CARLOS.   Not any more.
I know what I am worth. Karl can achieve
As much as Alba—Karl can do much more.
Why should the mercenary care what fate
Consumes the kingdom he will never own?   90
Why should he grieve when Philip grows grey-haired?
Your Carlos would have loved you. I feel dread
When I consider that you are alone,
Abandoned here in power.

KING [*his attention caught by the word, he stands contemplative and turned in on himself*].
                             Yes, alone.

CARLOS [*goes towards him with vivacity and warmth*].
You were before. Not now. Hate me no more,
I will love you so childishly and well,
Only hate me no more. It is so sweet
And a bewitchment when we feel ourselves
Exalted by another's grace, observing
Our joy contained in someone else's laughter,   100
Our sorrow moving someone else's tears.
It is so beautiful and glorious
To go with a beloved son, hand in hand,
Back down the vivid road to your young days
To live them through by sympathy again;
It is so sweet and noble to continue,
Immortal in the virtue of your child,
Bountiful to eternity! So lovely
To sow what a beloved son will gather,

Harvesting what will grow back richer still;   110
To think how high the fire of his thanks will climb!
Your monks were wise to keep you in the dark
About this earthly paradise.

KING [*not unmoved*].   My son,
You speak against yourself when you describe
A happiness you never offered me.

CARLOS. Let the Almighty judge that. It was you,
You who excluded me, both from your heart
And from the royal power—till today.
And tell me, father, was that good or wise?
I was a stranger here until today,   120
The heir to Spain in his own fatherland,
Imprisoned in the land that I would rule.
Was that correct or kind? I have blushed often,
Often, my father, hung my head in shame,
To learn the latest news from Aranjuez
From foreign emissaries or pamphleteers!

KING. The blood runs through you too impetuously.
You only know how to destroy.

CARLOS.   Then father,
Give me something to destroy. No wonder
The blood runs through me too impetuously,   130
For I am twenty-three and have done nothing
To win immortal fame, but now my calling
To be a king beats like a creditor
To drag me from my slumber and to force me
To pay the debt of wasted hours to heaven—
The great and sacred moment has arrived
When God at last demands the interest
Made from the talent that he gave to me.
My forebears and the story of the world
Both call me with their fame, and reputation   140
Drums like thunder—now the time has come
When I must throw the gates of glory open,
My King—so may I dare to ask the wish
That brought me here?

KING.   Another wish? What is it?

CARLOS. The news of the rebellion in Brabant*
　　Worsens each day. The rebels are determined
　　And must be met with courage and with cunning.
　　To overcome the fury of the rabble,
　　The Duke will lead an army into Flanders,
　　With royal powers, granted by the monarch—   150
　　This post is full of honour to my mind,
　　What better engine could there ever be
　　To lift your son into the hall of fame?
　　And I am not afraid to stake my life
　　On my belief in Flanders—

KING.   You are dreaming.
　　This post demands a man and not a youth.

CARLOS. I know it needs a man, it needs a human,
　　Which is the one thing Alba cannot be.

KING. Terror is the answer to rebellion.
　　Kindness would be insane. You are soft-hearted,   160
　　Whereas the Duke is feared. Take back your wish.

CARLOS. Send me to Flanders with the army, father,
　　Gamble on my soft soul—my name will fly
　　Before my flags—the Prince of Spain is coming!
　　And conquer what the hangmen of the Duke
　　Can only lay to waste. Upon my knees,
　　I beg you, save me, father, grant me this,
　　The first request that I have ever made;
　　Trust me with Flanders.

KING [looking at the INFANTE with a piercing expression].
　　　　　　　　　　　　　And with Flanders trust
　　My finest army to your lust for power—   170
　　Present my killer with a dagger?

CARLOS.   God!
　　Has nothing changed, and has this holy hour,
　　So long awaited, brought me only this?
　　　　　[After some reflection and with softened severity

Oh answer me more kindly—let me go
But not like this! This was an evil answer,
I wish to leave but not so sick at heart.
Treat me with honour, for my need is great,
And I can only make one last great effort—
I cannot think it, it destroys my reason
And makes me like a child, that you deny me   180
Everything, everything, everything, everything.
Now let me go, my just request denied;
My sweet anticipations taunt me now,
And so I leave your sight. Your Duke of Alba
And your Domingo will ascend in glory
The throne where now your child wept in the dust.
The courtiers in their crowds and the grandees
Who hover in the shadows, and the orders
Of monks made pale by their own sins, were witness
When you, with all due show and ceremony,   190
Granted this audience. Oh do not shame me!
The wound will be my death if you disgrace me,
And sacrifice me to the court's derision—
If strangers boast of favours from the King
While Carlos is denied his wish. But save me,
Show that you mean to honour me; despatch me
To Flanders with the army.

KING.   Repetition
Will win you only anger. Speak no more!

CARLOS. I risk your disesteem, and one last time
I beg you—give me Flanders to command.   200
I must and shall leave Spain. While I am here
I breathe as if the hangman stood by me—
The sky above Madrid is made of lead,
It is as if I knew about a murder.
Only a sudden change of sky can help me,
If you desire at all to save me, send me
To Flanders now, without delay!

KING [*with forced informality*].   Such illness
As you are suffering, requires great care.

You should be watched by doctors constantly.
You stay in Spain. The Duke shall go to Flanders.   210

CARLOS [*beside himself*]. Oh gather round me you good
    spirits—

KING.   Silence!
What do you mean by these expressions?

CARLOS.   Father,
    Is this decision never to be changed?

KING. It was the King that made it.

CARLOS.   It is over.
                    [*Exit in high emotion*

SCENE III

[*The* KING *remains standing for awhile, lost in dark
    thought. Eventually he walks a few steps up and
    down the hall.* ALBA *approaches meekly.*]

KING. The order for the army to depart
May come at any hour. Hold yourself ready.

ALBA. All preparations have been made, your Highness.

KING. Your signed authority lies sealed already
In cabinet. Meanwhile the Queen desires you
To take your leave of her. When you have done so   220
Proceed to bid farewell to the Infante.

ALBA. I saw him leave this chamber as I entered,
With the appearance of a man enraged.
Also your Royal Majesty is moved,
It seems to me, and not yourself at all.
Perhaps the matter of your conversation?

KING [*after pacing up and down*]. It was the Duke of Alba.
                    [*The* KING *stops in front of the* DUKE, *his eyes
                    fixed on him, and says darkly*
                                        That he hates

My councillors I love to hear. However,
I hate to hear that he despises them.
                    [ALBA *turns pale and moves to interject*
Make no reply now. But you are permitted   230
To reconcile yourself with him.

ALBA.   Sir!

KING.   Tell me,
Who was it I believed in the beginning
About my son's infernal plots against me?
I heard you then and never him. I wish
To test him now, to risk that. From now on
Carlos will be much closer to me. Go.
                [*The* KING *goes into the cabinet. Exit* ALBA
                through a different door

SCENE IV

[*An antechamber before the* QUEEN's *room.* DON
CARLOS *enters through the central door in
conversation with a* PAGE BOY. *The court attendants
who are in the antechamber disperse to the adjoining
rooms at his arrival.*]

CARLOS. A letter to me? And a key inside—
Delivered with such dreadful secrecy—
Come closer, now who gave you this?

PAGE.   The lady
Made me take note that she would rather be   240
Guessed than described.

CARLOS.   The lady—what?—and how?
Who are you anyway?

PAGE.   A noble boy
Belonging to her Majesty the Queen.

CARLOS [*shocked, he walks towards the boy and presses his
    hand to his mouth*].

Silence! No more! You have been sent by death.

> [*Hastily he breaks the seal and steps to the outermost end of the hall in order to read the letter. In the meantime the* DUKE OF ALBA *enters and goes past into the* QUEEN's *room, without being noticed by* CARLOS. CARLOS *begins to quiver and to blush, speechless for some time, his eyes rooted to the letter. Eventually he turns to the* PAGE BOY]

She gave you this herself?

PAGE.   With her own hand.

CARLOS. She gave you this herself? You play with me!
But I have never seen her handwriting,
I must believe you—if you swear to God!
If you were lying, say so openly,
And end this trickery.

PAGE.   What trickery?   250

CARLOS [*looks again at the letter and then considers the* PAGE BOY *with a doubtful, searching expression. After he has walked through the hall*]. Your parents are alive, yes?
Does your father
Honour the king, is he a son of Spain?

PAGE. My father fell in battle at St Quentin,*
He was a colonel in the cavalry
Serving Savoy, Alonzo, Duke Henarez.*

CARLOS [*takes him by the hand and looks at him meaningfully*].
Did you receive this letter from the King?

PAGE [*hurt*]. How have I earned this accusation, Prince?

CARLOS [*reads the letter*]. 'This is the key that will allow the holder
Into the back rooms of the Queen's pavilion.
The outermost of these conceals a chamber,   260
Within whose walls no spy has ever wandered.
Love can be uttered unrestrainedly,
And need no longer code its language there—

The fearful one will have a hearing there,
And the long sufferer a fair reward.'
This is no dream, and no delirium,
This is my right arm, this my sword of steel,
And these are words on paper—this is true,
I am beloved—I am—yes—I am loved!
> [*He storms through the room beside himself, his
> arms in the air*

PAGE. Come, let us go then, I will lead the way.   270

CARLOS. First let me pull myself together. See,
I tremble with the shock of happiness!
Even my greatest hopes were not this high!
Show me the man who can become a god
Effortlessly! What am I? And what was I?
This is a new sky, this is a new sun,
And I forget the way they were! She loves me!

PAGE [*moves to lead him away*]. Prince, Prince, you must not
say this here—remember.

CARLOS [*gripped by a sudden petrification*]. The King! My
Father!
> [*He lets his arms fall to his sides again and looks
> around self-consciously, beginning to collect
> himself*
> That is terrible.
Yes, you are very right, my friend. I thank you.   280
I think I was not quite myself just then.
That I must keep such happiness in silence,
Walled up inside, is an abomination.
> [*Takes the boy by the hand and leads him to one
> side*
What you have seen and what you have not seen
Must die and sink inside you like a coffin.
But leave me now. I go to meet myself.
No one must find us here. Go.
> [*The PAGE makes to leave*
> One thing more.

[CARLOS *lays a hand on the boy's shoulder and*
looks into his face seriously and solemnly

The secret that you bear is terrible,
And like strong poisons it may break its bowl—
Guard your expressions well, forbid your head   290
Ever to ask your heart what it remembers;
You are the trumpet that transmits a note
But never hears it—as you are a child,
So you must seem, and always laugh and play:
How wise the letter-writer was to choose
So young and innocent a messenger;
The King will not suspect his vipers here.

PAGE. And I am very proud to know myself
One secret richer than the King of Spain.

CARLOS. Fool, that is what should make you shake with fear.
If ever after this we meet in public,   301
Be shy, and act as if you do not know me,
Do not be forced by vanity to wave,
To show the world you are the Prince's friend.
My favour is an axe to flatterers,
It is a sin to know me. In the future,
Do not use words if you must speak to me,
Trust nothing to your lips, do not send news
With common thoughts along the open road;
Speak with your fingers or your eyelashes,   310
And I will hear by blinking and not answer.
The air we breathe, the light that wraps us round,
Are Philip's spies—he pays the walls to stand.
Someone is coming.
          [*The door to the* QUEEN's *room is opened and*
              ALBA *comes out*
                    We will meet again!

PAGE. My Prince! I only hope you find the room!
                                                        [*Exit*

CARLOS. It is the Duke. Yes, no, but, very well
I have to find that room.

SCENE V

[DON CARLOS, *the* DUKE OF ALBA.]

ALBA [*steps into his path*]. Great Prince, two words.

CARLOS. Of course! Why not? Another time, of course.
                          [*He makes to leave*

ALBA. I must agree, this place is not the best.
  Perhaps your Royal Highness would prefer   320
  To grant the favour of an audience
  In your own room?

CARLOS.   No, here. But please be brief.

ALBA. What really brought me here was the desire
  To thank your Highness.

CARLOS.   Thank me? To thank me?
  What could the Duke of Alba thank me for?

ALBA. No sooner had you left the Monarch's presence
  Than I was ordered to depart for Brussels.

CARLOS. For Brussels! Ah!

ALBA.   What can I owe this to
  But your most gracious intercession, Prince?

CARLOS. My intercession? No. Oh, truly not.   330
  You have to travel—God be with you, sir.

ALBA. Can that be all? It seems so very strange.
  Surely your Highness has some orders for me
  To take to Flanders?

CARLOS.   I am not so sure.

ALBA. And yet a while ago it seemed that country
  Required your personal attention, Prince.

CARLOS. That is correct—but things have changed since then.
  It is quite right, however, very proper.

ALBA. I listen with astonishment, my Prince.

CARLOS. You are a great commander, all confess.   340
   Envy itself would have to say as much.
   I am a young man, ask the King, he knows,
   And he is absolutely right of course.
   I understand and I am satisfied,
   So let that be an end of it. Farewell!
   I cannot now, as you too clearly see—
   I am a touch preoccupied—the rest,
   Leave to tomorrow, or another time,
   We will conclude on your return from Brussels.

ALBA. What?

CARLOS [*after a silence sees that the* DUKE *is still there*].
               You are leaving in a gentle season,   350
   Via Milan, through Lotharingia,
   And Burgundy and Germany—yes, no,*
   Yes, Germany—I think they know you there!
   Now it is April—May, June, and July,
   You will see Brussels by the very latest
   In early August. And I have no doubt
   That we will soon have news of your success.
   You never fail to vindicate our faith.*

ALBA. But can I do so when that faith is faint?

CARLOS [*after a silence, with dignity and pride*].
   You have good reasons to be hurt, good Duke.   360
   I own I did not scruple to employ
   The kind of weapons you could not reply to.

ALBA. I could not?

CARLOS [*stretches out his hand*].
               Now, farewell. It is a pity
   That I am not at present blessed with leisure
   To duel with the Duke till dawn. Farewell,
   Another time—

ALBA.   Prince, you misunderstand me.
  You act towards me as you see yourself
  Some twenty years from now. But I see you
  Just as you were that long ago.

CARLOS.   Indeed?

ALBA. And when I think of that I have to wonder   370
  How many nights now used and lost to time,
  Beside the beauty of the Portuguese,*
  The King's dead wife, your mother, he would give,
  To make an arm like this to give the crown.
  He should remember that a monarchy
  Is harder to assemble than a monarch—
  To give the world a king is very simple
  To give the King a world is not.

CARLOS.   Correct.
  And yet, Duke Alba, you—

ALBA.   And how much blood,
  The blood of your race, has to flow in pain   380
  To make a drop of yours worth anything.

CARLOS. Too true, by God, and very neatly put.
  This is the argument of work and merit
  Against good fortune. But be brief, Duke Alba,
  What do you wish to say to me exactly?

ALBA. Cursed be his gentle Highness in his cradle,
  Who mocks his nurse. It must be sweet to lie
  On the deep cushion of our victories
  And sleep in comfort. Pearls gleam on the crown,
  But not the wounds by which those pearls were won.   390
  This sword has written Spanish laws for strangers,
  And it has blazed before crusades and scarred
  Black furrows for the seeds of true belief
  To thrive in, in the blood of these domains.
  God judges heaven but I judge the earth.

CARLOS. God or the Devil, you were his right arm,
  Whichever one it was, I know that well.
  But now no more, I beg, your words revive
  Memories I would rather shelter from.
  My father's will is, as I said, my own.   400
  I know my father needs a Duke of Alba,
  And that the Duke is you is his misfortune.
  Are you a great man? It is possible,
  Sometimes I very nearly think you are.
  I only fear you come before your time,
  Long, long before; Duke Alba should appear
  When history is grinding to its end,
  When viciousness has worn out heaven's patience,
  When the rich harvest of the wicked stands
  Tall for the blade of an accomplished reaper.   410
  You are too soon, that time has not yet come,
  O God, my paradise on earth, my Flanders!
  But let that rest, that is another matter.
  I hear that you are wisely taking with you
  A large supply of signed death sentences,
  Whose names are blank. I praise you for your foresight.
  Thus burdensome reflection is pre-empted.
  O father, now I fully understand,
  I thought you hard because you would not set me
  The kind of task that suits the Duke of Alba—   420
  But now I see it was your love that spared me.

ALBA. Prince, I have not deserved this rancour.

CARLOS [flaring up].   What?

ALBA. Your status shields you from the consequence.

CARLOS [reaches for his sword].
  This calls for blood—see, Duke, my sword is out.

ALBA [coldly]. For what?

CARLOS [aggressively].   To run you through.

ALBA.   Well then—
                  [Draws his sword. They fight

SCENE VI

[*The* QUEEN, DON CARLOS, ALBA.]

QUEEN [*who comes out of her room, horrified*].
                                        What? Fighting!
                [*To the* PRINCE *indignantly and with a
                commanding voice*
No! Carlos, stop!

CARLOS [*beside himself at the sight of the* QUEEN, *lets his arm
    fall, stands motionless, and without sensation, then rushes
    to the* DUKE *and kisses him*].
                    Duke! Reconciliation!
Let us forgive each other!
                [*He throws himself silently at the* QUEEN's *feet,
                then stands up quickly and rushes away
                uncomposed*

ALBA [*standing utterly astonished*].
                                That is strange—
By heaven, that is very strange.—

QUEEN [*stands for a few moments disquieted and doubtful,
    then goes slowly back to her room. At the door she turns
    round again*].
                            Duke Alba!
                [*The* DUKE *follows her into her room*

SCENE VII

[*The chamber of* PRINCESS EBOLI. *The* PRINCESS,
*dressed beautifully but simply, plays the lute and
sings. The* QUEEN's *PAGE BOY enters.*]

EBOLI [*jumps up quickly*]. He comes!

PAGE [*zealously*].   Are you alone? How can it be?
I would have thought he would be here by now.   430

EBOLI. He wants to see me then. It is decided.

PAGE. He follows on my heels. O gracious Lady,
   You are so loved, loved more than anyone
   Has ever been or ever will be loved!
   What I have seen!

EBOLI [*pulls him towards her impatiently*].
                    What? Tell me quickly then.
   You spoke with him? What did he say? Tell me!
   How did he act? What were the words he used?
   Did he seem shy? Or was he horrified?
   And did he guess who sent the key? Oh speak!
   He did not guess at all—or guessed another—   440
   Well right or wrong? Can you not answer me?
   O Lord, you never were this slow before,
   You never were so maddening and wooden!

PAGE. Well if you let me speak I will, my Lady—
   I handed him the letter and the key
   In the Queen's antechamber—and he stood
   And stared at me as I pronounced the words
   'A Lady sent me.'

EBOLI.   Stared? He was astonished?
   Good, that was cautious! Come now, tell me more.

PAGE. I would have spoken, but his face turned pale,   450
   He tore the letter from my hand and glared,
   And said, with passion, 'I know everything,'
   And then began to tremble horribly—

EBOLI. Prince Carlos said that he knows everything?

PAGE. And asked me four times, was it really you
   Who sent the letter, was it you yourself?

EBOLI. Really myself? And did he say my name?

PAGE. Your name—no, no, he never said your name
   He said that spies were always creeping near
   To gather gossip for the King.

EBOLI.   He said that?   460

PAGE. And that the King would be extremely glad
  To have this letter in his hand.

EBOLI [*bewildered*].   The King?
  Are you quite certain that he said the King?
  Was that the actual word he used?

PAGE.   It was!
  He said the letter was a dreadful secret.
  And warned me to be careful of my speech
  And my expressions, as the slightest hint
  Can make the king suspicious.

EBOLI [*after recollection, full of amazement*].
                              Yes, it fits.
  How can it be? Carlos knows everything!
  Wherever did he get that information?   470
  But what can see so far as love's hawk eyes?
  But tell me more—when he had read the letter—

PAGE. The letter held such happiness, he said,
  That he could do no more than stand and tremble,
  And he had never dared to dream of this,
  But then unhappily the Duke appeared.

EBOLI. What in the world was Alba doing there?
  But never mind—what keeps the Prince from me?
  You were misled you see, you were mistaken,
  How full of bliss he would have been by now,   480
  How glad I could have made him in the time
  It took for you to say he wants to be.

PAGE. I am afraid the Duke—

EBOLI.   The Duke again!
  What does that man of valour want with me
  And my desire for peaceful happiness?
  The Prince can make him stand or make him go—
  Who in the world can disobey him? Really!
  Carlos, it seems, is no more swift to act

Once love is spoken, than he is to speak.
He does not know what minutes mean. But hush!   490
Someone is coming. It is Carlos! Go! [PAGE *runs out*]
Where is my lute? I must be calm and ready—
My song shall be the Prince's hunting cry.

SCENE VIII

[*The* PRINCESS *and soon after* DON CARLOS. *The*
PRINCESS *throws herself on to the ottoman and starts
playing her lute.*]

CARLOS [*bursts in and stands still as if struck by thunder*].
Good God! Where am I?

EBOLI [*drops the lute and comes towards him*].
                              Prince? Yes, it is you.

CARLOS. Where am I? This is madness, trickery—
This is the wrong room—

EBOLI.   Karl knows very well
The rooms where ladies can be found alone—
He notices these things.

CARLOS.   Princess, forgive me—
The door was open—

EBOLI.   How can this be true?
The door was locked, I turned the key myself.   500

CARLOS. So you believe, but how can you be sure?
You are mistaken. Yes, you wish you had,
That I admit, that I believe—and yet!
In truth it was not locked! I heard a lute—
Someone was playing—was it not a lute?
                              [*Looks around doubtfully*
Yes—there it is—that is what brought me here;
I love the lute, God knows, I love it madly,
More than you can imagine—to distraction!
I was all ears, I followed the sweet sound

To gaze into the eyes of the musician   510
Whose sweeping raptures moved me with such power.

EBOLI. A most bewitching curiosity—
Which was soon satisfied, I might point out.
                              [*After a pause, with significance*
Oh, but I should exalt the humble man
Who ties himself in such a web of lies
To save a woman from embarrassment.

CARLOS [*innocently*]. I only worsen what I mean to mend.
Princess, release me from this subterfuge—
It founders, and it will not bear me up.
You came in here to leave the world outside,   520
To listen to the quiet of your heart,
To tell the room your dreams, unheard by men—
Your calm is shattered utterly by me,
I am disaster's finest heir, forgive me,
And so I hasten to remove myself.

                                        [*Makes to leave*

EBOLI [*surprised and embarrassed, but soon composed again*].
Prince, that was cruel.

CARLOS.   Lady, I know well
What that look, in this chamber, signifies—
The virtuous confusion in your face
Moves me to honour. Woe betide the man
Who takes advantage of a woman's blush;   530
I die when women are confused by me.

EBOLI. Can this be true? Virtue beyond compare
For a young man whose father is the King.
Now I can ask you openly to stay—
Prince, now I beg you not to go, such goodness
Calms every girl's misgivings. Do you know,
What I was playing when your sudden entrance
Frightened me, was my favourite aria.
            [*She leads him to the sofa and takes up the lute
            again*

Now I will have to start again, Prince Carlos.
I sentence you to listen while I play.   540

CARLOS [*sits, not without reluctance, next to the* PRINCESS].
A punishment as pleasing as the crime.
And what I heard delighted me so much
That I could gladly hear it—twice again.

EBOLI. Prince, did you hear the whole of it? Oh dreadful!
I think it spoke of love.

CARLOS.   Of happy love.
Those words are strong and sweet and full of light,
And they were sung by one as fine as them,
But beauty can depart from truth, I think.

EBOLI. You think me false in my performance, Prince?

CARLOS. I think that truth will find itself excluded   550
When Carlos talk with Eboli of love.
                    [*The* PRINCESS *hesitates. He notices it and
                        continues with a lighthearted gallantry*
Look at this face as lovely as a rose;
Who could believe that you could ever love?
What chance is there that you could sigh unheard?
Yet only unrequited love can live.

EBOLI [*with the same jollity as before*].
Oh hush! That is so sad—but do you see,
This fate is yours above all other men,
And troubles you especially today.
                    [*Takes him by the hand with ingratiating interest*
You are unhappy, Noble Prince, you pine,
Yet by great heaven, how can it be so?   560
Why suffer when a happier vocation
Calls you so clearly—when the qualities
The generosity of nature lent you
Give you the right to all the joys on earth?
You—you are greater than a great King's son,
You—so much more—already in the cradle
Laden with gifts, so many and so bright
They doomed your status to obscurity.

Your goodness has corrupted all the judges
Of the stern court of women, who decide   570
Exclusively who is and is not worthy
Of fame, beyond appeal, among you men.
You, who have conquered where you merely looked,
You, who enrapture when you love a little,
Could play with heavens if you loved indeed,
For the inheritance of gods is yours.
Should he whom nature's artistry adorns
With happinesses few have ever had,
Be miserable in himself? O Heaven,
That you who gave him every cause for joy,   580
Should merely fail to add the gift of eyes
With which he might observe his own good fortune.

CARLOS [*who has all this time been sunk, distractedly, deep in
    thought, is brought suddenly to his senses by the silence,
    and starts up*]. Beyond compare! Superb! My Lady, please,
Sing me that part again.

EBOLI [*looks at him in astonishment*].
                         Where were you, Carlos,
While I was speaking then?

CARLOS [*jumps up*].   I thank you, Lady,
But I must go. You warned me just in time.
I must go now.

EBOLI [*holds him back*].
                Where to?

CARLOS [*in terrible trepidation*].
                         Away from here,
Into the clear air. Princess, let me go,
The world is turning into flames around me—   589

EBOLI. What is the matter? Why this strange behaviour?
            [CARLOS *stands still and becomes pensive. She
            takes the opportunity to pull him down on
            to the sofa*
Dear Karl, you are in need of peace—sit by me,
Be still, your blood is in an uproar now,

Shake off these sad delusions. To be honest,
Could your heart answer if your head should ask it,
In all sincerity, to name its trouble?
And if it could, is there not one, not one,
Of all the Knights and Ladies in this court,
Who could restore you—who could understand you?
Not one who could be worthy of that honour?

CARLOS [*quickly and without thinking*].
Perhaps the Princess Eboli.

EBOLI.   Oh really?   600

CARLOS. Write me a letter, praise me to my father,
   Do it! They say you have great influence!

EBOLI. Who says so? (So it was your jealousy
   Of that that made you curb your feelings for me!)

CARLOS. Doubtless the rumour is abroad already—
   I had a sudden itching to be gone,
   To try and win some glory in Brabant;
   My father has forbidden it; he feels
   That warfare may affect my singing voice.

EBOLI. Carlos, you play me false. Come now, admit it,   610
   Your mind is writhing like a bitten snake
   To find a means to get away from me—
   Look at me, hypocrite, look in my eyes!
   Could he who only dreams of valour, could he,
   I wonder, ever also sink so low
   As to steal ribbons dropped by accident
   By ladies—snatch them greedily and keep them,
   My Prince, forgive me—
            [*she whisks away his ruff and a hidden ribbon
               with a deft movement of her fingers
                        secretly and dearly?*

CARLOS [*steps back alienated*]. Princess, this is too much, I
      am betrayed;
   Nothing in hell or earth is hidden from you,   620
   You are in league with phantoms and with demons.

EBOLI. Carlos, you are surprised by this of all things?
  What shall the wager be, come, question me,
  I shall replenish your forgetfulness
  With stories, small events, slight histories;
  If I can sense the changes of a mood,
  And see a word half-spoken in the air,
  And glimpse a smile as sadness drops on it,
  If even gestures that escape from you
  When you are deep in thought and unaware,   630
  Do not escape me, you will know for sure
  That I see clearly what you want me to.

CARLOS. Well, it is dangerous indeed, dear Lady,
  But I will risk the wager—you propose
  To dig up secrets buried in my heart
  Which I am unaware of?

EBOLI.   Are you though?
  Remember better, Prince. Look all around,
  This is no chamber of her Majesty's
  With nothing but the speech of the observed
  For entertainment. Are you so amazed?   640
  You are all blushes suddenly. Of course,
  The horror of the thought of anyone
  Being so vicious as to spy on Carlos—
  What rank abandonment of all good taste!
  Who saw you when you left your dancing partner,
  The Queen, at the last ball, and forced yourself
  Into the couple dancing next to you,
  Leaving her Majesty to stand amazed,
  While you swept off the Princess Eboli?
  An act of impoliteness which the King,   650
  Arriving at that moment, also saw!

CARLOS [*with an ironic smile*]. The King himself? But hon-
    estly, my Lady,
  Of course it was not meant for him.

EBOLI.   Of course.
  Oh, and that sweet performance in the chapel,
  Which doubtless Carlos has himself forgotten;

You lay absorbed and motionless in prayer,
Stretched out beneath the Holy Virgin's feet,
When suddenly—and this was not your fault,
You heard the rustle of my dress behind you;
And then Don Philip's fearless son began   660
To tremble like a questioned heretic;
The prayer upon his pale lips, poisoned, died,
And in the fervour of religious fear,
Movingly improvised, if I may say so,
He gripped the icy fingers of God's mother,
And cried a storm of tears upon the marble.

CARLOS. You do me an injustice. They were pious.

EBOLI. Well, something else then, Prince. It was, of course,
Only the fear of losing which inspired
The wonderful dexterity with which,   670
Whilst playing rummy with the Queen and I,
Carlos removed my glove.
                    [CARLOS *jumps up in consternation*
                         But played it back,
Being a level fellow, as a card.

CARLOS. Oh God, oh heaven, what did I do then?

EBOLI. Nothing, I hope, that you would wish undone.
How very happily I was surprised,
To find a little letter in my hand,
Which you had sweetly hidden in the glove;
It was the most enchanting poem, Prince,
That I have ever—

CARLOS [*quickly interrupting her*].
                         It was poetry!   680
My mind is always blowing out these bubbles,
Odd things, that burst the moment they are born.
It was no more than that. No more of it.

EBOLI [*moving away from him in astonishment and contem-
    plating him awhile from a distance*].
I am exhausted. All I say is true,
And yet this snake-smooth stranger makes it lies.
                         [*She is silent for a moment*

And so—? Men's pride is bigger than a mountain,
And what if, simply to increase delight,
He fishes for me with this innocence?
>   [*She approaches the prince again and looks*
>   *doubtfully at him*

Prince, you must answer me directly now.
I stand before a secret locked by magic,   690
And all my keys have failed me shamefully.

CARLOS. I stand there also.

EBOLI [*she leaves him quickly, then walks a few times up and
    down the chamber, seeming to be considering something
    important. Eventually, after a long pause, solemnly*].
>   So it must be now.

Now I must speak at last and once for all.
I choose you for my judge. You are a Lord,
A Knight, a man, a very noble being.
I put my trust in you—Prince, rescue me,
For I am all alone. Take up my cry!
>   [*The* PRINCE *moves closer with expectant,*
>   *sympathetic astonishment*

An insolent adherent of the King,
Ruy Gomez, Earl of Silva, claims my hand.
The King desires it and the deal is made.   700
I am his creature's property.

CARLOS [*deeply stirred*].   What? Sold?
You have been sold, my Lady! Once again
The famous merchant of the South prevails.*

EBOLI. That is not all. To add to the disgrace
Of being sacrificed to politics,
My chastity is threatened. Look! This letter
Unmasks a so-called saint forever! Read it!
>   [CARLOS *takes the paper and hangs impatiently on*
>   *her story, without taking time to read the letter*

Who can I turn to for salvation, Prince?
Till now my pride has fought to keep my virtue,
But in the end—

CARLOS.   You fell? No! Did you fall?   710
    For God's sake, no—

EBOLI [*proud and noble*].
                    With whom would I have fallen?
    The feeble reasoning of men's great minds
    That treat the happiness of love like goods
    And bid for adoration with their wealth!
    It is the one thing in the bounds of earth
    That cannot be exchanged for anything
    But its own self. Love is the price of love.
    It is the only diamond I possess
    That I must either give away or hide;
    Much like the merchant, who, to spite a king,   720
    And since the whole of Venice could not pay,
    Returned his pearl to the enriching sea
    Rather than fix a price beneath its worth.*

CARLOS. (God of our fathers, she is beautiful.)

EBOLI. People may call it vanity, a whim,
    But I will not be shared among the many.
    The man I choose will be the only one,
    And I will give him all eternally.
    And he who has me will be made immortal,
    His happiness will make him God. A kiss,   730
    The distillation of divided souls,
    The deep indulgence of the lover's hour,
    The unforbidden witchcraft that is beauty,
    Are sister colours of a single flower
    Whose close-locked petals blend their many shades.
    Should I go mad and tear one shred away
    And lose the rest to give a broken part?
    Should I end woman's sacred majesty,
    And spoil the chosen refuge of our maker
    To help a glutton pass a drunken evening?   740

CARLOS. (Incredible. Madrid has such a girl,
    And I—and I discover her today,
    For the first time.)

EBOLI.   I would have left this court
  Long ago, left the world, entombed myself
  In piety, but one thing kept me here,
  The bond that ties me to the living earth,
  Perhaps a dream but worth so much to me—
  I love and it is not returned.

CARLOS [*approaches her full of fire*].
                              It is!
  As sure as we were made by God I swear
  You are—beyond all words—

EBOLI.   I am? You swear?   750
  Oh now I recognize my angel's voice!
  When you so freely swear it I believe it,
  And I am loved.

CARLOS [*embraces her tenderly*].
                      Oh passionate, free spirit,
  Worthy of adoration! You have opened
  My eyes and ears and filled me with enchantment!
  I am all wonder—who could look at you,
  Who under heaven could ever look at you
  And then say proudly, 'Love has never touched me'?
  Beloved of all the angels, why are you here,
  Among the priests and all their priestcraft, why?   760
  This is no climate for a tender flower—
  You want to break apart and so escape them—
  That is your wish; oh, I believe it gladly,
  But no, as long as I am living, no;
  I throw my arms around you, lift you up
  And bear you safely through the devil's armies.
  Yes, let me be your guardian angel.

EBOLI [*with a look full of love*].   Carlos!
  I never knew you—how could I have known?
  It was a long hard war to win your heart,
  But the reward is infinite.
                    [*She takes his hand and wants to kiss it*

CARLOS.   My Lady,   770
Where are you now?

EBOLI.   This hand is beautiful,
And rich beyond imagination. Prince,
This hand of yours has still two things to give,
The crown of empire and the heart of Carlos.
And must they both be given to one person?
They are a great and sacred gift, perhaps
Too great for one mere mortal to receive!
But what if you were to divide them, Prince?
Queens are for wearing crowns, and not for loving,
A woman who can love desires no empire.   780
So better to divide them, and right now,
Right now, my Prince—or is it done already,
Are they already shared? So much the better—
And do I know the lucky one?

CARLOS.   You will.
You are the girl to whom I can reveal it,
I can reveal it to this innocence,
To this untarnished nature—in this court
You are the worthiest, the only one,
My soul's discoverer, so you can be told,
I am in love.

EBOLI.   Oblique, elusive man,   790
Is the confession still so hard to make?
To love me, did you have to pity me?
I see how long I would have pined in doubt.

CARLOS. What did you say?

EBOLI.   You play such games with me!
Oh really, Prince, you are too cruel to me.
Denying that you had the key!

CARLOS.   The key!
                    [*After a dull realization*
Oh, that is how it is. Oh God! Oh God!
              [*He goes weak at the knees, holds on to a chair
              and covers his face*

EBOLI [*a long silence from both sides. The* PRINCESS *screams
    loudly and falls down*]. Oh horrible! Oh God, what have
    I done?*

CARLOS [*getting up, in an outburst of the most severe pain*].
    So deep from such a heaven to fall, God help us!

EBOLI [*hiding her face in a cushion*]. What have I said? Oh
    God, what have I told!   800

CARLOS [*thrown down in front of her*]. I am not guilty! It
    was only passion,
  A terrible misunderstanding—Princess,
  I am not guilty!

EBOLI.   Get away from me,
  For God's sake!

CARLOS.   I will not abandon you
  In this unbearable distress—how can I?—

EBOLI [*forcibly pushing him away*].
  I beg you of your magnanimity,
  Go far away from me or I will die.
  Be merciful. [CARLOS *makes to go*] Where is my letter,
    though?
  Give me the letter, and the key I gave you—
  Where is my other letter?

CARLOS.   What? What letter?   810
  What do you mean?

EBOLI.   The letter from the King.

CARLOS [*starting*]. From whom?

EBOLI.   The one I gave you earlier.

CARLOS. That letter was the King's?

EBOLI.   O heaven, heaven,
  I am tied fast and terribly—the letter!
  Hand it to me! Prince, I must have it now!

CARLOS. A letter from the King to you?

EBOLI.   The letter,
  In heaven's name!

CARLOS.   It was a knowing letter
  Of someone's stricken conscience, was it not?

EBOLI. Now I am dead—Oh give it me—

CARLOS.   The letter—

EBOLI. What have I put at risk so thoughtlessly?   820

CARLOS. Princess, that letter—it was from the King?
  Everything changes instantly. This letter
                    [*Holding up the letter gleefully*
  Is such a weighty and a priceless prize
  That in comparison all Philip's crowns
  Are matters of inconsequence—this, this,
  This I will keep.

                              [*Exit* CARLOS

EBOLI [*throws herself in his path*].
                  O great God, I am lost.

SCENE IX

[*The* PRINCESS. *Alone, she still stands stunned, beside
  herself. After he has left she rushes after him and
              tries to call him back.*]

EBOLI. Prince! one more word! Prince listen to me please!
  Oh he is gone, and he despises me;
  And now I stand most fearfully alone,
  Rejected, undermined,
              [*She sinks down into an armchair. After a pause*
                  No, not rejected,   830
  But left unchosen, firmly pushed aside
  By a rival. That he is in love with someone
  Is now beyond all doubt. He has confessed.
  But who attracts his passion? What is clear

Is that he loves where love is a disgrace.
He fears discovery. Before the King
His love goes cringing to its hiding place—
Why before he who wants his son to love?
Or is this fear of Philip not the fear
A son feels of a father? When I told him   840
About the Monarch's amorous intentions,
His face lit up, true happiness returned,
His imitated virtue disappeared,
And why? Why then? What can he hope to gain
From Philip's infidelity?

> [*She stops suddenly, surprised by a thought. At
> the same time she tears the ribbon given to
> her by* CARLOS *from her bosom, looks at it
> quickly and then recognizes it*
>   Oh madness!

I have been blind but now my eyes are open!
Yes, long before the Monarch married her
They loved each other, it is common knowledge.
When the Prince saw her I was always there,
So I believed the warm, the infinite,   850
The so true adoration was for me.
A subterfuge beyond imagination—
And I confessed my frailty to her! [*Silence*]
But could he love without a breath of hope?
It is not likely. In these close-fought battles
Love without hope dies in the early stages.
To take his pleasure where the Highest Monarch
In the whole world has fallen out of favour!
And truly, unrequited love has never
Been known to make such sacrifices. Yes!   860
I felt her in his kiss—he drew me to him,
To the thunder of his heart that beat for her,
It was romantic love testing its strength,
Hoping for no response. He takes the key,
Which he decides to think the Queen has sent—
He trusts that love will take such twelve-league steps—
That Philip's wife has lost her mind tonight—
But how could he have dared that infamy

Without the strong persuasion of a sign?
It came to light. He has been heard. She loves him!   870
The saintly woman has a heart, by heaven!
She is so fine! I tremble, even I,
Before the face of such unheard-of virtue;
A higher being towers over me,
I am eclipsed by Glory. Holy beauty
Crushed me with envy of its calm, its freedom
From all the yearnings of our mortal nature,
But what was this tranquillity concealing?
She eats her fill at two majestic tables,
She has the nerve and arrogance to parade   880
Godliness and restraint, while all the time
She tastes the secret pleasures of the damned.
And will this fine charade of hers continue?
Who gives her licence? Shall she go unnoticed
For lack of an avenger? No by heaven,
I worshipped her, and that demands revenge.
The King shall know he is betrayed. The King?
                                        [*After some thought*
Yes, certainly—he will be very grateful.
                                                  [*Exit*

SCENE X

[*A room in the royal palace.* DUKE ALBA,
FATHER DOMINGO.]

DOMINGO. What did you wish to tell me of, Toledo?

ALBA. A strange discovery I made today,   890
   That I would offer for interpretation.*

DOMINGO. What are you saying? What discovery?

ALBA. I and Prince Carlos met at noon today
   Outside an antechamber of the Queen's.
   I was insulted, we exchanged strong language,
   The argument grew loud—we drew our swords.
   Hearing the noise, the Queen burst from her room,

Stepped in between us and addressed the Prince
With a commanding but familiar look—
It was a single look, but instantly   900
His arm was still, he fell upon my neck,
Kissed me, implored forgiveness, and was gone.

DOMINGO [*after a silence*]. This is suspicious, Duke, most
     certainly.
It brings to mind some very awkward thoughts
That have been growing in me for a while.
I fly such thoughts as these—I never tell them,
They are the kind of sword that wounds the wielder,
Untrustworthy acquaintances. I fear them.
To know what people think is difficult,
To know the reasons why, impossible.   910
A word unloosed is a companion lost,
And so I keep my secrets to myself,
And let time's trowel bring them to the light.
To serve a king is often dangerous,
Your best-aimed shot can miss and the rebound
Crush your own battlements. I only wish
That swearing on the Holy Sacrament
Could make my thoughts convincing. But a word
Carelessly said, and caught, an eyewitness,
A tiny scrap of paper, tip the scales   920
More surely than my oaths. It is a curse
That we are standing on the soil of Spain.

ALBA. Why not stand here?

DOMINGO.   In every other court
Passion is left to sing itself to sleep.
Here it is kept from sleeping by bright laws—
Which makes it hard for Queens of Spain to sin;
Hardest of all to undertake that crime
Whose revelation would promote us most.

ALBA. Hear more. Don Carlos had an audience
This morning, with the King, an hour in length.   930
He asked the King for the Vice-Regency
Of Flanders—begged with all his heart and voice,

I heard him from the Cabinet. His eyes
Were red with weeping when I met him leaving.
But when we met at noon he was triumphant,
Delighted that the King had chosen me,
And very thankful. Things are different now,
He said, and better. He does not dissemble,
So how can I resolve these contradictions?
The Prince was glad to have been overlooked,   940
And I was given honour by the King
With all the signs of rage. What can I think?
This post looks more like banishment than favour,
Quite frankly, now.

DOMINGO.   And has it come to this?
One blast of chaos scatters to the winds
What cost us years of sacrifice to build.
Yet you are calm. What will become of us
When this young man is king? Do you not know him?
I am no enemy of his, believe me,
Other anxieties than him disturb me,   950
I grieve already for the throne and for
God and his Church. I know this young man's soul;
What he intends is terrible. Toledo,*
He has the mad idea to be the regent,
And to exist without our creed's assistance;
His heart is yearning for a bright new virtue,
That, buttressed by outrageous self-belief,
Will beg no creed for guidance—and he thinks!
Strange fantasies are burning in his mind,
He honours all humanity as one.   960
Is this man fit to be our king, my friend?

ALBA. It is a shadow in his soul, no more,
And youthful pride must play a part in it.
If he is fated to command one day,
He cannot choose but let these visions go.

DOMINGO. I doubt it. Irresponsibility
Is his chief joy—he will not curb his freedom,
Not even to constrain the lives of others.

Is this man suited to our throne? His mind,
Like a mad giant, will plough random lines   970
Through the symmetry of our statecraft. I have tried,
In these times, vainly, to subvert the rebel
To lascivious ways—no test can overwhelm him.
When such a mind inhabits such a body,
The soul is uncontrollable. And Philip
Will soon be sixty years of age.

ALBA.   Your vision
Reaches afar.

DOMINGO.   Karl and the Queen are one.
The poison of innovation creeps unseen
Through both their bodies; and before too long
Will be within a bowshot of the throne.   980
I know these Valois and we must expect
Unrestrained vengeance from that quiet opponent,
If ever Philip should allow her power.
Luck is still ours. So let us strike home now,
And catch them in a single noose. One hint
Made to the King at present, can do much,
Whether a fact or our imagination,
If it can make him pause, and win us time.
As for ourselves, we are both free of doubt;
Persuasion is the gift of the persuaded,   990
And we are certain to uncover more
By being certain more can be uncovered.

ALBA. And now the hardest question of them all—
Which of us shall be bold to tell the King?

DOMINGO. Neither of us. Now, learn what I intend,
The secret aim and seed of all my plans,
The inspiration of my silent work.
The league that we comprise is incomplete,
The third and most important one is absent.
King Philip loves the Princess Eboli,   1000
My hopes have grown as I have fed this passion,
I am the go-between, and I have taught
The good Princess the workings of our plan.

If all goes well we have, in this young woman,
A confidante who will become a Queen;
And it was she that called me to this room.
I hope for glory—all these Valois lilies*
May be uprooted by a Spanish Maiden
In one short night.

ALBA.   This is incredible!
    Can it be true? I am amazed, dear heaven!   1010
    The final blow is struck, and we have won!

DOMINGO. Quiet, who comes? Yes, it is she we speak of.

ALBA. I will be near—

DOMINGO.   Good. I will call her in.

SCENE XI

[PRINCESS, DOMINGO.]

DOMINGO. Princess, your servant.

EBOLI [looking at the DUKE curiously].
                              We are not alone.
    I see you have a witness near.

DOMINGO.   My Lady?

EBOLI. Who left the room just then?

DOMINGO.   The Duke of Alba,
    Who asks to be the next received, my Lady.

EBOLI. What does he want with me? The Duke of Alba?
    What can he want? Perhaps you can inform me.

DOMINGO. But not before I know what great event   1020
    Has brought my Lady Eboli to me.
                    [Pause, while he awaits her answer
    Perhaps a situation has arisen
    That smiles upon his Majesty's desires?
    May reason hope that reconsideration

Has shone a kinder light upon an offer
A moment of contrariness rejected?
I came here full of joyful expectation.

EBOLI. Have you conveyed my answer to the King?

DOMINGO. I have withheld a wound that would be deadly.
There is still time, Princess, for you to soften.   1030

EBOLI. Then you may tell the King that I await him.

DOMINGO. Dare I believe that this can be, my Lady?

EBOLI. I think I would not say those words in fun.
You scare me though, Almighty God in heaven,
What have I done if even you turn pale?

DOMINGO. Princess, this sudden change, from doubt to
    triumph
Beggars my understanding.

EBOLI.   It is well.
I have no wish for you to understand,
Ever. Enough for you that it is so.
So you may spare your searching mind the pain   1040
Of rooting out the cause or of enquiring
To whose persuasiveness you should be grateful.
But let me add, to ease your priestly mind:
Your conscience has no part in this disgrace,
Nor does the Church, though you have stated cases
In which the Church for its high purposes
Has used even the bodies of its young daughters
And thought the policy no sin. No matter.
There is no blame, although I have to say,
Those pious explanations are beyond me.   1050

DOMINGO. One can discard them if one does not need them,
And then with pleasure, Princess.

EBOLI.   Beg the King
Not to mistake my motives in this matter,
Nor to neglect my interests in this business.

I am what I have always been, but things
Are very different from the way they were.
When I rejected his approaches proudly,
And vainly, I believed him to be happy
In his possession of a gracious Queen—
I thought her good and worth my self-denial.   1060
I thought that then, but now I know much better.
Things are much clearer now.

DOMINGO.   Princess, continue,
   I hear you and we understand each other.

EBOLI. She is exposed. I will not shelter her.
   Enough! The clever thief is in the open.
   The King and all of Spain has been deceived.
   She is in love—I know she is in love,
   What I can prove will murder her composure.
   The King has been betrayed, but I swear now
   By God he shall not suffer unavenged.   1070
   I will tear from her the intractable
   And so unearthly veil of her denial,
   To bare the horror written on her brow;
   And I must pay a dreadful price for this,
   But I will triumph through my suffering.
   The Queen's defeat is greater.

DOMINGO.   All is ready.
   One moment while I call the Duke, my Lady.

                                                    [*Exit*

EBOLI [*astonished*]. What will he do?

SCENE XII

[PRINCESS, ALBA, DOMINGO.]

DOMINGO [*leading* ALBA *in*].   Our news is out of date,
   The lady Eboli reveals to us
   The secret that we meant to break to her.   1080

ALBA. Doubtless my presence does not shock you then.
  I trust your observations more than mine—
  A woman's eyes are sharper in these matters.

EBOLI. Now let us speak of revelations.

DOMINGO.   Lady,
  When to your mind would be the fitting time,
  And where the best place—

EBOLI.   I have thought of this.
  And we shall meet again at noon tomorrow.
  I have good reasons to desire no longer
  To be the hiding place of indiscretions.
  I wish to tell the King and let him bear them.   1090

ALBA. That was what brought me here. I feel the Monarch
  Must learn of this at once—and learn from you,
  I think it has to be from you, my Lady,
  For whom could he believe more readily
  Than the alert companion of his wife?

DOMINGO. Who more than she who when she wishes to
  Can bind him to her with a casual glance?

ALBA. I am the Prince's open enemy.

DOMINGO. And I am held to be so. But not you.
  Openly to accuse is not our duty,   1100
  But frankness is your office. What you scatter
  Will flourish in the monarch's mind, and then
  He will be ours.

ALBA.   But it must happen soon.
  The present would be best, each hour is precious,
  Each moment brings my marching orders closer.

DOMINGO [turning after some thought to the PRINCESS].
  Is there a means to lay one's hand on letters?
  Letters from the Infante, naturally.
  They would be most effective. Yes, of course!
  I think you share a chamber with the Queen?

EBOLI. I sleep next door to her, but what of that?   1110

DOMINGO. Someone who knows the ins and outs of locks.
    Or do you even know the hiding place
    In which her Highness keeps her casket's key?

EBOLI [*thinking*]. Yes, that could work. I think it could be
    found.

DOMINGO. Letters need bearers. If we could but scent
    Their trail, among the Queen's large retinue.
    Gold can do much—we must try everything.

ALBA. Does the Infante have a confidante?
    Has it been noticed?

DOMINGO.   Carlos speaks to no one,
    No one in all Madrid.

ALBA.   That is so strange.   1120

DOMINGO. You can depend on it that he despises
    Everyone in the court: my source is certain.

ALBA. And yet, when I emerged not long ago
    From the Queen's chamber, he was standing there
    Conferring with a page boy, and they spoke
    As if exchanging secrets.

EBOLI.   That was nothing—
    That was another matter—

DOMINGO.   So you think,
    But can we know? To me it seems suspicious.
    Duke, did you recognize the page?

EBOLI.   A child!
    It was a game—what else could it have been?   1130
    I know about it. We shall meet again
    Before I see the King. And in the mean time
    Much can be learned.

DOMINGO [*leads her to one side*].
                        And so the King may hope?*

And may I tell him when the hour may be
That shall fulfil his dearest wish at last?

EBOLI. In a few days from now I will fall ill.
And I will then be parted from the Queen;
That is the usual practice, as you know;
My illness will confine me to my room.

DOMINGO. Most fortunate. Then the great game is won.   1140
The devil take all Queens!

EBOLI.   Be Quiet! Listen!
Someone is calling me. It is the Queen.
Goodbye.

                                                    [*Exit*

SCENE XIII

[ALBA, DOMINGO.]

DOMINGO [*after a pause, in which he has followed the*
    PRINCESS *with his eyes*].
              These roses, and your struggle, Duke—

ALBA. I wait for your great God to strike us down!

SCENE XIV

[*In a Carthusian monastery.* DON CARLOS, PRIOR.]

CARLOS [*as he enters, to the* PRIOR]. He has been here and
    gone?

PRIOR.   He has been here
Three times today. He left an hour ago.

CARLOS. Will he return? Oh did he leave no message?

PRIOR. He will be here by noon, your Majesty,
That was his promise, I know nothing more.

CARLOS [*steps to a window and looks around*].
The setting is precisely as I wished;   1150

Your monastery set back from the road,
The towers of Madrid just visible;
The peaceful Manzanares flowing here,
Is as it should be, quiet as a secret.

PRIOR. Or as the door into another world.

CARLOS. I have entrusted what I hold most sacred,
My dearest treasure, to your love of silence.
Reverend sir—no mortal must suspect
Who met me here or that it was in secret.
I have important reasons for denying   1160
The man I am to speak with, to the world,
And so I chose these cloisters. We are safe,
Surely, from ambush or betrayal here.
You do remember what you swore to me?

PRIOR. Good sir, do not be anxious. The suspicion
Of kings does not extend beyond the living.
The ear of curious duplicity
Is pressed against the door of happiness
And passion, not the cells of this poor place.

CARLOS. You think the conscience that my caution hides   1170
With so much fear, must be a guilty one?

PRIOR. I do not think.

CARLOS.   You are in error, father,
You wander from the truth. I fear the judgement
Of Godless men, but I am loved in heaven.

PRIOR. My son, we make no condemnations here.
This sanctuary is for everyone,*
The guilty and the innocent. Your heart
Must judge if your intentions are for good
Or tend towards the devil and disgrace.

CARLOS [with warmth]. Our secret is no trouble to your God—
It is His own work; and indeed, to you,   1181
To you at least I can reveal it—

PRIOR.   Why?
I wish for no such burden, Prince. The world

And its devices lie the other side
Of my great journey, strongly sealed by time.
Why break it in the little that remains
Before departure? On the way to heaven
The spirit needs to carry very little.
Now I must go to pray, I hear the hour.

[*Exit* PRIOR

SCENE XV

[DON CARLOS. MARQUIS OF POSA *enters*.]

CARLOS. Oh finally, Roderigo!

MARQUIS.   What a test   1190
For any friend's impatience! Since your fate
Was fixed, the sun has set and risen twice,
And only now am I to hear the news.
So, are you reconciled?

CARLOS.   With whom?

MARQUIS.   The King!
And is the Flanders question settled, Karl?

CARLOS. The Duke is leaving in the morning, yes.
That has been settled.

MARQUIS.   But it cannot be.
Can all Madrid believe a lie? They say
You had a private audience—the King—

CARLOS. Stands firm. We will be far apart for ever,   1200
And henceforth even further than before.

MARQUIS. You shall not go to Flanders?

CARLOS.   No! No! No!

MARQUIS. Oh all my hopes!

CARLOS.   But, leaving that aside,
Roderigo, oh, since we last saw each other
I have had such experiences that

I need your wisdom more than anything.
I must see her—

MARQUIS.   Your mother? No! What for?

CARLOS. I have been given hope again. Be calm!
I should be happy and I will be happy.
But more of that another time. For now,   1210
Advise me how to get to speak to her.

MARQUIS. What has brought on this new delirium,
What does this mean?

CARLOS.   It is no fever, friend,
By God above, I am as clear as day!
            [*Pulls out a letter from the* KING *to* EBOLI
The truth is hidden in this piece of paper.
The Queen is free; free in the eyes of men
And by the will of God. To understand,
Wonder no more, but read.

MARQUIS [*opening letter*].   What can this be?
Good God, but this is written by the King!
                        [*After he has read it*
To whom is it addressed?

CARLOS.   To Eboli.   1220
A page boy of the Queen's
Brought me a letter by an unknown hand
Two days ago, and, sealed with it, a key,
Which, so he said, would usher me within
A chamber in the left wing of the palace,
Where the Queen lives; and there a lady waited,
Who was in love with me; I understood,
Or so I thought, and went at once—

MARQUIS.   You went!
Madman!

CARLOS.   I did not recognize the hand.
I only knew one lady who could think   1230
That she is loved by Carlos. So I fly,
Dizzy with rapture, to the place described;

Heavenly music reaching from within
Comes to me from the room to be my guide;
I push the door, and whom do I discover!
Imagine my despair.

MARQUIS.   I see it clearly.

CARLOS. I would have been beyond all hope of rescue,
   If it were not that she to whom I wandered
   Was like an angel. Sad misunderstanding!
   Reading the words of love my mad looks wrote,   1240
   She led herself into the sweet delusion
   That it was she I prayed to for an answer.
   Touched by my silent agony of spirit,
   Her generosity of heart unwisely
   Convinced itself to give me love for love.
   Respect appealed to her to keep her silence,
   But then she found the bravery to break it,
   And so the beauty of her soul lay open—

MARQUIS. How can you speak of this disaster calmly?
   She has seen through you, there can be no doubt   1250
   That she has looked upon your darkest secret,
   She knows you love—you have rejected her,
   And she controls the King.

CARLOS [*confidently*].   But she is honest.

MARQUIS. She is—for love—I know this honesty,
   And greatly fear it. It is not that virtue
   That grows in us without self-interest,
   That brings forth freedom from the fertile soul,
   The only food of beauty and just pride,
   And flowers into generosity
   Without the help of any gardener!   1260
   It is a strange plant from a harsher climate
   Grafted onto our south; and it is trained
   And educated to be innocent,
   And virtue is a principle it holds;
   Fighting with all its strength against its mind
   It brings its overheated blood to good;

Think, Carlos, how can she forgive the Queen?
The chastity she fought so long and hard
To keep for you, goes unrewarded, and
You burn in hopelessness for Philip's wife.   1270

CARLOS. But do you really know her?

MARQUIS.   I do not.
I have not seen her more than twice perhaps.
Yet I must tell you how she seemed to me.
She wears her virtue like a coat of arms.
Rather, her self-restraint is like a sword.
And in comparison, the Queen—oh Carl,
What an entirely different character!
Her glory is a gift she bears in silence,
Effortlessly, and free of care; decorum,
And all its rules, are followed but forgotten;   1280
Equally far from recklessness and fear,
She simply wanders with heroic footsteps
Down the right road, which is the decent one,
Quite unaware of all the love she stirs;
She never dreams that she deserves applause.
And can my Carl by peering in this mirror
Ever see Princess Eboli? The Princess,
Because she loved, guarded her chastity;
Love, and the hope of love, upheld her virtue,
But unrewarded she will fall.   1290

CARLOS [*with some fire*]. No! No!
          [*After he has walked up and down agitatedly*
                      If you could only see the elegance
With which your eloquence sets out to steal
His faith in human nature from your friend!

MARQUIS. My soul's first love, that I do not deserve;
That I do not wish, no, by God in heaven!
Oh, this Princess would be a beam of light,
Made of perfection, I would bow before her,
Like you, as if before a stainless angel,
If she could only keep your deathly secret.

CARLOS. How vain your fears are! How can she reveal it?
The only evidence she has condemns her,   1301
And will she buy the pleasure of revenge,
A dreary joy, with her dear hoard of honour?

MARQUIS. Often before now, to erase past blushes,
Many have chosen to disgrace their present.

CARLOS [stands up forcefully]. No, that is too harsh, she is
    honourable,
And proud. I know her and I do not fear her.
In vain you try to frighten off my hopes.
I shall speak to my mother.

MARQUIS.   Now? But why?

CARLOS. Now I have nothing left on earth to lose,   1310
And I must know my destiny. Think only
How I can speak to her.

MARQUIS.   And show her this?
Do you intend to show this letter to her?

CARLOS. Do not ask that, but only tell me now
How I may find a way to speak to her.

MARQUIS [with significance]. You tell me that you love her—
    love her, Carl,
And yet you plan to make her read this letter.
            [CARLOS looks to the ground and is silent
I can see something that I do not know
In your expression; something new to me.
You look away. Why do you look away?   1320
So it is true. I guessed right. Let me read—
        [CARLOS gives him the letter. MARQUIS tears it up

CARLOS. What! Are you mad? [With measured sensitivity] In
    truth I have to say
I meant that letter to do much.

MARQUIS.   I know.
And so I tore it up.

[*The* MARQUIS *looks searchingly at the* PRINCE,
*who returns the gaze doubtfully. Long
silence*

Speak now, please tell me,
What has a trespass in the royal bedroom
To do with your—your love, and tell me also,
How are your reckless hopes affected by
The dereliction of a husband's duties?
Is Philip now no longer any danger?
He is unfaithful to the one you love.   1330
Now truly I begin to understand you.
How little I have understood your feelings.*

CARLOS. What do you mean? What do you think, Roderigo?

MARQUIS. I see what I must grow accustomed to.
    Once it was different—once you were so rich,
    So open, that the circle of the earth
    Could turn with ease within your heart. But now
    All has been withered by a single passion,
    Shrunk to a single selfish interest,
    The dead star of your heart. No tear remains   1340
    For the destruction of the provinces,*
    Not one, not one—oh Carl, now you are poor,
    You are far poorer than the poorest beggar
    When you love nothing but your own desire!

CARLOS [*throws himself into an armchair. After a while with
    barely concealed sobbing*]. I see that you no longer care
    for me.

MARQUIS. No, Carl, I know the chaos that you suffer,
    The conflict of emotions that are good.
    The Queen belonged to you, the Monarch stole her,
    But up to now you humbly told yourself
    The right was his, if he was worthy of her.   1350
    The final judgement and the full conclusion
    You dared not think too clearly. But that letter
    Set your mind free. You are more worthy of her.
    With proud joy now you saw that in the end

Fortune is tyranny and robbery.
Now you were glad to be the sufferer,
For guiltless souls, torture is flattery.
But your imagination was confused,
Your pride found satisfaction in this pain,
And out of that your heart concocted hope.   1360
You see—I knew—this time you were misled,
This time you failed to understand yourself.

CARLOS [*moved*]. Ah no, Roderigo, there you are mistaken,
   I think less nobly, very much less nobly
   Than you would have me and yourself believe.

MARQUIS. Am I so little understood here? Carl,
   If you should lose your way, a hundred faults
   Can never hide the virtue underneath.
   I think we see ourselves more clearly now.
   You shall speak to the Queen now, yes, you must.   1370

CARLOS [*falls on his knees*]. I am not worthy to stand next
   to you!

MARQUIS. You have my word. Now leave the rest to me.
   A happy thought is rising in my mind
   A lovelier mouth shall speak it to you, Carl.
   I will break through to see the Queen. Tomorrow
   Perhaps our goal will hove at last in view.
   Until that time, believe, my friend, remember,
   'A scheme that reason brings into the world,
   That can reduce the suffering of man,
   Although it fails a hundred thousand times,   1380
   Must never be forgotten or abandoned.'
   And think of Flanders always!

CARLOS.   I remember
   Everything virtue and yourself have taught me.

MARQUIS [*goes to the window*]. Our time is up. Your entourage is coming.
                                              [*They embrace*
   Once more the vassal and the prince my Lord.

CARLOS. Where will you go? Back to the city?

MARQUIS.   Yes.

CARLOS. But one word more. How easy to forget
  Things of great moment: Letters from Brabant
  Are opened by the King. Be on your guard!
  The Post has secret orders, I know well—   1390

MARQUIS. How did you learn this?

CARLOS.   Don Raimond of Taxis,
  The Postmaster, is my good friend.

MARQUIS [*after a minute*].   This also.
  So they will travel via Germany!

                              [*Exeunt different ways*

ACT THREE

SCENE I

[*The* KING's *bedroom, on the night table two burning candles. In the background several page boys on their knees, having fallen asleep. The* KING, *from the waist up half undressed, stands in front of the table, one arm bent over the armchair, in a contemplative pose. In front of him lie a medallion and some papers.*]

KING. That she has always been a dreamer, no one
  Can truthfully deny. I could not love her,
And yet she never seemed downcast. So now,
It has been proved, and she is false.
     [*Here he moves in such a way as to bring himself
     to his senses. He looks up, confused*
                           Where was I?
Am I my only watchman? What is this?
The candles almost out, yet still no light?
I have lost out on sleep again. Well nature,
Take what I give. There is no time for Kings
To get back lost nights. Well, I am awake,
And so it shall be day!
        [*He puts the candles out and opens a curtain.
        Whilst he paces up and down he notices the
        sleeping boys and stays standing in front of
        them silently for a while. Then he rings the
        bell*
                  Are all asleep?   . 10
Even the watchers in my antechamber?

SCENE II

[*The* KING, COUNT LERMA.]

LERMA [*with consternation on seeing the king*].
  Your Majesty is ill?

KING.   There was a fire
In the pavilion. Did you not hear them shouting?

LERMA. Your Majesty, I did not.

KING.   What? I dreamt it?
It cannot be coincidence—the Queen
Sleeps in that wing?

LERMA.   She does, your Majesty.

KING. This dream has not a little frightened me.
The guard is to be doubled in that place,
As soon as evening comes; but secretly,
With subtlety. It is not my desire—   20
Why are you eyeing me so carefully?

LERMA. I see a burning eye that pleads for sleep.
May I presume to draw my King's attention
To a dear life so precious to its people,
Who would be very troubled in their thoughts
To see the traces of a night watched through
Upon their monarch's features. Two short hours
Of sleep, and in the morning—

KING.   I shall sleep
When I am in the Royal Vault. In sleep
The King forgoes his crown, in sleep the man   30
Has lost his wife. No! No! It is a lie!
It was a woman whispered this to me;
I call that woman Falsehood. Let a man
Give her words force, and then I will believe.
        [To *the page boys, who have in the mean time
            woken up*
Summon the Duke of Alba. [*Exit pages*] Count, come closer.
Is it the truth?
        [*He comes to a standstill before* LERMA, *searching
            his features*
                Oh to know everything
For the duration of a heartbeat. Swear.
Am I betrayed? Is that the truth, is it?

LERMA. My great, my best King—

KING.   King! they cry, King, King,
  I only get this echo for an answer,   40
  Fevered, I thirst, I strike the stones for water,
  They pour forth molten gold.*

LERMA.   My King, you ask,
  'Is it the truth?' Is what the truth?

KING.   Go. Leave me.
      [*The* COUNT *makes to go, but the* KING *calls him
          back*
  You have a wife, Count, and you are a father,
  Is that not so?

LERMA.   It is, your Majesty.

KING. Married, and yet you dare to spend the night
  Guarding your master? You have silver hair,
  Yet you persist in the self-flattery
  Of thinking that your wife is virtuous?
  Go home, she kisses in your own son's arms,   50
  And their embrace shall curse your lineage.
  Believe your King, and go. You stand amazed?
  You look at me as if to say—that I,
  I also have a touch or two of grey.
  Fool, think. A queen does not besmear her virtue.
  Damn you to hell if you do not believe me.

LERMA [*heatedly*]. Who could not? Who is so impertinent,
  Of all the subjects of my King's domains,
  As to breathe forth the poison of suspicion
  Upon the stainless virtue of that angel?   60
  So to insult the best Queen—

KING.   Best? The best?
  And she is your best also, obviously.
  She sees to it that friends of hers surround me.
  That must have cost her—must have cost her more,
  As far as I know, than she has to spend.*
  You are dismissed. And let the Duke come in.

LERMA. I hear him in the antechamber—

[*He is about to go*

KING [*in a milder tone*].   Count,
  What you so kindly noted must be true,
  My head is pounding from a night awake;
  Forget the ramblings of my waking dream.   70
  You hear? Forget. I am your noble King.

       [*Holds out his hand to be kissed.* LERMA *goes,
       opening the door for* ALBA

SCENE III

[KING. DUKE OF ALBA.]

ALBA [*approaching the* KING *with an uncertain expression*].
  The call was unexpected at this hour—

       [*He hesitates and looks at the* KING *more closely*
  And what can this severity express?

KING [*has sat down and picked up a medallion from the
    table. He looks at the* DUKE *for a long time, silent*].
  So it is true—I have no faithful servants.

ALBA [*stands still, self-conscious*].   What?

KING. I have sustained a wound that cannot heal.
  It was foreseen, but I was left unwarned.

ALBA [*with an expression of astonishment*].
  An insult to the King escaped my notice?

KING [*shows him a letter*].
  Whose is this hand?

ALBA.   It is the Prince's writing.

KING [*pause, in which he watches* ALBA *intently*].
  Did you not warn me that he was ambitious?
  Do you have no suspicions? Was it only   80
  Ambition I was to expect from him?

ALBA. Ambition is a broad bed, and within it
    Innumerable other sins can slumber.

KING. And is there nothing in particular
    You can reveal to me?

ALBA [*after a silence, with an impenetrable expression*].
                    Your Majesty
    Made me the watchful shepherd of your empire.
    I serve the empire with my intuition,
    And all my secrets are the empire's servants.
    But my unproved suspicions are my own.
    A slave can keep his feelings from a king,   90
    It is his only right, and one that subjects
    Share in no less. Not everything I know
    Exists within me with such clarity
    That it is ready for my King to hear.
    And if he must be answered, I must plead
    That he asks not as my master.

KING [*gives him the letter*].   Read.

ALBA.   What madman
    Had the idea to put this wretched letter
    Into my King's hand?

KING.   What? You know this letter?
    You know whom it refers to? For the name,
    I know, is not there.

ALBA [*stands back embarrassed*].
                    I was over-hasty.   100

KING. You know?

ALBA [*after some thought*].
                    Then it is out. My master's orders—
    I cannot hide it or deny it now.
    I know the one to whom these words refer.

KING [*stands up with a terrible gesture*].
    O God of terror and revenge help me
    To find a new way for a man to die!

The whole world knows it and it is so clear,
So loudly spoken and so understood,
That anyone is certain who it is
At a first glance, without the need for thought!
That is too weighty, that I did not know.   110
I am the very last in all my empire
To find this out—

ALBA.   Yes, I admit my guilt,
My noble monarch, I am deep in shame,
The wisdom that convinced me to be silent
Was cowardly: the honour of my King,
And truth and justice thundered all the while
That I should speak. But things will tend to stillness,
And beauty often silences a man;
But speech must now be risked, though I know well
How easily affection for a son,   120
And the endearments of a family,
Tears of a wife, can overcome—

KING.   Stand up.
You have my royal guarantee. Stand up.
Speak without fear.

ALBA.   Your Majesty remembers,
An incident in Aranjuez—the Queen
Was happened on alone, without her Ladies,
In a fraught state in a secluded arbour.

KING. Tell me of that! Continue!

ALBA.   The Marquise
Of Mondecar was banished from the Empire,
Because she found the generosity   130
To sacrifice her standing for her Queen
Without the slightest thought or hesitation.
But now we learn that the Marquise performed
As ordered; why? Prince Carlos had been here.

KING [exclaims terribly]. So, after all that—

ALBA.   Footprints in the sand
Led from the left-hand entrance of the arbour

To a small grotto where a handkerchief
Was lost—Don Carlos has been looking for it.
This has aroused suspicions, obviously.
And at the moment when your Majesty   140
Stood questioning the Queen, a gardener
Happened to see Don Carlos in the grotto.

KING [*returning out of deep contemplation*].
And how she wept when questioned. In the eyes
Of all my court, made me the cruel demander;
And in my own eyes also! God in heaven,
I shrank before her virtue like a sinner.

> [*A long and deep silence. He sits down and*
> *covers his face*

Yes, you are right, Duke Alba, this could bring
Terrible actions. Leave me for awhile.

ALBA. This evidence alone is inconclusive,
My King—

KING.   And is this also inconclusive?   150
And this, and this too? And the deafening
Hubbub of unconflicting ways to damn her?
Oh, this is clearer than the light of noon,
And I first saw it when it was the dawn.
Sin rose when I received her from your hands,*
Here in Madrid. Oh I can see her now,
As pale as if she sees or is a ghost,
She casts her terrified eyes on my grey hair.
And then the fraud commences.

ALBA.   For the Prince,
A mother was the tombstone of a bride.   160
They were already coupled in their minds,
And had achieved a passionate understanding
That their new status overruled. Young shyness
And all the fear that hinders love's expression,
Had stood aside already, and seduction
Spoke without shame through mutual recollections
Permitted by the circumstance. Their thoughts,
Set to the tune of youth, became one song,

And, angered by the sudden new restriction,
They saw few reasons for resisting passion.   170
Politics cancelled their instinctive closeness,
But are we to believe that she would bow
To the power of the state in everything?
Could she resist the ruling of temptation,
And love the ruling of the cabinet?
She was determined to be loved, instead—
Was crowned.

KING [*insulted and with bitterness*].
                    A very statesman-like distinction.
Your honesty is admirable, Toledo,
I thank you for it. You are right of course,
                              [*Standing up, proud*
The Queen was wrong to hide these letters from me,   180
And to deny me knowledge of the blameful
Presence of the Infante in the garden.
Her kindness has misled her very badly.
I think I know how best to punish her.
                              [*He rings the bell*
Who else is in the antechamber? Alba,
I have no further need of you. Please leave me.

ALBA. Have I through diligence offended you
A second time, my King?

KING [*to* PAGE].   Let in Domingo.
                                   [*Exit* PAGE
You are forgiven, Duke. For two harsh minutes
You made me live in fear of what I know   190
Can only happen to a man like you.
                                   [*Exit* ALBA

SCENE IV

[KING, DOMINGO.]

KING [*walks up and down several times to collect his
    thoughts*].

DOMINGO_ [*enters a few moments after* ALBA *has left,
    approaches the* KING, *whom he considers a while in
    solemn silence*].
How very pleasantly I am surprised
To see Your Majesty so calm.

KING.   Surprised?

DOMINGO. Thanks be to providence, that after all
My doubts and fears should be without foundation.
Now I may give my hopes free rein.

KING.   Your fears?
What did you fear?

DOMINGO.   That I have known of secrets
Is all I dare to say, Your Majesty.

KING [*darkly*]. And have I mentioned a desire to share them?
Who is this man who faces me so glibly?   200
Rare courage, God!

DOMINGO.   My King, the place, the time,
At which these revelations came to me,
The seal on which their certainty was sworn,
Acquit me of the charge of speaking lightly.
They are a gift of the confessional,*
Given to me as weights of wickedness
That crushed the tender conscience of their witness,
Forcing her to appeal to God for ease;
Though she does not desire it, what she tells
Must compromise the Queen.

KING.   In truth? Good heart,   210
You guess the reason for your summons well.
You are the guide to bring me from the maze
To which my eagerness has led me blind.
Speak to me often. I expect from you
Nothing but truth. What am I to believe?
What to conclude? The truth is your profession.

DOMINGO. Sir, if the sacred mildness of my office
Did not entail a duty to protect you,

I would advise Your Highness to be calm,
Plead with you for your own sake not to look,   220
But to allow this secret to depart,
For it can never come to any good.
What you have learnt so far you can forgive,
And all the Queen's misdeeds, should you desire,
Can vanish with a word. The will of kings
Creates the virtue of its favourites;
And only your contentment, widely known,
Can quell the rumours vileness multiplies.

KING. Rumours of me? Among my people? Rumours?

DOMINGO. Damnable lies! All lies! I swear by heaven!   231
   But there are always cases, are there not,
   In which a nation wishing to believe
   Can give a lie the weight of truth.

KING.   By God!
   And this is an explosive theme—

DOMINGO.   The priceless
   And only gift a people can compete
   On the same level as a Queen to keep,
   Is a good name.

KING.   I hope that there at least
   We have no need to fear.
                  [*His eyes rest uncertainly on* DOMINGO. *After a
                  silence*
                        But speak on, Chaplain,
   I know that you have something dark to say.
   Do not hold back. Your tone is ominous   240
   And I have borne its tenor long enough.
   Tell me your tale whatever it may be,
   Keep me no longer twitching on the rack!
   What are the people thinking?

DOMINGO.   Once again
   I say the people can be wrong—and are.
   What they believe must not affect the King,

Only, that what they say should go so far
Already, as to credit that—

KING.   Oh God,
What? Must I plead for every drop of poison?

DOMINGO. The people still recall that month of fear   250
That brought your Majesty so near to death;
Thirty weeks after that they were to read
Of the good birth—

        [*The* KING *stands up and rings the bell,* ALBA
        re-enters

DOMINGO [*embarrassed*]. I am amazed!

KING [*approaches* ALBA].   Toledo!
You are a man. Oh shield me from this priest.

DOMINGO [*he and* ALBA *look sheepishly at one another. After
    a pause*].
If we had known beforehand that this news
Would earn its bringer punishment—

KING.   A bastard!
You say that I was little more than dead
When the Infanta was conceived. But that,
If I am not mistaken, was the time
When all your churches blessed St Dominic   260
For the great miracle performed in me!
Is it a wonder and a sign no more?
Did you lie then or are you lying now?
Which version would you rather I believed?
Oh I see through you now. If your black plot
Had been prepared and fit for action then,
St Dominic would not have got your thanks!

ALBA. Our plot!

KING.   Can you appear before me now,
In harmony, your stories one another's,
And not be in collusion? It is I,   270
Your King, whose mind you struggle to confuse.
Should I be blind to the inhuman hunger
With which you fall upon your prey? I know you.

And how could I be blind to the delight
With which you feed upon my agony
And my increasing rage? Should I not see
The eagerness with which the Duke there burns
To seize the glory meant to raise my son?
And with what ecstasy the priest employs
My giant anger in his little grudge?   280
You see me as a dumb but mighty bow
That can be strung at will by any man.
But I will have my will and if I doubt,
You will permit me to begin with you.

ALBA. Our changeless loyalty did not foresee
    Such misinterpretation.

KING.   Loyalty!
    Loyalty warns of things that are to come,
    Lust for revenge uncovers guilt gone by.
    How may I profit from your labours—say!
    If what you tell is true, and is avenged,   290
    What will be left me but the pain of loss?
    The empty triumph of revenge? Oh no,
    You only bring me fears and waverings,
    And death-cold doubts—you lead me down to hell
    And run away and leave me standing there.

DOMINGO. What stronger evidence could we provide,
    Unless your eyes could see what we have seen?

KING. I will assemble all my noblemen
    And seat myself above them as their judge,
    And you will stand before them if you dare,   300
    And then accuse her of adultery!
    And there will be no mercy—but mark this,
    If she can clear herself, that fate is yours.
    So will you honour truth with sacrifice?
    Make up your minds, my friends. You hesitate.
    You will not. So, the bravery of liars.

ALBA [who has stood silently in the background. Coldly and
    quietly].
    I will.

KING [*turns round astonished and stares at the* DUKE *a while*].
        Brave man! But it occurs to me
That you have often in the heat of battle
Risked your existence for much slighter causes,
Gambled it lightly for the dream of fame.   310
The blood of royalty will not be sold
To one whose only hope is to exchange
A wretched life for a remembered end.
Your offer is rejected. Go now. Go.
Await my orders in the antechamber.
                 [*Exeunt* ALBA *and* DOMINGO

SCENE V

[KING *alone.*]

KING. Now, Providence, good Providence, send me
A man. You have been generous to me,
Now bless me with a man. You are alone,
Because unaided you see everything,
I beg you for a friend because my eyes   320
See little by themselves. You sent me servants,
I see them as they are, their petty evil,
Broken and harnessed, serves my purposes,
As storms impose your order on creation.
I am in need of truth. I need a helper,
Kings may not dig for truth where it lies buried.
Find the uncommon man whose heart is open
And pure, whose soul is clear, whose eyes unblinkered,
For he will help me seek it out. I shuffle
The destinies. Among the many thousands   330
Who flutter to the flame of royalty,
Let that one find me.
      [*He opens a casket and takes out a writing block.*
        After he has leafed through
                Empty names are here,
Nothing but names, and not a single mention

Of how they earned their places on the table.
And who is more forgetful than a debtor?
But on this other table here I read
Endless offences noted down in detail.
What! Vengeance has a better memory.
This is not good.

                                        [*Reads further*
            Count Egmont? No, no, no,
The honour of his triumph at St Quentin   340
Has long been lost. I set him with the dead.
            [*He erases the name and writes it on the other
              list. After he has read further*
Marquis of Posa? Posa? Posa? no,
I have no recollection of the man.
And yet I see his name scored under twice,
Which means that I was set on raising him.
Can this be possible? And all this time
He has been elsewhere, hiding from the eyes
Of him who owes him royal gratitude.
By God—within the borders of my empire
There is a man who does not seek my favour.   350
If he had any greed or lust for power
He would have come here long ago, beguiling.
Shall I explore this mystery? This man
Might speak the truth, if he depends on no one.

SCENE VI

[DON CARLOS *in conversation with the* PRINCE OF
PARMA. *The* DUKES OF ALBA, FERIA, *and* MEDINA
SIDONIA. COUNT LERMA *and other grandees with
documents in their hands. All wait for the* KING.]

MEDINA SIDONIA [*obviously avoided by all around him, he
turns to the* DUKE OF ALBA, *who stands alone, preoccupied, pacing up and down*]. Duke, you have spoken to
his Majesty.
How did he seem?

ALBA.   Your presence and your news—
　Neither are welcome to him.

MEDINA SIDONIA.   In the fire
　Of the English cannons I was happier
　Than standing on these stones.
　　　　　　　　[CARLOS, *who has looked at him with quiet*
　　　　　　　　sympathy approaches now and shakes his
　　　　　　　　hand
　　　　　　　　　　　　　　My Prince, warm thanks
　For this greathearted sympathy; you see,   360
　They shun me, and their looks confirm my downfall.

CARLOS. Hope for the best, both from your innocence,
　And the King's mercy.

MEDINA SIDONIA.   I have lost a fleet,*
　The like of which the seas have never seen;
　How can a little head like this compare
　To seventy galleons sunk? But Oh My prince,
　Five sons, as hopeful for their lives as you,
　That breaks my heart.

SCENE VII

　　　[*The* KING *comes out. Others as before. All take off*
　　　their hats and retreat to either side, thereby forming
　　　a semicircle round him. Silence.]

KING [*briefly surveys the semicircle*]. Cover your heads!
　　　　[DON CARLOS *and the* PRINCE OF PARMA *approach*
　　　　first and kiss the KING's *hand. He turns with*
　　　　some friendliness to the latter, without wanting
　　　　to notice his son
　　　　　　　　　　　　Nephew, your mother asks*
　If you have pleased the people in Madrid.   370

PARMA. That she should wait to know until the outcome
　Of my first battle.

KING.   Be content for now.
Your turn will come when these stout oaks are felled.
                              [*To the* DUKE OF FERIA
What news there?

FERIA [*bows before the* KING].
                    The Grand Master of the order
Of Calatrava passed away this morning.*
Here is his Knight's Cross, which returns to you.

KING [*takes the medal and looks round the circle*].
Who is the worthiest to follow him?
            [*He motions to the* DUKE OF ALBA, *who falls on
            one knee in front of him, and hangs the medal
            round* ALBA's *neck*
Alba, you are my finest general.
Never be more, and grace will never fail you.
                              [*He notices* MEDINA SIDONIA
Ho there, my Admiral!

MEDINA SIDONIA [*approaches gingerly and kneels before the*
    KING *with bowed head*].
                    This, my great King,   380
Is all the ships and all the youth of Spain
That the Armada has returned to you.

KING [*after a long silence*].
God rules above me. You were sent to fight
Men, and not storms; the English, not the weather.
And you are welcome in Madrid.
                    [*He gives him his hand to be kissed*
                    I thank you,
You brought back one good man at least—yourself!
My Lords, this lord is honoured, honour him.
            [*He motions to* MEDINA SIDONIA *to stand up and
            cover his hand. Then he turns to the others*
Who else is there?
                [*To* DON CARLOS *and the* PRINCE OF PARMA
                Princes, I thank you both.

[*They exit. The remaining grandees come closer
and hand over their papers to the* KING. *He
looks through them briefly and hands them to
the* DUKE OF ALBA

Present them to me in the Cabinet.
No more?

[*No one answers*

Why is it that among my nobles   390
One never sees a certain Marquis of Posa?
I know that he has served me with distinction.
Perhaps he stands no longer with the living?
Why does he not present himself?

LERMA.   The Knight
Has only recently returned from travels
That took him through the length and breadth of Europe.
He is at present in Madrid and waits
Only for the appropriate occasion
To kneel before his lord as is his duty.

ALBA. Marquis of Posa? Yes, the Knight of Malta,   400
Your Royal Majesty, whose reputation
Is spread by tales of such inspired achievements.
When, summoned by the Master of the Order,
The Knights assembled to defend their island,
Besieged by Suleiman, this youthful student,*
Eighteen years old, no more, was suddenly
Missed at the University of Alcala.
Unsummoned, he was at Valetta, saying*
'The cross was bought for me, now I must earn it.'
He was among the band of forty men   410
Who countered the attacks of Mustafa,
Hassem, Piali, and Ulluciali*
On the Castle of St Elmo. It was stormed
Four times, and in the heat of noon; at last,
When he observed that all but he were dead,
He jumped into the sea and made his way,
The sole survivor, to besieged Valetta.

Some two months later, when the siege was raised,
The Knight returned at once to Alcala
To turn himself once more towards his studies.   420

FERIA. And it was Posa who alone uncovered
The fearful plot in Catalonia,*
And won that vital province for the crown,
Through his quick-wittedness.

KING.   I am astonished.
What kind of man can do these wondrous things,
And then, of three I ask to tell me of them,
Not one betrays the slightest hint of envy?
His character is either other-worldly
Or negligible. I must speak to him,
He is a modern wonder. [to ALBA] After mass   430
I wish to see him in the Cabinet.
                              [Exit ALBA. The KING calls FERIA
Sit for me in the secret council, Feria.
                                        [Exit the KING

FERIA. His Majesty is well disposed today.

MEDINA SIDONIA. Call him a god. He has forgiven me.

FERIA. But you are worthy of this happiness.
And I am truly glad for you.

ONE OF THE GRANDEES.   And I.

A SECOND. And I, in truth.

A THIRD.   My heart is full again—
Such a fine admiral.

THE FIRST.   His Majesty
Showed you no mercy—only common justice.

LERMA [to MEDINA SIDONIA suddenly, while leaving].
How suddenly a word can raise the dead!
                                        [Exeunt

SCENE VIII

[*The* KING'S *cabinet.* MARQUIS OF POSA *and the* DUKE
OF ALBA.]

MARQUIS [*as he enters*]. He wants to see me? Me? This is not
    so.   441
You have the wrong name. Why in all the world
Should he want me?

ALBA.   He wants to get to know you.

MARQUIS. Just curiosity—and then regret
For wasted time. And life goes by so fast!

ALBA. I hand you over to your destiny.
The King is in your hands. So use this moment
As best you may, and if it comes to nothing,
The fault is all your own.

                                [*Exit*

SCENE IX

[MARQUIS, *alone.*]

MARQUIS.   Good Duke, well spoken.
An opportunity as rare as this*   450
Must not be lost. It is a useful lesson
This courtier gives me, though I will not use it
As he would do, but after my own fashion.
                   [*After some pacing up and down*
How am I here? Is it coincidence
That sets my image in these mirrors now?
What struck the King and stirred his crowded mind,
And from the myriads contained therein
Plucked me, precisely the unlikeliest?
Only coincidence? It may be more;
What is coincidence but rough-hewn stone   460
That comes to life beneath the sculptor's hands?

Coincidence is providence—its purpose
Is ours to fashion. What he wants of me
Should not concern me—what I want of him,
That is quite clear. The King alone with me!
If I can spark a flicker of truth's fire
In the cold tyrant's soul . . . but done with skill,
And it will blaze! So, what appeared bizarre
Becomes, through thought, predictable and useful.
And if it should prove otherwise—no matter,   470
What can I do but act on my belief?

> [*He walks up and down in the room a few times
> and finally comes to a standstill in front of a
> painting. The* KING *enters the adjacent room,
> where he gives a few orders. Then he enters,
> stands in the doorway and watches the*
> MARQUIS *for a while without being noticed by
> him*

SCENE X

> [*The* KING, MARQUIS OF POSA. *As soon as he notices
> him,* POSA *walks up to the* KING *and falls to his
> knees before him, stands up and remains standing in
> front of him without looking confused.*]

KING [*contemplates him with a look of surprise*].
  So you have spoken to me in the past?

MARQUIS. No.

KING.   You have earned the royal gratitude.
  But you deny the opportunity.
  Why? Though my memory is full of men,
  God's mind alone is faultless. You yourself
  Ought to have drawn attention to your merit.
  Why did you not?

MARQUIS.   Sir, I returned to Spain
  Only two days ago.

KING.   It is my custom
Not to remain indebted to my servants.   480
Ask me a favour.

MARQUIS.   I enjoy the laws.

KING. So does a murderer.

MARQUIS.   Then the fair-minded
Are all the more contented. I am one, sir.

KING [to himself]. Astonishing self-confidence, by God!
But that can be expected. I commend
Arrogance in a Spaniard. I am happy
To hold my peace when that cup overflows.
I hear you left my service?

MARQUIS.   I withdrew
To give a better man a chance to shine.

KING. Sad. When a mind like yours decides to rest,   490
The loss to my domains is great indeed.
Perhaps you fear that you will be employed
In spheres unworthy of your skill?

MARQUIS.   No, sir,
I am aware that your experience
In your wide field, the weighing-up of souls,
Can tell you at a glance, if you desire,
What I am useful for, if anything.
I sense with very humble gratitude
The honour that your Royal Majesty's
Gracious opinion of me heaps upon me.   500
And yet—

                              [He pauses

KING.   You doubt?

MARQUIS.   I have, I must confess,
Not yet arranged my latest ruminations,
Thoughts of a citizen of everywhere,
In forms of speech befitting to your subject.

Indeed, when I had finished with the crown,
I thought I had escaped the obligation
Of setting forth my reasons for departing.

KING. Are they so feeble that you fear to say them?

MARQUIS. If I win time enough to speak my mind,
   You will be wearied, and my life endangered.   510
   However, I will leave the truth alone,
   If you deny me that too-great reward.
   To choose between disgrace and your contempt,
   Is now my fate, but I would rather leave
   An outlaw than a fool.

KING.   Well, then, go on.

MARQUIS. I cannot pledge allegiance to a lord.
          [*The* KING *looks at him in astonishment*
   I will not sell myself on false pretences.
   If you should think me worthy of your favour,
   It would be only for my stirring actions.
   You need my skill at arms, my strength in battle,   520
   My mind in council. All that I would do
   Should be to win the favour of the crown,
   And for no other purpose. But my aim
   Is to serve virtue and no human master.
   What good you did through me would be my own,
   My motive would be my desire, not duty.
   And is this what you want? Could you abide
   Another maker of your own creations?
   And should I be content to be the brush
   When I can be the artist? I think not.   530
   I love mankind, and in a monarchy
   My only love can be for my advancement.

KING. This fire is admirable. Your desire
   Is to do good. The way to do it is
   The same for sages as for patriots.
   Seek out in all my empire for yourself
   The post that seems most suitable to you
   For your desire's fulfilment.

MARQUIS.   There is none.

KING. What?

MARQUIS.   Is it common human happiness
  That you intend to spread through me, my King?   540
  Is it the happiness I wish to give,
  Through openness and love, to humankind?
  Your Majesty would fear that happiness
  If you could see it. No! What you provide
  Is a new product of crown policy,
  Whose distribution it can still afford,
  That makes new feelings in the hearts of men
  For its new happiness to satisfy.
  The crown permits its coins to bear this stamp,
  The only kind of truth it can abide;   550
  All other superscriptions it discards.
  But what the crown can tolerate—is that
  Enough for me? Can my humanity
  Allow itself to chain humanity?
  If they can't think, I cannot call them glad.
  Let me not be the chosen advocate
  Of the serenity you force on men.
  I must refuse to be so generous.
  I cannot pledge allegiance to a lord.

KING [*a little abruptly*]. You are a Protestant, I think.

MARQUIS.   Your creed
  Is also mine, sir. [*after a pause*]
                  You misunderstand me.   561
  I was afraid of this. You see my hand
  Suddenly reaching out to pluck away
  The veil that hides the secrets of the King.
  What can convince you that I still revere
  What frightens me no more? I am a threat
  Because I am a servant of myself.
  But King, I threaten no one. My desires
  Die here, where they are born.
                          [*Laying his hand on his breast*

                              The ludicrous
Passion for newness that can never break   570
Oppression's chains, but only strengthens them,
Will never fire my blood. This century
Is far from ripe for my designs. I live
Among the citizens that are to come.
How can this image trouble your composure?
Breathe once and it is gone.

KING.   Am I the first
To know this side of you?

MARQUIS.   This side of me?*
Yes.

KING [*stands up, takes a few steps and then comes to a stand-
       still opposite the* MARQUIS. *To himself*].
           Well, my God, a new noise anyway!
Flattery has collapsed. To simulate
Erodes a man of spirit. But for once   580
To try the challenge of the opposite—
Why not? Surprises often bring good fortune
And put like that, yes, I can find a way
To redirect this errant strength of mind
To benefit the crown.

MARQUIS.   Sir, I have heard
That you are scornful of the worth of man,
And see the artistry of flatterers
Even in free speech—I can tell you now
What has encouraged you to think this way.
Men, men have done it. Of their own free will   590
They have demeaned themselves, deliberately
Abandoned their nobility, and struggled
To be beneath you. They avoid in fear
The ghost of what was once the good in them,
Take pleasure in their poverty of soul,
And beautify their chains with sophistries,
Wise cowardice, and call their customs virtues.
Thus you have overcome the world. And thus
The world was yielded up to your great father.

And whom, in all this sorry mutilation   600
Of manhood, could you find to honour?

KING.   Yes,
There is some truth in this.

MARQUIS.   A sad disaster!
As you received from the creator's hand
The men your own hand rearranged, and gave
As God, yourself, to these newfangled creatures,
You overlooked one thing: that you yourself
Remained a human being, that you retained
The weaknesses God gave you, you continued
To suffer as a mortal, to desire.
You need compassion, and a man can only   610
Offer himself to, pray to, tremble before
A god; you are no substitute for that,
You pervert nature—when you orchestrate
Mankind to perform the music of your will,
Who shares the harmony with you?

KING.   (By God,
He reaches to my soul!)

MARQUIS.   This sacrifice
Means nothing to you, though; in compensation,
You are unique. You are your own small species.
And at that price you are a god indeed.
If you were not—how sad a travesty!   620
If even at the price of the destruction
Of the content of millions, you were nothing!
If that same freedom that you have extinguished
Was the one thing that could fulfil your wishes!
I beg you, Sir, dismiss me, my great theme
Has carried me away. My heart is full.
To stand before the only man on earth
To whom my thoughts desire to be revealed,
Is far too much for me to bear.
                    [COUNT LERMA *enters and speaks a few words*
                    quietly with the KING. *The* KING *indicates for*

LERMA *to go and remains seated in the*
previous position

KING [*to the* MARQUIS *after* LERMA *has left*].
                        Continue!

MARQUIS [*after some silence*].
    Sir, I am sensible of the great—

KING.   Finish!   630
    I think you had some more to tell me.

MARQUIS.   Sir!
    I just returned from Flanders and Brabant;
    So many rich and healthy provinces!
    A people great and strong—and also good.
    To be a father to a race like this,
    Is to be God on earth, I thought, and then
    I saw the heaps of blackened human bones.
        [*He falls silent. His eyes come to rest on the* KING,
        who tries to return his gaze, but casts his eyes
        embarrassed and confused on the ground
    You are right. And what you do is necessary.*
    That you can do what you decide you must,
    Fills me with cold and terrible respect.   640
    And it is sad that, kneeling in his blood,
    The victim is too weak and transient
    To sing the praises of the sacrificer.
    It is a pity that our history
    Is written not by gods but by ourselves,
    For they can see that kinder centuries
    Will bury Philip's time, that milder wisdom
    Will come—the happiness of citizens
    Will thrive upon the greatness of their Lords,
    And when the state will use its people well,   650
    Necessity will have a human face.

KING. When do you think your human centuries
    Would ever come to pass if I fall down
    Before the curse of this one? Look around,
    In Spain my subjects prosper and increase

Under a cloudless sky—and this will last,
And this is what I wish to bring to Flanders.

MARQUIS [*quickly*]. The undisturbed contentment of a
    graveyard.
And do you hope to end what you began?
To trample on the universal spring,*   660
Halting the present changes in religion?
The world is growing younger day by day,
And you alone in Europe fling yourself
Into the path of the great world-fate's wheel,
That runs unstoppably at full speed on!
To jam its spokes with your thin human arm!
You will not. Many thousands have already
Fled from your kingdoms, poor but overjoyed;
The citizen you lose for his religion
Is your best man. With open mother's arms   670
Elizabeth receives your refugees,*
And all the craftsmanship of your domains
Is building England fearfully. Grenada,
Emptied of its industrious new Christians,
Lies fallow—and with joy all Europe watches
Your heart's blood flowing from the wound you gave it.
      [*The* KING *is moved. The* MARQUIS *notices it and
        steps closer*
You want your garden to flower eternally
But the seed you sow is death. An institution
Built upon fear will not survive its founder.
You have established deep ingratitude.   680
In vain you battle to the death with nature;
And you have sacrificed your royalty
To projects of destruction for no reason.
Humanity is more than you imagined.
It will escape the bondage of long sleep
And once again demand its sacred rights.
Your name will be cast down to lie with Nero*
And Busiris—and this is very sad,*
For you were good once.

KING.   Are you sure of that?

MARQUIS. Yes, by Almighty God, I say you were,   690
  Oh give us back what you have taken from us.
  Be strong, and bountiful, let happiness
  Flow from your fingers. Souls will grow immortal
  In your world house. Give back what you have taken,
  And make your citizens a million kings.

          [*He approaches boldly, while directing firm and
            fiery looks at the* KING

  I wish the exhortation of the thousands
  Whose destinies depend on this great hour
  Could crowd into my words and raise the gleam
  Beginning in your eyes, into a blaze!
  Tear from your face the evil mask of Godhead,   700
  Beneath whose eyes we perish. Be the image
  Of truth and everlastingness. For never
  Has any mortal man possessed so much,
  To do such good with. All the kings of Europe
  Honour the name of Spain above all others.
  A single word of yours can suddenly
  Create the world anew. Give us the freedom
  To think.

                    [*Throws himself at the* KING's *feet*

KING [*surprised, his face averted and then turned back to rest
  on the* MARQUIS].
            The strangest dreamer. But, stand up.

MARQUIS. Look all around at nature's mastery—
  Founded on freedom. And how rich it grows,   710
  Feeding on freedom. The creator makes
  Dewdrops bear worms, and even in the chambers
  Of still decay, sets free the self-delighting.
  But your creation, oh how thin, how poor!
  The King of Christendom is terrified
  By a wind-shaken tree, and you must tremble
  Whenever virtue smiles. But he, the other,
  Rather than lock away one speck of freedom,
  Allows the ghastly armies of the devil
  To swagger through the universe unhindered.   720
  He, the creator, men are not aware of,

Because eternal laws are wrapped around him,
A free mind sees the laws and not their maker.
Who needs a God, it says, the world is all.
And this free spirit's blasphemous respect
Is praise far greater than a Christian's anthems.

KING. And would you undertake to emulate
This wild ideal in the mortality
Of all my earthly states?

MARQUIS.   Yes, you can do it.
Commit to human happiness your power   730
That has for so long raised itself alone;
Give back nobility to humankind.
Your subjects must be what they were once more,
The crown's unique concern. Can there be any
Holier duty than equality?
If men should recognize themselves again,
Be given back themselves, then freedom's proud,
Exalted virtues will be everywhere,
And when your kingdoms are the happiest
In the whole world, your duty will be clear—   740
Then you must make an empire of it all.

KING [*after a long pause*]. I let you reach the end. I understand
That how your mind portrays the world to you
Is not how others do—so I refrain
From thinking of you in the light of them.
I am the first to whom you have disclosed
Your innermost ideas. That I believe,
Because I know it. For the sake of this
Reserve, and for the sake of these opinions
Delivered with such fire, until today   750
Kept hidden, and because I see your wisdom
Is humble, I will overlook, young man,
What I have heard you say, and in what manner.
Stand up. I wish to disagree with you,
Who have so overreached your youth, not as
The King, but as an old man. This I wish
Because I wish it. Clearly every poison

Can, in a nature that is well-disposed,
Transform itself to something good. However,
Be wary of my Inquisition. It would   760
Make me most sad—

MARQUIS.   But would it? Would it really?

KING [*lost in thought looking at him*]. No, I have never met
    a man like this.
No, Marquis, there you go too far. You hurt me.
I have no wish to be another Nero.
I would not choose to seem like that to you.
I shall not wither every happiness,
For you yourself at least shall still survive,
Beneath my eyes, a human.

MARQUIS [*quickly*].   And your subjects?
Sir, I have not been pleading for myself.
What of my fellow human citizens?   770

KING. You know so well how future times will judge me,
Show them yourself, for you are the example
Of how I acted when I found a man,
With mercy.

MARQUIS.   Oh! The most impartial King
In the whole world cannot so suddenly
Become the blindest. In your provinces
There are a thousand better men than I.
No, if I may now say what I observe,
You can perceive the kinder face of freedom,
Now for the first time ever.

KING [*with milder earnestness*].
                        Brave young man,   780
No more of this. Once you know men as I do
Your mind will change. But if this is to be
Our final meeting, I will grieve indeed.
How may your King proceed in your acquaintance?

MARQUIS. Let me be what I am. I will be useless
If you corrupt me like the rest of them.

KING. This pride is too much! Sir, as from today
 You are in my employment. No appeal!
 This is my wish.

                                        [*After a pause*
                What was my true desire?
 It was the truth I wanted, was it not?   790
 And here is honesty and more. You found me,
 Marquis, upon my throne, and understood me—
 What if you saw me in my house?
                [*As the* MARQUIS *seems to be considering*
                    something
                                    I know.
 I understand you. And yet surely I,
 The most unlucky father of them all,
 Could be a lucky husband?

MARQUIS.   If a son
 Who is the joy and hope of all who know him,
 And a fair wife so worthy to be loved,
 Can earn a man the right to be described
 As lucky here on earth, then you are so,   800
 Through both of these.

KING.   No, Marquis, I am not.
 And it is clearer to me now than ever
 That I am not.
        [*Rests his eyes with an expression of melancholy*
            on the MARQUIS

MARQUIS.   The Prince is noble-minded
 And good. I never found him otherwise.

KING. But I have found him otherwise. No crown
 Can compensate for what he took from me—
 The virtue of my Queen!

MARQUIS.   Who dares to say so?

KING. I and the rumours of the world dare say so.
 Evidence lies before me to condemn her
 Beyond all rational defence—still more   810

Is near to hand that makes the worst seem certain.
But it is very hard for me to credit
A fraction, never mind the whole of it.
For who are her accusers? If her honour
Is capable of self-annihilation,
How easy to believe that such a fragile
And wind-blown soul as Eboli can falter?
Of course the priest abhors my son and her.
And Alba thinks of nothing but revenge.
My wife is worth far more than any of them.   820

MARQUIS. And something lies within the woman, sir,
    That is above all tricks of circumstance
    That rumours use for tinder—it is called
    Feminine virtue.

KING.   Yes, I say so too.
    It costs a woman dear to sink as low
    As some would have me think the Queen has. Honour
    Cannot devour itself as painlessly
    As they would like me to believe. Good Marquis,
    You know the ways of men. I have been searching
    For such a man as you, for far too long.   830
    Your goodness is unwearied by your knowledge;
    So I have chosen you—

MARQUIS [*surprised and shocked*].
                    You choose me, Sir?

KING. You stood before your Lord and asked for nothing—
    This I have never known. You will be just.
    Passion will never break your concentration.
    Get near my son. Inquire into the Queen,
    You have the right to speak to her in secret.
    But leave now.

                    [*He rings the bell*

MARQUIS.   May it be with one prayer answered?
    If so, this is the most triumphant day
    Of my entire life!

KING [*gives him his hand to kiss*].
                It is by no means   840
The least in mine.
              [MARQUIS *stands and goes*. LERMA *enters*
              This Knight shall be admitted
From this day on, whenever he desires,
Unannounced.

ACT FOUR

SCENE I

[*Hall in the* QUEEN's *quarters.* QUEEN, DUCHESS
OF OLIVAREZ, EBOLI, COUNTESS FUENTES,
and other ladies.]

QUEEN [*standing up, to the chief lady-in-waiting,* OLIVAREZ].
The key has not been found? Well then, break open
The casket, quickly.
      [*she becomes aware of* EBOLI, *who approaches
her and kisses her hand*
               Welcome, dearest Lady.
I am so glad to see you well again,
Though still a little pale.

FUENTES [*a touch spitefully*].
                 The wicked fever
Does jolt the nerves, is that not so, Princess?

QUEEN. I dearly wished to visit you, my friend,
But I could not, for it is not allowed.

OLIVAREZ. Loneliness did not trouble the Princess.

QUEEN. Good. But you tremble. Are you not yet well?

EBOLI. Yes, it is nothing, really nothing, Queen.   10
But may I beg permission to retire?

QUEEN. You are more ill than you would have us think.
Standing is torture. Sit upon this stool;
Assist her, Countess.

EBOLI.   I will soon recover
In the cool air.

                              [*Exit*

QUEEN.   A sudden deep depression!
Follow her, Countess!
      [*A page boy enters and speaks to the* DUCHESS,
      who then turns to the QUEEN

OLIVAREZ.   Majesty, the Marquis
  Of Posa—from his Majesty the King.

QUEEN. Let him come in.
            [*Exit page boy to open the door to the* MARQUIS
            OF POSA

SCENE II

            [MARQUIS OF POSA. *The others as before. The*
      MARQUIS OF POSA *goes down on one knee before the*
            QUEEN, *who signals him to get up.*]

QUEEN.   Can my good master's orders
  Be spoken openly?

MARQUIS.   My Queen, his message
  Is for your Royal Majesty alone.   20
            [*The ladies remove themselves after a signal from
            the* QUEEN

SCENE III

            [QUEEN, MARQUIS OF POSA.]

QUEEN [*full of astonishment*].
  What, Marquis—can I trust my own two eyes?
  The King has sent you here?

MARQUIS.   Your Majesty,
  Does that seem strange? It is not so to me.

QUEEN. Well then, the world is turning in reverse.
  I must confess, the King and you, my friend—

MARQUIS. It has a doubtful sound; and well it may,
  The age is rich in miracles and signs.

QUEEN. But none as wonderful as this, I think.

MARQUIS. Suppose that I have let myself be won,
  That I was weary of my character   30

As the outsider here at Philip's court;
And what can the outsider hope to do?
He who would be the servant of mankind
Must first discover how to speak to it.
And why do monks announce their faith with clothes?
Tell me who is so free of vanity
As not to long to lecture and persuade.
Suppose I was to put myself about
To set my own opinions on a throne?

QUEEN. No, Marquis, even as a pleasantry   40
   I cannot let you speak such senselessness.
   You are no dreamer who will give himself
   To what can never come to anything.

MARQUIS. Whether it could or not is just the question.

QUEEN. What would be unforgivable of you,
   Marquis, and what would make me hate you, would be—

MARQUIS. Equivocation. Yes.

QUEEN.   Dishonesty;
   It would be that. His Majesty's desire
   Is not, I think, to send for me by you,
   Nor to speak through you.

MARQUIS.   No.

QUEEN.   Can your good cause   50
   Transform the evil of its means to honour?
   How can your pride—forgive me for the question—
   Hire itself out for this unpleasantness?
   I hardly can believe it—

MARQUIS.   Nor can I—
   If all that matters is to cheat the Monarch;
   But that is not my aim in this endeavour.
   I mean to bring more vision to my duty,
   And serve him with more honour than he looks for.

QUEEN. I recognize you there. So, let it be.
   What does he want?

MARQUIS.   The King? How suddenly   60
My sharp-eyed judge reminds me of my place.
But what I do not hasten to relate,
Your Majesty is in no haste to hear,
I truly think. And yet it must be heard.
The King desires to ask your Majesty
Kindly to grant the French ambassador
No further audience today. Your Highness,
This is my message.

QUEEN.   Is that all he sends me?

MARQUIS. That is the reason for my presence—almost.

QUEEN. And I am very happy not to know   70
What must perhaps remain unsaid to me.

MARQUIS. It must, my Queen. Were you not as you are,
I would divulge to you without delay
Numerous things, and tell you to beware
Several people—but the need is slight,
Since you are you. The tempest will arise
And rage around you and despair and die
Without you ever knowing it was there.
Danger is not so pressing as to tempt me
To break the sleep that crowns an angel's brows.   80
And it was not that threat that brought me here.
Prince Carlos—

QUEEN.   How is he?

MARQUIS.   My Queen, he suffers,
Like the unique philosopher an age
Forbids to worship truth. He is as ready
To die for love as the philosopher.
For truth. I bring few words, but they are his.
                              [*He gives the* QUEEN *a letter*

QUEEN [*after she has read it*]. He says he has to see me.

MARQUIS.   So say I.

QUEEN. And will it make him happier to see
With his own eyes, that his despair is mine?

MARQUIS. No, but your misery will spur him on   90
  And strengthen his resolve.

QUEEN.   To what endeavour?

MARQUIS. The Governor of Flanders has been chosen.
  It is the Duke of Alba.

QUEEN.   I have heard.

MARQUIS. We know the King. The choice will not be altered.
  But for his life, the Prince must not stay here;
  Not here, not now, no matter what, and Flanders
  Must not be sacrificed.

QUEEN.   Can it be saved?

MARQUIS. Possibly, though the means I have in mind
  Almost outdreads the loss it would pre-empt.
  It is a plot as brave as desperation.   100
  But I can see no other.

QUEEN.   Tell me of it.

MARQUIS. To you alone I dare disclose my plan.
  From you alone must Carlos hear of it.
  Only from your lips could the word be sweet,
  For, to be frank, it horrifies the ears.

QUEEN. Rebellion.

MARQUIS.   He must turn against the King,
  And travel secretly at speed to Flanders.
  The Flemish will receive him openly,
  The news of his arrival will explode,
  And the delivered Netherlands will rise.   110
  The King's own son will lift the cause of justice,
  His power will appal the throne of Spain,
  And what his father has denied him here,
  He will concede in Brussels readily.

QUEEN. You spoke to him today, yet you are sure
  That such a change could ever come about?

MARQUIS. I know because I spoke to him today.

QUEEN. Your plan both tempts and terrifies me, Marquis.
  In my belief the scheme is not misguided.
  Its boldness draws me, I will ponder on it.   120
  Does the Prince know of this?

MARQUIS.   It was my hope
  That yours would be the lips he heard it from.

QUEEN. There is no doubt that the idea is mighty.
  The Prince is young, however.

MARQUIS.   Have no fear.
  Orange and Egmont will advise him there,
  The warriors of Charles the Emperor,
  As wise in council as severe in war.

QUEEN [*with vivacity*]. No! The idea is grand and beautiful.
  The prince must act. I feel it earnestly.
  The role one sees him given in Madrid   130
  Would make me wretched. I will promise him
  France, and Savoy as well. I am entirely
  Of your opinion, Marquis. He must act.
  We shall need money.

MARQUIS.   There is much already
  At our disposal.

QUEEN.   I will add my own.

MARQUIS. So may I once more raise my Prince's hopes?
  When shall he see you?

QUEEN.   I will give it thought.

MARQUIS. Carlos is very anxious for an answer,
  And I have promised to return with knowledge,
  My Queen.
              [*He passes his writing block to her*
  Two lines will be enough for now.   140

QUEEN. And Marquis, shall we also meet again?

MARQUIS. Whenever you desire, my Queen.

QUEEN.   Whenever?
  How am I to interpret this largesse?

MARQUIS. With innocence, which is your character.
  It is enough for us that we have stolen
  Brief freedom. For my Queen it is sufficient.

QUEEN. Marquis, I hope that in the end all Europe
  Will feel this freedom, and that you provide it.
  You may depend on my support, though silent.

MARQUIS [*with fire*]. Oh how I knew that here I would be
  heard!   150
            [DUCHESS OF OLIVAREZ *appears at the door*

QUEEN [*in a distant manner to the* MARQUIS]. Anything spoken
  by the King my master
  I honour as the law. Assure my husband,
  When you return to him, of my submission.
            [*She gives him a signal. Exit* MARQUIS

SCENE IV

[DON CARLOS *and* COUNT LERMA.]

CARLOS. What is it that you wish to say to me?
  Speak, we will not be heard.

LERMA.   Your Royal Highness
  Is not without a friend here in the Court.

CARLOS. The opposite is my experience.
  What do you mean?

LERMA.   I ask to be forgiven
  If I have learnt more than I should have done,
  But let me reassure your Majesty—   160

The source of my intelligence is true,
Which is to say, in short, I am the source.

CARLOS. Whom does your news concern?

LERMA.   It is the Marquis
Of Posa.

CARLOS.   Well? What of the noble man?

LERMA. If he should know more secrets than is wise
About yourself, your Highness, which I fear—

CARLOS. What do you fear?

LERMA.   I saw him with the King.

CARLOS. So?

LERMA.   They conferred in secret for two hours.

CARLOS. Really?

LERMA.   They did not speak of trivia.

CARLOS. That I can well believe.

LERMA.   Your name was mentioned,
Prince, more than once.

CARLOS.   I hope with commendation.   171

LERMA. And furthermore, in the King's bedchamber,
Her Majesty the Queen was spoken of
In strange terms in the early hours.

CARLOS.   Count Lerma?

LERMA. And when the Marquis left the royal presence,
I was commanded that from this day on
He is to be admitted unannounced.

CARLOS. Generous grace.

LERMA.   There is no precedent,
In all my years of service to the crown.

CARLOS. These are great things. But what was that you said,
  How was the Queen referred to?

LERMA [*stepping back*].   No, my Prince,   181
  That is against my duty.

CARLOS.   Very strange!
  You tell me one thing but you hide another.

LERMA. The first was yours. I owe it to the Monarch
  To hide the second.

CARLOS.   You are right.

LERMA.   The Marquis
  Has always been an honourable man,
  I know that.

CARLOS.   Then you know him very well.

LERMA. But every man is good before the test.

CARLOS. And many sometimes after.

LERMA.   To enjoy
  A great King's favour is to occupy   190
  A questionable position. Many virtues
  Have gaped and died upon that hook of gold.

CARLOS. Too true.

LERMA.   It is no folly to disclose
  What cannot be kept secret.

CARLOS.   No! No folly!
  And yet you say that you have known the Marquis
  To be an ever-honourable man!

LERMA. If he is still, my doubts will do no harm.
  And you are twice the richer.

                                    [*Makes to go*

CARLOS [*follows, moved, and shakes his hand*].
                        Noble man,
  In truth my gain is threefold in this case,
  I keep the friend I had and find another.   200

                                    [*Exit* LERMA

SCENE V

[MARQUIS OF POSA *comes through the gallery.*
CARLOS.]

MARQUIS. Karl! Karl!

CARLOS.   Who calls? Ah, it is you, thank God!
Follow me to the monastery soon,
I go there now.

MARQUIS.   Two minutes' speech with you.

CARLOS. But we may be surprised.

MARQUIS.   No fear of that,
What I must say will not take long. The Queen—

CARLOS. You have been with my father?

MARQUIS.   I was summoned.

CARLOS [*full of expectation*]. Well?

MARQUIS.   It will happen. You shall speak to her.

CARLOS. But tell me of the King. Why were you summoned?

MARQUIS. Him? He was simply curious, I think,
Wanting to know what kind of man I am,   210
At the suggestion of some helpful friend.
I do not know the reason for my summons.
He offered me some trivial position.

CARLOS. Which you refused, of course?

MARQUIS.   Oh certainly.

CARLOS. How did you part?

MARQUIS.   On amicable terms.

CARLOS. Did you discuss me?

MARQUIS.   You? Of course we did,
Broadly.

            [*He pulls out his writing tablet and gives it to
            the* PRINCE

But in the meantime, look, and read,
It is a message from the Queen herself.
I will find out tomorrow, when and how—

CARLOS [*reads very distractedly, puts the writing block
    away, and moves to leave*]. So you will meet me at the
    monastery—   220

MARQUIS. No one is coming. Wait a bit. Why run?

CARLOS [*with a forced smile*]. Our roles have truly changed
    I see. Today
All my affairs are under your control.

MARQUIS. Why is it strange today? What is the matter?

CARLOS. What is my letter from the Queen about?

MARQUIS. Did you not read it just this moment now?

CARLOS. I? Yes, oh yes.

MARQUIS.   What is the matter with you?

CARLOS [*reads what is written once again. Delighted and
    passionate*]. Angel of God! My only true desire
Is to be worthy of you. Now I know,
The love of great souls never shall be conquered,   230
Though it may be beyond their comprehension.
I am obedient to her command.
She tells me that a very great decision
Will test me soon, and that I must be ready.
What does she mean by that? Can you explain?

MARQUIS. Well if I can, is now the moment, Karl?

CARLOS. Did I insult you? I was far away.
Forgive me, please, Roderigo.

MARQUIS.   What upset you?

CARLOS. It was—I do not know. This writing tablet,
It is for me?

MARQUIS.   No—on the contrary,   240
I have to take your own.

CARLOS.   Mine! For what reason?

MARQUIS. And any other small and telling items
That you may have, that could be lost or stolen,
And fall into the wrong hands—such as letters,
Or any thoughts you may have jotted down;
In short, whatever your portefeuille contains.

CARLOS. Why?

MARQUIS.   To forestall misfortunes of all kinds.
No one will look for things of yours on me.
Give them to me.

CARLOS.   But this is very strange.
Why this alarm so suddenly? Explain.   250

MARQUIS. For peace of mind. This is a wise precaution
Before the risk. There is no great new danger
Behind this act, that I am hiding from you.
I did not mean to frighten you, believe me.

CARLOS [gives him the portefeuille].
Look after it.

MARQUIS.   I will do that.

CARLOS [looks at him with significance].
                         Roderigo!
I have entrusted you with much today.

MARQUIS. Not with as much of yours as is already
In my safekeeping. That is everything.
And now, farewell, farewell.

                              [He makes to go

CARLOS [struggles inwardly with his doubts. Eventually calls
him back].
                         Give me the letters.
There is among them one she wrote to me   260
When I lay near to death in Alcala.*
I always keep it near my heart. To live
Without that letter would be hard for me.

Leave me that letter, you may take the others.
      [*He takes the letter out and gives the portefeuille
      back to* POSA

MARQUIS. Karl, this is very foolish, what concerned me
Was just that letter.

CARLOS.   Farewell.
            [*He walks away slowly and silently, stops for a
            moment at the door, turns round again and
            brings the letter back to* POSA
                              It is yours.
            [*His hand trembles, he begins to weep, falls
            around* POSA's *neck and presses his face to*
            POSA's *chest*
My father cannot do this. Am I right?
Tell me he cannot do this, my Roderigo.
                                          [*Exit quickly*

SCENE VI

MARQUIS [*gazes after him in amazement*].
   Can it be true that I do not yet know him?
   Not properly? Can I have failed to notice   270
   Such a forbidding shadow on his spirit?
   Yet it is true—he doubts his greatest friend.
   No! I am thinking like his enemy;
   What evil has he ever done to me,
   That I should think him shallow and distrustful?
   I would behave like him, I can believe
   That he would feel excluded. But to hide
   In reticence—he never has before.
   But there is no kind way. I must torment
   Your noble spirit, Karl, a little longer.   280
   The King believes the vessel he has chosen
   To bear his holy secret, to be worthy.
   I must be grateful for his faith in me.
   And even if I told you everything,

The whisperers would make you suffer, Karl,
Force you to doubt your friend. Why show the sleeper
The thundercloud that hangs above his head?
Better to lead it silently away,
To give him perfect weather when he wakes.

                                          [*Exit*

SCENE VII

[*The* KING's *office.**]

[*The* KING *is sitting in an armchair. Next to him the*
INFANTA CLARA EUGENIA.]

KING [*after a deep silence*]. No, she is still my daughter, to
    breed lies   290
Is not a capability of nature.
My own eyes find that these blue eyes are mine,
And in these features that repeat their father
I see my own lost childhood rediscovered.
Surely the love that made you was for me,
And that is why my heart's blood draws you to me.
                       [*He interrupts himself and pauses*
My blood! It is the worst I can imagine.
My face, that I see here, is also his face.
        [*He has taken the medallion into his hand and
        looks alternately from the picture to the
        mirror opposite. Finally he throws the
        medallion to the floor, stands up quickly and
        pushes the* INFANTA *away*
Go, go! Before this chasm drags me in.

SCENE VIII

[COUNT LERMA, *the* KING.]

LERMA. Her Majesty the Queen has just appeared,   300
And she is in the antechamber.

KING.   Now?

LERMA. She seeks the honour of an audience.

KING. No, this is not the proper time at all,
Tell her I cannot speak to her, not now—

LERMA. And yet, her Majesty is here already.

[*Exit*

SCENE IX

[*The* KING. *The* QUEEN *enters. The* INFANTA. *The*
INFANTA *flies towards the* KING *and cuddles up to
him. The* QUEEN *falls at his feet. The* KING *stands
silent and confused.*]

QUEEN. My Master and my husband, I am forced
To kneel before you as a suppliant.

KING. What do you mean?

QUEEN.   I find I am unworthy
In this court's eyes, of any dignity.
My jewel casket has been stolen from me.   310

KING. What?

QUEEN.   A few things of worth to me alone
Have vanished.

KING.   Things of worth to you alone?

QUEEN. And since there is a false significance
The kind of person who could know no better
Might give these objects—

KING.   False significance?
What kind of person? Stand.

QUEEN.   Husband, I shall,
When you have bound your honour by a vow
To lend the power of your royal arm
To my unveiling of this criminal.

If you do not, I must dismiss my household,   320
Since it sees fit to hide a thief.

KING.   But stand!
In this position how can I—stand up—

QUEEN [*stands up*]. That he is noble we may surely know,
Because my casket held at least a million
In pearls and diamonds, but he was content
With letters.

KING.   Tell me—

QUEEN.   Husband, yes of course.
They were some letters and a gold medallion
Sent me by the Infante.

KING.   Sent by him?

QUEEN. Yes, by your son—

KING.   To you?

QUEEN.   Most certainly.

KING. You are prepared to say this to my face?   330

QUEEN. Why should I not, my husband?

KING.   With no shame!

QUEEN. What are you thinking? Surely you remember
The letters that with both crowns' full permission
Don Carlos wrote to me at St Germain?*
And whether sending me his picture too
Was bolder than this licence would have liked,
Was the indulgence of a rashful hope,
That stepped too far, it is not mine to say.
If it was foolish it can be forgiven,
So I declare! For he was not to know   340
That she to whom in love he sent his picture
Would one day be his mother.
                    [*Sees the agitation of the* KING
What is wrong?
              What are you—

INFANTA [*who has in the meantime found the medallion on the floor and is playing with it, brings it to the* QUEEN].

Mother, look a lovely picture—

QUEEN. What is it, my—

[*She recognizes the medallion and stays standing still, speechless. The* KING *and* QUEEN *eye each other suspiciously. After a long pause*

Oh, sir, can this be true?
To choose this way to put me to the test
Strikes me as noble and monarchical,
But let me ask one question if you please—

KING. I am the questioner.

QUEEN.   And I the suspect,
But innocence will not be hurt by that.
If I was robbed at your command—

KING.   You were.   350

QUEEN. Then no one can be charged with this disgrace,
And I have no one to forgive and pity
But you, my King and Lord, whose wife was never
The kind of woman traps like this are for.

KING. I know the way you talk too well; but madam,
You cannot take me twice with this performance.
I learned my lesson in Aranjuez,
I know now what this Queen of Angels is,
And what she covers with her eloquence.

QUEEN. What do you know?

KING.   So be it. If I must,   360
I shall not spare you. Is it true, still true,
That you conversed with no one in the garden?
Madam, is that entirely true, with no one?

QUEEN. I spoke with the Infante, yes, with Carlos.

KING. Yes? So it sees the light, and you are happy!
In what contempt you hold my honour!

QUEEN.   Honour?
  If any honour was in danger there,
  I fear a greater trembled on the edge
  Than his who gave me for a wedding present
  Castile.*

KING.   You hid the fact that you had talked.   370

QUEEN. Is it my custom to allow myself
  To be examined and to answer questions
  Before my courtiers, sir, like a delinquent?
  The truth is something I will never hide,
  When it is sought for with respect and grace,
  But that was not your tone in Aranjuez,
  Was it, your Majesty? Perhaps a queen
  Should make account for all her private acts
  In the grand setting of a court of law?
  I met the Prince, I made this rendezvous,   380
  Which he requested very urgently,
  Because I wished to, and will not allow
  Etiquette to disservice innocence.
  Because I did not wish to speak of freedom,
  And argue with the King before my servants,
  I hid this meeting from your Majesty.

KING. Madam, you argue boldly, very boldly.

QUEEN. And I will add—because the Prince your son
  Does not enjoy his father's fair appraisal,
  And the good standing in your heart he merits.   390

KING. Merits?

QUEEN.   I will not lie. I value Carlos.
  I love him dearly as a relative.
  He was found worthy once to be for me
  What is worth most. And I have not yet learned
  Why he who was my dearest in the past
  Should for that reason be a stranger now.
  Though statesmen's wisdom will make marriages
  Where it sees fit, to break them when it likes
  Is somewhat harder. I will not feel hate

Because I should, and now that finally
I have been forced to let my conscience out,
I shall not let you bury it again,
Never again!

KING.   Elizabeth! Take care!
Times you have seen me weak now make you bold.
You often test the limits of your power
Against my strength, but you should learn to fear:
What makes me weak can also make me mad.

QUEEN. Tell me what I have done.

KING [*takes her hand*].   If it should be—
If it still is—and is it not already?
If the vast burden, the impending mountain   410
Of accusations that you bear increases
By so much as the weight of half a whisper,
If I have been deceived—[*lets her hand drop*] but even this,
The final shame, a man can overcome.
He can and will. But woe to you and I,
Elizabeth!

QUEEN.   Tell me what I have done!

KING. Then blood will flow, well if it will, it will,
Why should I care?

QUEEN.   So it has come to this.
Oh God!

KING.   I cannot recognize myself.
I honour no tradition any more,   420
The voice of nature speaks of emptiness.
What should I want with treaties, schemes, and aims?

QUEEN. Oh how I pity you, my Lord.

KING.   You, pity?
The comfort of a whore.

INFANTA [*startled, clings to her mother*].
                        The King is angry,
Beautiful mother cries.
            [KING *knocks the child roughly from the* QUEEN

QUEEN [*calmly and with dignity, but in a quavering voice*].
                    While I am living,
This child shall not be treated in this fashion.
Come, daughter, come with me,
                    [*She picks her up into her arms*
                            now we must go,
Because the King has no desire to know you,
And look for help across the Pyrenees,
Someone to cope for us.
                    [*She makes to leave*

KING [*embarrassed*].   Elizabeth—   430

QUEEN. This is too dreadful. I can bear no more.
          [*She tries to reach the door and falls with the
          child at the threshold*

KING [*rushes to her, full of consternation*].
  God! What has happened?

INFANTA [*calls out fearfully*]. Oh, my mother bleeds!
                    [*she runs out*

KING [*busying himself about the* QUEEN].
  No, this is wrong. Blood. Most unfortunate.
  I should not have to suffer this! Stand up!
  People are coming! Pull yourself together!
  We will be seen—stand up, stand up, stand up!
  Shall my whole court be feasted on this sight?
  Or must I beg you on my knees?
                    [*She pulls herself up assisted by the* KING

                    SCENE X

          [*The former.* ALBA *and* DOMINGO *enter shocked.
                    Ladies follow.*]

KING.   You there—
  The Queen is sick. Assist her to her chamber.
          [*Exit the* QUEEN *accompanied by ladies.* ALBA *and*
          DOMINGO *step closer*

ALBA. The Queen in tears, and bloodstains on her face—   440

KING. Does that surprise the devils who misled me
  And tempted me to this!

ALBA, DOMINGO.   Us?

KING.   You who told me
  Nothing for certain, but enough to draw me
  Into a fury of bewilderment?

ALBA. We gave you what we knew—

KING.   May hell repay you.
  Now I have done what I regret. Oh heaven,
  Were those the pleadings of a guilty conscience?

MARQUIS [*still offstage*]. May I consult the King?

KING [*starting up at the sound of his voice, walks a few steps
    towards* POSA].   Oh! It is you!
  Marquis, you are most welcome to me now.
  I have no further need of you, Duke Alba.   450
      [ALBA *and* DOMINGO *look at each other in silent
      amazement and leave*

SCENE XI

[KING, MARQUIS OF POSA.]

MARQUIS. Sir, the old man who fearless for your sake
  Stepped to the edge of death in twenty battles,
  Will find it hard to run from you like this.

KING. The thought becomes you and the action me.
  What you have done for me in half a day
  He could not do for me in many lives.
  I shall not hide the thing that pleases me.
  The seal of royal favour you have earned
  Will shine upon your forehead to the world.
  Him I befriend, I want to see them envy.   460

MARQUIS. Although to carry out successfully
  The services that make him worth that name,
  He must rely upon a cloak of darkness?

KING. What have you brought?

MARQUIS.   I heard a dreadful rumour
  As I was coming through the antechamber,
  That I cannot believe—about a conflict,
  A harsh exchange of words—blood—and the Queen—

KING. You came from there?

MARQUIS.   It would be terrible
  If any action of your Majesty's
  Had influenced events. Discoveries   470
  That I have made have changed the state of things.

KING. Well then?

MARQUIS.   I seized an opportunity
  To take some papers from your son's portefeuille;
  They will, I hope, make things a little clearer.

KING [taking the letters]. A letter from the emperor my father.
  I never knew that such a thing existed.
  The plan of some defences—of a fortress;
  Fragments of Tacitus—and what is this?*
  I think I ought to know this hand! This letter
  Is from a lady—let me see—'This key—   480
  Entrance into the Queen's pavilion—'
  Ha! What is this? 'Love—unrestrainedly
  And the long sufferer a fair reward.'
  Demonic treachery! I know her now
  So it is her—this is her hand—

MARQUIS.   The Queen's?
  Impossible!

KING.   The Princess Eboli's!

MARQUIS. So what the boy confessed to me is true,
  The page who bore the letter and the key,
  Henarez—

KING.   I am in the grip of evil.
Marquis, I wish it to be known, this woman   490
Stole letters from the casket of the Queen;
She warned me first—and is the monk behind her?
I am defeated by a damned charade!

MARQUIS. But it may come to good.

KING.   Oh Marquis, Marquis,
I fear I have oppressed my own dear wife,
And punished her for nothing terribly.

MARQUIS. If there were secretive communications
Between Don Carlos and the Queen, their nature
Was very far from what has been suggested.
I know for sure that the Infante's wish   500
To lead the army to the Netherlands
Was kindled by the Queen.

KING.   I always thought so.

MARQUIS. The Queen has her ambitions, certainly,
But, if I may say more, she is insulted,
She is appalled to see her proud hopes fail,
And feels herself denied a share of power.
The Prince's inexperience is useful
To her farsighted schemes. As for her feelings,
I do not think she loves the Prince.

KING.   I tremble
Before her power-scheming not at all.   510

MARQUIS. But is she loved, and should we ask ourselves
If we should fear the worst from the Infante?
These questions merit my investigation,
His case demands the greatest watchfulness.

KING. I put him in your hands.

MARQUIS [after some consideration]. Your Majesty,
If I am to be trusted with this office,
I ask that it shall be without control,
Free of all supervision.

KING.   It shall be.

MARQUIS. Without one aide, no matter what his name,
   To interrupt me in my undertakings,   520
   No matter what I have to do.

KING.   Not one.
   Nothing will hold you back, I promise you.
   You are my guiding spirit in this night,
   I thank you for the gleams you have revealed.
          [*To* LERMA, *who has entered on these last words*
   How did you leave the Queen?

LERMA.   Still faint, but better.
          [*He looks at the* MARQUIS *doubtfully, and leaves*

MARQUIS [*after a pause, to the* KING]. A wise precaution is
      required, my King.
   I fear the Prince may very easily
   Learn our intentions—he has friends enough,
   Perhaps among the rebels in Brabant.
   He may be pushed to an extreme reaction   530
   If suddenly alarmed. In my opinion
   Steps must be taken and swift measures planned
   For this eventuality.

KING.   Correct.
   But how is one to plan for such a crisis?

MARQUIS. A secret warrant for your son's arrest
   Must be drawn up, and placed in my safekeeping,
   Which I will use the instant danger threatens.
                    [*As the* KING *seems to consider*
   It would remain a secret of the state
   Until its use, of course.

KING [*goes to the desk and writes out the warrant*]. Uncom-
      mon danger
   Calls for strange measures, and the very empire   540
   Is under threat. You I need not advise
   To act with caution, Marquis, using this.

MARQUIS. We are the last defence, my King.

KING.   Now go,
  Go, my dear Marquis, quickly, and return
  Sleep to my nights and quiet to my heart.

SCENE XII

[*Gallery.* CARLOS *enters in the greatest fear.* LERMA
walks towards him.]

CARLOS. I have been seeking you, my friend.

LERMA.   My Prince,
  I have been seeking you.

CARLOS.   For God's sake, tell me,
  Is it the truth? Is it?

LERMA.   Is what the truth?

CARLOS. That she was carried bleeding from his chamber.
  He drew a dagger on her—answer me,   550
  What is the truth, by all the saints in heaven!
  What am I to believe?

LERMA.   No more than this:
  She fainted and in falling cut herself.

CARLOS. There was no greater danger, on your honour?

LERMA. Not for your Queen, but much I fear for you.

CARLOS. But she is safe. My mother, safe, thank God!
  Horrible rumours reached me, that the King
  Was raging at the mother and the child,
  And that a secret had been brought to light.

LERMA. That may be true.

CARLOS.   But tell me how. What secret?   560

LERMA. My Prince, I have advised you once today,
  And you rejected what I said outright.
  But you must use the second warning well.

CARLOS. What do you mean?

LERMA.   If I am not mistaken,
  I saw, my Prince, a day or two ago,
  A velvet, gold-embroidered blue portefeuille,
  In your possession.

CARLOS [*a little disconcerted*]. It is mine. Go on.

LERMA. And on the lid, set round about with pearls,
  A silhouette.

CARLOS.   Correct, you have described it.
  What of it?

LERMA.   When I entered unannounced   570
  The cabinet, not long ago, I saw,
  So I believe, the very article
  In the King's hand. And with him was the Marquis
  Of Posa.

CARLOS [*after a short silence in which he freezes, vehemently*].
                No! It is impossible!

LERMA [*hurt*]. Then I am nothing but a slanderer.

CARLOS [*looks at him for a long time*]. You are, precisely.

LERMA.   I forgive you that.

CARLOS [*walks up and down in terrible agitation and
    eventually comes to a standstill before* LERMA]. What
    evil has he ever done to you?
  What has our harmless friendship done to you
  That you proceed with hellish diligence
  To rend it and to crush it utterly?   580

LERMA. Prince, I respect the pain that makes you rage.

CARLOS. Oh God, oh God, let me not be suspicious!

LERMA. As I stepped in, his Majesty was saying,
  'I thank you for the gleams you have revealed.'

CARLOS. Tell me no more.

LERMA.   They say the Duke is down.
  And that the seal is taken from Ruy Gomez
  And given to the Marquis.

CARLOS [*lost in deep thought*]. Why not tell me?
  Why keep this from me?

LERMA.   He is held in awe
  By the whole court, as the first minister,
  And the omnipotent crown favourite.   590

CARLOS. He was a friend to me and loved me well.
  That has been pledged and proved a thousand times.
  But am I dearer than his fatherland,
  Worthier than a million citizens?
  In his almighty heart a friend is nothing,
  His love is too far-reaching for my life.
  And he is not to blame, but it is certain,
  Now it is very certain, I have lost him.
                    [*He goes to one side and covers his face*

LERMA [*after a silence*]. But my best Prince, what can I do to
    help you?

CARLOS. It is your turn, go sell me to the King,   600
  I have no more to lose.

LERMA.   But hold to hope.
  Who knows where this may lead?

CARLOS [*leans on the railing and looks vacantly straight ahead*].
                    Yes, I have lost him.
  And now I am forsaken utterly!

LERMA [*approaches him, moved to sympathy*]. You must
    consider how to save yourself.

CARLOS. To save myself? Oh you goodhearted man!

LERMA. And is there not another you should fear for?

CARLOS [*jumps up*]. God! What you bring to mind—of course,
    my mother!

The letter that I would not let him keep,
But which I gave him back. Oh God in heaven,
            [*He walks up and down, wringing his hands*
Does she deserve all this? He should have spared her,   610
He should have spared her, Lerma, shouldn't he?
                            [*Quickly, decided*
Who shall I send? Can there be no one, no one?
Ah yes, thank God, I still have one true friend,
And there—the worst has been revealed already.
                                    [*Exit quickly*

LERMA [*follows him calling*]. Prince, where to now?

SCENE XIII

[*One of the* QUEEN's *rooms. The* QUEEN, ALBA,
DOMINGO.]

ALBA.   If we may be permitted,
    Great Queen—

QUEEN.   What brings you?

DOMINGO.   Our anxiety
    Would not permit us to stand by in silence
    While danger threatens your exalted person.

ALBA. So we precipitously rushed to you,
    To bring to nothing with a timely warning,   620
    A plot that aims to wound you.

DOMINGO.   And to offer
    Your Majesty our unrestricted service.

QUEEN [*looks at them in astonishment*]. I am astounded, truly,
        I suspected
    No such devotion in the Duke of Alba,
    Or in Domingo; great Duke, reverend sir.
    I think I know how I may value it.

But speak, you tell me of a plot against me,
May I enquire, whose is it?

ALBA.   We implore you,
Be on your guard against a certain Marquis
Of Posa, whom the monarch has entrusted   630
With secret dealings.

QUEEN.   I am glad to hear it.
His Majesty has chosen well. The Marquis
Has often been described to me as good,
Even, at times, as great. The royal favour
Was never more judiciously extended.

DOMINGO. Judiciously? But we know otherwise.

ALBA. It has been common knowledge for some time
What Posa will permit himself to do.

QUEEN. You have intrigued me; tell me what, speak on.

DOMINGO. When did my Queen last look into her casket?

QUEEN. What?

DOMINGO.   Are you missing anything of value?   641

QUEEN. Why do you ask me that? What I have lost
The whole court knows. But tell me how the Marquis
Of Posa is connected with the matter.

ALBA. Closely, your Majesty, extremely closely.
The Prince has also lost important papers,
And we must tell you, they were seen this morning
In the King's hand, when he was with the Marquis
In secret council.

QUEEN [after some reflection]. That is very strange.
By heaven that is curious. I find   650
An enemy I never dreamt I had,
And two old friends I don't remember liking.
          [As she fixes a penetrating gaze on them

But that was soon to change, I must confess; I was about
   to offer you forgiveness
For the disservice you have done me, friends.

ALBA. Us?

QUEEN.   You.

DOMINGO.   Duke Alba, us!

QUEEN [*still directing her eyes fixedly on them*]. But it is
   sweet
   To see in time the rashness of my feelings,
   And to destroy them. Anyway today
   I planned to urge his Majesty to face me
   With my accuser. Now my case is stronger,   660
   For I can ask you for a testimony,
   Duke Alba.

ALBA.   I, my Queen? A testimony?

QUEEN. Why not?

DOMINGO.   But it would scatter to the wind
   All that we have achieved in secret for you.

QUEEN [*with pride and gravity*]. What have you ever done
   for me? Duke Alba,
   What could the king's wife wish to say to you,
   Or, for that matter, priest, to you, please tell me,
   That she would wish her husband not to hear?
   What am I? Innocent or guilty? Say!

DOMINGO. Horrible question!

ALBA.   What if it should be   670
   That he himself, the King, has been unjust,
   Till now—

QUEEN.   Then I must wait for his good judgement
   To reassert its rule. When that day comes,
   God bless all those who stand to gain by it.
        [*She bows to them and exits. They exit the other
        way*

SCENE XIV

[PRINCESS EBOLI *and immediately afterwards*
DON CARLOS.]

EBOLI. So the bizarre and terrifying news
That has already filled the court, is true—

CARLOS [*enters*]. I'll be as gentle as a child. Be calm.

EBOLI. Prince, this surprise—

CARLOS.   Have you forgiven me?

EBOLI. Prince—

CARLOS.   Are you still offended? Still? I beg you,
Tell me.

EBOLI.   What is this questioning about?   680
What do you want? Prince, you forget yourself.

CARLOS [*takes her hand impulsively*]. Sweet girl, you cannot
     hate eternally.
Love can and must forgive the insolent.

EBOLI. Oh what are you reminding me about!

CARLOS. Your gentleness and my ingratitude.
Oh I know well that I have wounded you,
Torn your mild heart and turned your angel's gaze
Into the anguish of the damned. And even now
I have not come to speak about regret—

EBOLI. Prince, you must leave immediately—I—   690

CARLOS. No, I have come because my very life
Depends upon the beauty of your soul.
I have no friend but you in all the world,
Once you were kind to me, you will not hate me
Until the end, you will be reconciled.

EBOLI. Enough! For God's sake, Prince, no more, no more!

CARLOS. I will remind you now of how you were,
Of when you loved me, of that golden time.

You will remember all your love for me,
Against which I rebelled. I will reward   700
And realize your dreams of love for me,
I will be once more what I was to you,
Exactly as your heart imagined me.
Once more and only once I shall appear
Before your soul as I was to you then,
And you must give this shadow what to me,
To me, you cannot give, and never will.

EBOLI. Oh Karl, you play so horribly with me!

CARLOS. Be greater than your sex. Forget my insults,
Be what no woman ever was before,   710
Do what no woman ever will again,
I ask the inconceivable of you,
Let me—upon my knees I beg you—let me
Speak with my mother!

SCENE XV

[*The former.* MARQUIS OF POSA *bursts in, behind him
two officers of the royal guard.*]

MARQUIS [*intervenes, breathless and beside himself*]. What
  has he confessed?
Do not believe him!

CARLOS [*still on his knees, with a raised voice*].
                      Blessed God in heaven!

MARQUIS [*forcefully interrupting him*]. He is insane. Do not
  believe the madman!

CARLOS [*loudly, more urgently*]. Our lives depend on what I
  have to say!
I beg you, take me to her.

MARQUIS [*pulls the* PRINCE *forcibly away*]. Hear his words,
  And you will die. [*to one of the officers*] Count Cordua,
  the King

Binds you: [*he shows the arrest warrant*] Don Carlos is
   your prisoner.   720

> [CARLOS *stands frozen, as if struck by lightning.*
> EBOLI *screams and makes to flee, the officers*
> *are astonished. A long pause.* POSA *is seen*
> *trembling violently and maintaining his*
> *composure only with difficulty. To the* PRINCE

Give me your sword, please. Princess Eboli,
Remain. [*To the officer*] Now listen closely to your duty.
His Highness shall not speak to anyone,
Your life is lost if he is not kept silent.

> [*He continues to speak to the officer quietly, then*
> *he turns to the other officer*

I go at once to kneel before the King,
To tell my Lord what I have done and why.

> [*To* CARLOS

And then to you. Expect me in one hour,
Prince, at the longest.

> [CARLOS *lets himself be led away without a sign*
> *of consciousness: only in passing he lets a dull,*
> *dying gaze fall on* POSA, *who covers his face.*
> *The* PRINCESS *tries to flee again. The* MARQUIS
> *leads her back by the arm*

SCENE XVI

[*The* PRINCESS OF EBOLI, MARQUIS OF POSA.]

EBOLI. Oh God in heaven let me leave this place!

MARQUIS [*leads her downstage with terrible gravity*].   730
   What did he say to you, unblessed woman?

EBOLI. Nothing—release me—

MARQUIS.   What have you discovered?
   You will not tell your tale to anyone
   In this world.

EBOLI [*looks with fright into his face*]. Do you plan to murder
   me?

MARQUIS [*draws a dagger*]. I am most sorely tempted. Now,
  be short.

EBOLI. I? Gracious God, what crime have I committed?

MARQUIS [*looks to heaven, lays the dagger to her breast*]. Your
    lips have not yet spread their poison, only
  Shatter the vial, and all is as before.
  A woman's life against the fate of Spain—
            [*He remains doubtfully in the same position*

EBOLI [*has sunk down on him and looks firmly into his face*].
  Why hesitate? I do not ask for mercy.
  No, I deserve to die and I desire to.   740

MARQUIS [*lets his hand sink slowly, after a short reflection*].
  No, it would be a crime and cowardly.
  Ah, but, thank God, there is another way!
            [*He drops the dagger and rushes out. The*
            PRINCESS *stumbles out another way*

SCENE XVII

[*One of the* QUEEN'S *rooms.* QUEEN, COUNTESS
        FUENTES.]

QUEEN [*to* COUNTESS FUENTES]. What is that uproar in the
    palace, countess?
  Every commotion frightens me today.
  Would you enquire, and come to me again?
            [*Exit* FUENTES. EBOLI *bursts in*

SCENE XVIII

[*The* QUEEN, PRINCESS EBOLI.]

EBOLI. Queen, help me, he is taken!

QUEEN.   Who is taken?

EBOLI. He has been thrown in prison by the Marquis,
  By order of the King.

QUEEN.   But who?

EBOLI.   The Prince.

QUEEN. Are you insane?

EBOLI.   They led him off just now.

QUEEN. Who took him?

EBOLI.   It was Posa, Majesty.   750

QUEEN. Thank God it was the Marquis anyway.

EBOLI. How can you be so calm and cold my Queen?
  God, you have no idea, you do not know—

QUEEN. Why he has been imprisoned? He is surely
  Guilty of some imprudent undertaking,
  Some accident, which is in character,
  The youth is very prone to such mistakes.

EBOLI. No, no! My Queen, I know the circumstances,
  Devilish, horrid, godforsaken act!
  There can be no reprieve now: he will die.   760

QUEEN. Carlos will die?

EBOLI.   And I have murdered him!

QUEEN. What are you thinking? Why will Carlos die?

EBOLI. And oh the reason why the Prince will die;
  If I had known that it would come to this!

QUEEN [takes her hand]. Princess! You are beside yourself, be
    calm,
  And tell me what has happened quietly,
  Not terrifying me. What do you know?

EBOLI. Spare me this saintly sympathy, my Queen!
  Spare me this kindness, hellfire in my mind.
  I have no right to look you in the eyes,   770

My own are damned and will not lift themselves
In grateful admiration at your words.
Punish the viper writhing at your feet,
Already torn and half destroyed by shame.

QUEEN. What is it that you would confess, poor woman?

EBOLI. Glorious saint! Angel of endless light!
 You do not know yet, and you may not guess
 That you have smiled and jested with the devil.
 Well you must learn today, for evermore.
 The thief that robbed you of yourself was I.   780

QUEEN. You?

EBOLI.   I betrayed your letters to the King,
 And I accused you.

QUEEN.   You could do that? You?

EBOLI. It was the madness of revenge and love,
 I hated you because I loved the Prince.

QUEEN. So it was love for him that made you do it.

EBOLI. I spoke my love and it was not returned.
 That was my reason.

QUEEN.   Now at last some light
 Breaks through the maze. You loved the Prince. Stand up.
 You are forgiven. This has been forgotten.
 Stand up.

EBOLI.   No! No! I have a worse confession.   790

QUEEN. Speak then, what further truths must I endure?

EBOLI. The King—seduction—I—you look away,
 Oh I can see rejection in your eyes
 The crime that I revealed as yours was mine.
                [*She presses her glowing face to the floor. Exit
                the* QUEEN. *After a long pause the* DUCHESS
                OLIVAREZ *comes out of the cabinet into*

which the QUEEN *went, and finds the*
PRINCESS *still lying in her previous position.*
She approaches her silently, but the PRINCESS
hears and jumps up like a madwoman as she
can no longer see the QUEEN

SCENE XIX

[EBOLI, OLIVAREZ.]

EBOLI. She turns from me for ever, it is over.

OLIVAREZ [*steps closer*]. Princess of Eboli.

EBOLI.   Oh yes, I know,
  Countess, what you have come to say to me.
  The Queen has sent you to pronounce my sentence.
  Speak it then, quickly!

OLIVAREZ.   The Queen has ordered me
  To take your cross and keys into my keeping.*   800

EBOLI [*takes a golden nun's cross from her bosom and places it*
      in OLIVAREZ'*s hands*]. Is it permitted that I kiss the hand
  Of my best Queen once more?

OLIVAREZ.   What is decided
  You will be told when you are in the cloister.

EBOLI [*bursting into tears*]. So will I never see her face again?

OLIVAREZ [*embraces her with face turned away*]. Live hap-
    pily and long.
              [*She goes away quickly.* EBOLI *follows her to the*
                door of the cabinet, which is closed
                immediately behind the DUCHESS. *For a few*
                moments she stays silent and motionless on her
                knees before it, then she gathers herself up and
                hurries away with her face covered

SCENE XX

[QUEEN, MARQUIS OF POSA.]

QUEEN.   You come at last,
  Marquis, how fortunate!

MARQUIS.   Your Majesty,
  Are you alone? Can we be overheard?

QUEEN. No, we cannot. Why? What have you to say?
            [*She looks at him more closely and steps back,
                shocked*
  Marquis, your face is changed, you frighten me,
  What can it be? The terror in your face   810
  Is that of someone close to death.

MARQUIS.   You know now,*
  Presumably.

QUEEN.   That he has been imprisoned?
  And, as I hear, by you? It is the truth?
  And I would not believe this if I heard it
  From any lips but yours, good Marquis.

MARQUIS.   Yes,
  It is the truth.

QUEEN.   And it was you who did it?

MARQUIS. Yes, it was me.

QUEEN [*looks at him doubtfully for a few moments*].
                    I honour all your actions,
  Even the few beyond my understanding,
  But now—forgive the terrors of a woman;
  The dangers of the game you play appal me.   820

MARQUIS. And it is lost.

QUEEN.   O help us, God in heaven!

MARQUIS. Be calm, my Queen, his safety is ensured.
  I only shall be lost.

QUEEN.   What must I hear?

MARQUIS. But who was it but I that chose this way,
   Risking so much on such a doubtful throw?
   Thinking to deal on equal terms with heaven?
   Who was the man who fearlessly proposed
   To pilot fate without omniscience?
   I was so clever! Why was I so clever?
   Each moment of our life sustains the weight   830
   Of the whole life. And maybe even now
   My last few drops are falling from the hand
   That held them cupped; the judge is weary of me.

QUEEN. Why are you speaking in these terms? The judge?
   What do you mean? I do not understand,
   But these are fearful words.

MARQUIS.   But he is saved!
   No matter that the price is very great.
   But not for long—he only has a moment,
   And he must use it well and fly from Spain.

QUEEN. At once? Tonight?

MARQUIS.   Arrangements have been made.
   A coach is waiting in the monastery,   841
   For a long time our friendship's hiding place.
   Here is the wealth the world has given me,
   Add what is lacking. There are many things
   That he should know, my heart would tell my Karl,
   But if I tried to settle all with him,
   My time would soon run out. But you, tonight,
   Will speak to him, and so I speak to you.

QUEEN. Please, for my peace of mind, explain things to me,
   Marquis, do not continue in this way,   850
   Speaking in riddles, terrifying me.

MARQUIS. There is one more important testimony
   For you to safeguard. I have had the luck,
   As few have had, to love a royal prince,
   Pledged to one person, set on him alone,
   My heart was able to embrace a world!

I made his soul a paradise for millions!
The beauty of my dreams could rival heaven,
But heaven sees fit to summon me away
Before the lovely harvest time has come.   860
Soon his Roderigo will exist no more,
The friend will vanish, leaving the beloved
Here, on the altar of his dearest church,
In his Queen's heart, I leave my parting gift.
It will be there when I shall be remembered.
                [*He turns away, his voice choked with tears*

QUEEN. This is the speech of the condemned. I hope,
Merely a passing fit of terror, Marquis.
Or is there meaning in it?

MARQUIS.   Tell the Prince
Not to forget the sacred oath we swore
Upon the sacrament in better times.   870
I have been true to that, unswervingly,
And faithful to our friendship unto death.
Now he must honour his part.

QUEEN.   Unto death?

MARQUIS. The Prince must give the vision life—oh tell him;
The fearless vision of another order,
Born out of our devotion. He himself
Must set his chisel to the unhewn stone.
That he may not achieve what he intends
Should not deter him. He must start the work.
And after centuries have hurried by,   880
Chance will provide another man like him,
And set its champion on an equal throne,
With the same dreams and the same strength of mind.
Tell him that when he is a man and King
He must respect the dreams he had when young,
And guard his sacred gentleness of heart
Against the disenchanting touch of reason.
He must not stumble when the dust of thought
Threatens to choke his passion, heaven's gift.
As I have told him often—

QUEEN.   Told him what?   890
Where is this leading?

MARQUIS.   Tell him furthermore,
The happiness of man is in his hands;
That I entrust its fragile life to him,
That I, who have deserved its touch, demand
With my last words, that he is true to it.
It would have suited me to be the bringer
Of a bright new beginning to the empire.
The Monarch took me to his inmost heart,
Called me his son, gave me his seal to bear.
And all his Albas vanished suddenly.   900

[*He pauses and looks for a few moments silently
at the* QUEEN

Beautiful soul, I know this weeping well.
Its cause is joy. But it is over. Over.
The choice was terrible and swift. Myself
Or Karl. The fate of one of us was sealed,
And it was to be mine, much rather mine.
Oh question me no more.

QUEEN.   Oh I begin
To understand. Poor man, what have you done?

MARQUIS. I have surrendered two short evening hours*
To save the glory of a summer's day.
Now I have given up his Majesty,   910
But I am not the man to serve a King,
In these dry fields my roses will not grow.
The fate of Europe rests upon my friend,
Now it is his, it ripens in his mind,
And Spain should trust its destiny to him,
Till then it must weep blood at Philip's hands.
But if my sacrifice should be betrayed,
If he should ever be unworthy—no!
I know my Carlos, that will never be,
You are the guarantee of that, great Queen!   920

[*After a silence*

I saw the slight beginning of this love,
I saw disaster stirring in his veins,

And I could well have crushed the passion then,
But I did not, instead I helped it grow,
For it was no catastrophe to me.
Others may judge according to the world,
My heart does not condemn me. I saw love
Where they saw death. And in this hopeless love
There was a gleam of hope for something else.
I wanted him to learn from excellence,   930
For highest beauty to uplift his soul.
Language denied me words, mortality
Transcendence, so I turned to you, my Lady.
And this was my intention, nothing more:
To show him what love is.

QUEEN.   But you misled him.
He occupied your thinking so entirely
That you forgot my human imperfection.
Am I so far removed from other women
That you could think to make an angel of me,
And turn his passion into stainless virtue?   940
This you forget—that when we give such feelings
Exalted names, we can no longer limit
The sacrifice our hearts will offer to them.

MARQUIS. That would be true of any other woman.
One thing I know—but tell me truly now,
Are you ashamed to be the inspiration
Of a heroic virtue? If your picture
Affords a soul in the Escorial
Immortal feelings, does that hurt King Philip?
Can the deaf owner of a lute complain   950
If others take the pleasure of its sound?
He has the right to break it if he likes,
But not the skill to call its music out,
Blending the strings like streams into a song.
The truth is for the wise, and they will find it,
Beauty is always with the pure at heart,
You two are one another's utterly,
Prejudice may not change my faith in that.
Promise to love that man eternally,

And never to reject him, to be empty,   960
Through terror or mistaken heroism.
Love him unchangingly, eternally.
Queen, do you promise, do I have your promise?

QUEEN. My heart alone shall choose my love for ever.
I promise that—no other judge can rule it.

MARQUIS [*pulls his hand back*]. Then I can die in peace, my
work is done.
[*He bows to the* QUEEN *and makes to leave*

QUEEN [*accompanies him silently with her eyes*]. Marquis,
you must not leave before I know
If we shall—when we are to meet again.

MARQUIS [*comes back, his face turned away*]. For certain we
shall meet again, and soon!

QUEEN. Posa, I understand you very well.   970
Why have you done this to me?

MARQUIS.   He or I.

QUEEN. No, no! This horrible catastrophe,
That you so nobly praise, you wished for it!
I know you—you have waited for this moment
Year after year. To feed your depthless pride,
A thousand hearts can break, it is no matter!
Your one desire is to be wondered at!

MARQUIS [*hurt, to himself*]. This I was not prepared for—

QUEEN [*after a silence*].   Marquis, think,
There must be hope.

MARQUIS.   No hope.

QUEEN.   Impossible!
Can I do nothing?

MARQUIS.   Nothing can be done.   980
Not even you can help.

QUEEN.   But I have courage,
You do not know me.

MARQUIS.   Yes I do. I know you.

QUEEN. There must be something.

MARQUIS.   No.

QUEEN [*leaves him and covers her face*]. Then leave me, leave
   me.
There is no hope of honour any more.

MARQUIS [*prostrate before her, highly moved*]. There is no
   man I honour any more.
       [*He jumps up and exits quickly. The* QUEEN *goes
       into her cabinet*

SCENE XXI

[*The* KING's *antechamber.* DUKE OF ALBA *and*
DOMINGO *walk up and down silently and
preoccupied.* COUNT LERMA *comes out of the* KING's
cabinet. Then DON RAYMOND OF TAXIS, *the chief
postmaster, enters.*]

LERMA. So, has the Marquis not yet shown himself?

ALBA. Not yet.
                [LERMA *makes to go back in*

TAXIS [*enters*]. Count Lerma, I must see the King.

LERMA. The King is not to be disturbed.

TAXIS.   His Highness
Will be most grateful for the news I bring.
Tell him I have to see him, Lerma, hurry,   990
I will not stand delay.
              [LERMA *goes into the cabinet*

ALBA.   He will not see you.
You must learn patience, Taxis.

TAXIS.   What? Why not?

ALBA. You should have asked permission from the Marquis,
Who holds both son and father in his hand.

TAXIS. What? Posa? That is what has brought me here.
It was from him that I received the letter.

ALBA. The letter?

TAXIS.   That I was to send to Brussels.

ALBA [*attentive*]. Brussels?

TAXIS.   But I will hand it to the King.

ALBA. To Brussels! Chaplain, do you hear? To Brussels!

DOMINGO. That is suspicious.

TAXIS.   And the furtiveness   1000
With which he gave it to me!

DOMINGO.   Furtiveness—

ALBA. To whom is it addressed?

TAXIS.   To the Prince of
Nassau and Orange.

ALBA.   That is treason. Chaplain,
William of Orange!

DOMINGO.   Yes, most certainly.
It can be nothing else. Of course this letter
Must hurry to the King. You serve your monarch
With great attention, sir, deserving honour!

TAXIS. Reverend sir, I only do my duty.

ALBA. You have done well.

LERMA [*comes out of the cabinet. To* TAXIS]. The King will
see you now.
                              [TAXIS *goes in*
You have not seen the Marquis?

DOMINGO.   He is looked for.   1010

ALBA. This is too strange. The Prince has been imprisoned,
The King does not know why. Extraordinary!

DOMINGO. But has the Marquis brought no explanation?

ALBA. What is the King's reaction?

LERMA.   There is none.
  He has not said one word.

ALBA.   Be quiet! Listen!

TAXIS [*coming from the cabinet*]. Count Lerma!

ALBA [*to* DOMINGO].   Chaplain, what is happening?

DOMINGO. His voice was shaking. What was in the letter?
  I fear the worst.

ALBA.   He asks for Lerma only,
  Though he knows well that we are waiting here.

DOMINGO. Our day is gone.

ALBA.   But am I not the man   1020
  For whom all doors sprang open? Where is he?
  Everything has transformed itself around me.

DOMINGO [*has approached the cabinet door quietly and stays
    standing in front of it, eavesdropping*]. Listen!

ALBA.   Dead stillness. I can hear them breathing.

DOMINGO. The double tapestries absorb the noise.

ALBA. Someone is coming! Back!

DOMINGO [*leaves the door*].   I am afraid,
  And overwhelmed, as if this was the moment
  When destiny for ever is decided.

SCENE XXII

[PRINCE OF PARMA, DUKES OF FERIA *and* MEDINA
SIDONIA *enter with a few other grandees. The
others as before*]

PARMA. May I consult the King?

ALBA.   No.

PARMA.   Who is with him?

FERIA. Posa, no doubt.

ALBA.   He is expected soon.
  We wait for him.

PARMA.   We were in Saragossa,*   1030
  We only just returned. So is it true?
  Throughout Madrid the shock is palpable.

DOMINGO. It is the truth.

FERIA.   A Knight of Malta holds
  The Prince in chains?

DOMINGO.   Indeed.

PARMA.   But why? What happened?

ALBA. A mystery to which his Majesty
  And Posa only can supply the answer.

PARMA. They did not think they should consult the Cortes?*

FERIA. Cursed be all those who emulate or aid
  This crime against the state.

ALBA.   Cursed be all those.

MEDINA SIDONIA. Cursed be all those.

THE OTHER GRANDEES.   It must be stopped at once.

ALBA. I will proceed into the cabinet,   1041
  Who will go with me? I will throw myself
  At the King's feet.

LERMA [*bursts out of the cabinet*]. Duke Alba!

DOMINGO.   Oh, thank God!
  At last!

LERMA [*breathless, in great agitation*]. Our master is alone
    no longer.
  When Posa comes, the Marquis must wait here
  For the King's summons.

DOMINGO [*to* LERMA, *while everyone else crowds round in
    curious expectation*].   You are pale as death,
  Count, what has happened?

LERMA.   Oh, too devilish!

PARMA, FERIA. What is?

LERMA.   King Philip wept.

DOMINGO.   Wept!

ALL [*simultaneously, moved and astonished*].
                                      The King wept!
        [*A bell is heard in the cabinet.* LERMA *rushes in*

DOMINGO [*follows him, trying to hold him back*]. Count,
    one more word, forgive me—he is gone.
  And here we stand like victims of Medusa.   1050

SCENE XXIII

[PRINCESS OF EBOLI, FERIA, PARMA, MEDINA SIDONIA,
            and other grandees.]

EBOLI [*hurriedly, beside herself*]. Where is the King? I have
    to speak to him!
                                      [*To* FERIA
  Duke, take me to him.

FERIA.   No, the King is troubled.
  No one may be admitted.

EBOLI.   Is he signing
  The death sentence? But I can prove deception,
  He has been lied to—

DOMINGO [*gives her a significant look from a distance*].
                              Princess Eboli!

EBOLI [*goes to him*]. Priest, you here too? Good, you can
    help my cause,
  I need you to confirm my explanation.
              [*She grabs his hand and makes to pull him into
              the cabinet with her*

DOMINGO. Princess, I think you are beside yourself.

FERIA. Stay out. The King no longer honours you.

EBOLI. But he must listen. Were he ten times God   1060
  He has to hear the truth I have to say.

DOMINGO. Go! You are risking everything!

EBOLI.   Poor man,
  The anger of your God appals you still,
  But I have nothing left on earth to lose.
              [*As she enters the cabinet,* ALBA *bursts out again*

ALBA [*his eyes sparkle, triumph in his gait. He rushes up to*
    DOMINGO *and embraces him*]. Let every steeple in the
    land resound
  With the Te Deum. Victory is ours.*

DOMINGO.   Ours?

ALBA [*to* DOMINGO *and all the other grandees*]. Now go in
    and kneel before the master.
  Me you shall hear from presently again.

ACT FIVE

SCENE I

[*A room in the royal palace separated by a large iron grille gate from a forecourt, in which guards walk up and down.*]

[CARLOS, *sitting at a table, his head in his arms as if sleeping. At the back of the room some officers, who are locked in with him.* MARQUIS OF POSA *enters without being noticed by* CARLOS, *and speaks quietly to the officers who then remove themselves. He himself steps up close in front of* CARLOS *and looks at him for a few moments silently and sadly. Finally he moves, waking* CARLOS. CARLOS *stands up, becomes aware of* POSA, *and jumps with surprise. Then he looks at him for a while with large, staring eyes, and runs his hand over his forehead, as if trying to recollect something.*]

MARQUIS. Karl, it is I.

CARLOS [*giving him his hand*]. Your kindness is undying,
And even now you visit me.

MARQUIS.   I thought
That you would need a friend here.

CARLOS.   Did you really?
You truly thought that? See, that comforts me,
More than you can imagine. Ah, my friend,
I knew that you would always care for me.

MARQUIS. I have deserved that thought.

CARLOS.   Of course you have.
We have not ceased to understand each other.
That makes me happy. This protectiveness,
This gentleness, befit great souls like ours.   10

Though it may be that one of my demands
Was reckless, were they all to be denied?
Virtue is sometimes hard, but never harsh,
Never unkind. I know it cost you dearly,
Oh yes, I know, I know too well, how deeply
Your heart was wounded by itself, preparing
Your victim for the altar.

MARQUIS.   Carlos, Carlos,
What are you saying?

CARLOS.   You yourself will finish
What I set out to do and failed, Roderigo.
It will be you that brings the golden days   20
This land had hoped for from its Prince in vain.
For me it is all over and for ever,
As you have recognized. Oh, dreadful love
Has gathered all the flowers of my soul,
And keeps them. For your vision I will die.
You had to give my secret to the King,
To gain his trust, and you will be his angel,
Led to his side by chance or destiny.
For me, his son, there can be no reprieve,
Perhaps for Spain there can. I did no wrong,   30
Only I have been criminally blind,
For I could never see until today
That you are great as well as gentle.

MARQUIS.   No!
This I did not foresee. How could I know
That you, led on by generosity,
Would be more sly and subtle in your schemes
Than I by thinking? I forgot your heart,
And all my clever structures fall to nothing.

CARLOS. Yet, if it had been possible for you
To save her from this fate, my gratitude   40
Would have been inexpressible! My friend,
Why could I not have borne this load alone?
Why did there have to be another victim?

But silence on this subject would be wiser,
I will not add reproaches to your burden,
What is the Queen to you? You do not love her.
My little love should not distract your virtue
With its complaints; forgive me, I was wrong.

MARQUIS. You were, but not the way you think you are.
  If I have wronged you once, I always wronged you,   50
  And if I had I would not stand before you.
                          [*He takes out his portefeuille*
  Here are some letters that you gave me—take them,
  I kept them safe for you.

CARLOS [*looks with astonishment first at the letters, then at
    POSA*].   What? How is this?

MARQUIS. They will be safer in your keeping now,
  So I return them to you.

CARLOS.   Can this be?
  You did not hand them to the King?

MARQUIS.   These letters?

CARLOS. You did not show them all, you kept these hidden?

MARQUIS. Who told you that I showed him any of them?

CARLOS [*very surprised*]. This is too strange. Count Lerma.

MARQUIS.   He said that?
  Yes, now I see, whoever could have known?   60
  Lerma. That man has never learned to lie.
  But no, a part of what he says is right,
  The rest of them are in the King's possession.

CARLOS [*looks at him for a long time in speechless astonish-
    ment*]. Then what has put me in this cell?

MARQUIS.   Precaution.
  It was my plan, to keep you from confessing
  A second time, to Eboli.

CARLOS [*as if waking from a dream*]. Oh heaven!
  At last I see. It is as bright as day.

MARQUIS [*goes to the door*]. Who comes?

SCENE II

[*The former*, DUKE OF ALBA.]

ALBA [*approaches the* PRINCE *respectfully, turning his back
   on the* MARQUIS *throughout the scene*]. Prince, you are
  free, the King himself requested
  That I should bring this message, and the honour   70
  That he accords me makes me very happy.

CARLOS. One locks me up, the other lets me out,
  And neither has the grace to tell me why.

ALBA. My Prince, it seems it was an accident,
  To which some bad adviser tricked the Monarch.

CARLOS. So I am here by order of the crown?

ALBA. His Majesty's misunderstanding, yes.

CARLOS. Forgive me, but the King himself must mend,
  In person, what the King's mistake has broken.
      [*He seeks the eyes of the* MARQUIS *and sees there
       a proud condescension towards the* DUKE
  The world describes me as Don Philip's son;   80
  A subject of its curiosity,
  I have no wish to seem to thank his grace
  For what his Majesty must do as duty.
  Otherwise I am very much prepared
  To stand before the judges of the Cortes.
  I will not take my sword back from this hand.

ALBA. There will be no objection from the King,
  And if your Highness will thus honour me,
  I will go with you to him.

CARLOS.   I remain,
  Until the King or his Madrid shall come   90
  To take me from my cell. That is my answer,

Take it to him.
> [*Exit* ALBA. *He can still be seen for a while in the forecourt, giving orders*

SCENE III

[CARLOS *and the* MARQUIS OF POSA.]

CARLOS [*as the* DUKE *has left, full of expectation and astonishment to the* MARQUIS]. But what is this about? Explain it to me. Are you not in power?

MARQUIS. I was, but as you see I am no longer.
> [*Walking towards him, very moved*
Oh Karl, it has succeeded, it has triumphed,
Praise the omnipotence that let this be,
The work is done.

CARLOS.   What has been done? What triumph?
I do not understand.

MARQUIS [*gives him his hand*]. Your life is saved.
And you are free, and I—

CARLOS.   And you?

MARQUIS.   And I
Can hold you for the first time to my heart   100
With a supreme right. Everything I love
I have exchanged for this—and Karl, this moment,
How very great it is—I am content.

CARLOS. How suddenly you changed, your eyes are shining,
And I have never seen you so exalted.

MARQUIS. Karl, we must say farewell. Do not be frightened.
Oh be a man. Whatever they may say,
Promise me not to make this worse for me
By giving way to agony, unworthy
Of great souls. Karl, you are about to lose me   110
For a long time, so long the foolish call it

For ever.

> [CARLOS *withdraws his hand and stares at him without answering*

Be a man, you have to be,
I count on you, for I will spend the hour
Men sourly call the last, with you. But Karl,
Shall I confess it? I have longed for this
For a long time. Let us sit down, I weary,
And I am drained of words.

> [*He moves close to* CARLOS, *who is still in deadly shock and who lets himself be sat down without resisting*

Where are you now?
You cannot answer. I shall not speak long.
We spoke together at the monastery
For the last time. That was the day before   120
My summons to the King; you know the outcome,
As does Madrid, but what you do not know,
And must know now, is that you were betrayed,
Your letters to the Queen were used against you,
I heard this from the King himself—and further,
You do not know that I—confided in him.

> [*He pauses to hear* CARLOS'S *answer.* CARLOS *remains doggedly silent*

Yes, my own lips undid my loyalty!
And I contrived the plot that was your downfall.
What had been found by then seemed all too clear.
It was too late, I could not set you free,   130
So I became the King's avenging angel,
I turned against my friend to serve him better.
Karl, do you hear?

CARLOS.   Go on, go on, I hear.

MARQUIS. Till now I am unblamed. But very soon,
The unfamiliar sunshine lets me down,
The new-found favour of the King betrays me.
You learn of it as I supposed you would,
But I, by mad pride goaded to complete
The daring scheme without endangering you,

Hid from our friendship my terrific secret   140
That lit the fuse! Oh I had blundered badly,
I know that now. My confidence was madness.
Forgive me—I was made impetuous
By our eternal friendship.

> [*He falls silent.* CARLOS *comes out of his*
> *petrification and becomes very*
> *animated*
> > Very quickly

My fears were realized. Invented facts
Filled you with terror, rumours of the Queen
Beaten and bleeding, echoed everywhere.
Lerma's unfortunate good services,
And my unfriendly silence mystify you;
You faltered and you gave me up for lost.   150
But in yourself too noble to admit
Your friend's disgrace, you dress it up as greatness,
You can believe in his disloyalty
When it becomes a hero's villainy.
Abandoned by the only one you trusted,
You turned to Princess Eboli, surrendered
Your fortune to the guidance of the devil.
Poor fellow, she betrayed you, and I saw you
Running to her—a dreadful premonition
Filled my whole mind, I followed, but too slowly,   160
To find you sprawled before her, the confession
Had stepped across your lips, a precipice—
And then for you there can be no reprieve.

CARLOS. No, no! You are mistaken, she was moved,
    I know that!

MARQUIS.   Midnight drips into my mind.
    Nothingness—no way out from nothingness—
    No hope of help from anything alive.
    Despair became the fury of a beast,
    I held a dagger to a woman's throat,
    But sudden sunlight sweeps across my soul—   170
    What if I could mislead the King's suspicions
    To thinking that the guilty one is me?

Probable or improbable, enough
That it is evil to convince this King.
More than enough. And therefore it shall be.
Maybe a sudden thunderclap from nowhere
Will be enough to make the tyrant stumble,
I ask no more, he stops, he thinks, and Carlos
Has won the time to steal away to Brussels.

CARLOS. And you have done this?

MARQUIS.   I have sent a letter   180
To William, Prince of Orange, telling him
That I have loved the Queen, but have by chance
Avoided the suspicions of the King,
Because his jealous eyes were set on you.
I added that the King himself provided
The means by which I saw the Queen alone,
But that, presuming I had been discovered,
Because you sought the Princess Eboli,
Knowing about my passion, and intending,
I have to fear, to warn the Queen through her;   190
Leaving you safe in prison bars behind me,
I have decided to escape to Brussels.

CARLOS [interrupts him fearfully].
Did you entrust this letter to the Post?
You know that letters to Brabant and Flanders—

MARQUIS. Are given to the King. No doubt by now
Taxis has done his duty.

CARLOS.   We are lost!

MARQUIS. Why are you lost?

CARLOS.   I drag you down with me.
How can the King forgive you for these lies?
No! He will not be reconciled.

MARQUIS.   What lies?
You are confused. Who tells him they are lies?   200
Think now.

CARLOS [*stares into his face*]. Who tells him? Can you ask me
   that?
Who else but I?

                           [*Makes to go*

MARQUIS.   Stay. Have you lost your mind?

CARLOS. No, I must go, for God's sake, let me go,
He will be hiring killers even now.

MARQUIS. So much the wiser not to waste the time.
We still have much to say to one another.

CARLOS. What? While we wait for him to slaughter us!
     [*Again he makes to leave, but* POSA *takes him by
     the arm and looks at him hard*

MARQUIS. Was I so anxious to announce the truth
That time you bled for me when we were boys?

CARLOS [*stands in front of him, moved and full of admiration*].
 O providence of heaven.

MARQUIS.   Save yourself,   210
For Flanders' sake. To rule is your vocation,
To die for you was mine.

CARLOS [*walks up and takes him by the hand, full of deepest
   emotion*].   He cannot hate us,
How can he punish such nobility?
No, no, he will not, we will go to him,
A friend has done this, father, I will say,
To save his friend, and he will cry warm tears,
Believe me, he is cold but not inhuman,
He will admire us, and he will forgive us.
      [*There is a shot through the grille door.* CARLOS
      jumps up
Who was that for?

MARQUIS.   I think it was for me.
                        [*Sinks down*

CARLOS [*falls with a cry of pain next to him on the floor*].
O God have mercy on us.

MARQUIS [*with breaking voice*]. It is swift—   220
The King—I hoped for longer—Karl, escape,
Hear me, escape—your mother knows the rest,
I can no longer—
                    [CARLOS *stays lying, as if dead, next to the
                    corpse. After a while the* KING *enters,
                    accompanied by many grandees, but steps
                    back, embarrassed, at the sight. A
                    universal deep silence. The grandees align
                    themselves in a semicircle around the
                    two, and look alternately at the* KING *and
                    his son. The latter still lies without any
                    sign of life. The* KING *contemplates him
                    in silence*

SCENE IV

[KING, CARLOS, DUKES OF ALBA, FERIA, MEDINA
SIDONIA, PRINCE OF PARMA, COUNT LERMA,
DOMINGO, *and many grandees.*]

KING [*in a benevolent tone*]. Infante, what you ask for has
    been granted.
I come, with all the great ones of my empire,
To give you back your freedom, wrongly taken.
                    [CARLOS *looks up and looks around, like someone
                    woken from a dream. His eyes fix first on the*
                    KING, *then on the dead man. He does not answer*
Take back your sword, our actions were misguided.
                    [*He approaches him and helps him to stand*
Stand up. My son is not where he should be.
And be received into your father's arms.
                    [*He receives his father's embrace without
                    consciousness, but suddenly becomes
                    aware of himself, stops, and looks at
                    him more closely*

CARLOS. You smell of murder, I cannot embrace you.   230
    [*He pushes him away. The grandees make a
        commotion*
How have I shocked you? Touched the Lord's anointed?
Horrible act! Fear not, I will not harm you.
Look at the mark God stamped upon my forehead.

KING [*makes to go*]. Gentlemen, follow me.

CARLOS.   Where are you going?
    Stay here!
        [*He holds on to him forcibly with both hands,
        but gets hold of his sword, that the* KING *has
        brought, with one hand. It comes out of its
        sheath*

KING.   You draw a sword against your father!

GRANDEES [*drawing their swords*]. Protect the King!

CARLOS [*holding the* KING *firmly with one hand, the bare
    sword in the other*].   Put up your stupid swords.
You are mistaken if you think me mad.
And it would not be prudent if I was
To tell me by your gestures that his life
Rests on my swordpoint. Keep away, however,   240
Unstable natures such as mine need caution,
So keep away. My business with the King
Does not concern your oaths of fealty.
Oh see his crooked fingers, how they bleed,
Look at him closely, do you see him now?
Then cast your eyes a little over there—
This is the artist's latest masterpiece!

KING. All of you, step back—do not shake with fear,
Are we not son and father? We shall see
If he shall break the laws of nature.

CARLOS.   Law?   250
There is none, if our nature is to murder.
You have unravelled nature's ancient ties,
You have destroyed its roots in all your Kingdoms,
Until today there never was a murder.

Is there no God? Oh look, look over there.
Or was creation made for Kings to ravage?
Only one man has less deserved to die
Since mothers first bore children. Where is God?*
What have you done? No, no, you do not know
That you have basely stolen from the world   260
A life that was more precious and more noble
Than you and all your subject generations!

KING [*with a conciliatory tone*]. If I have acted hastily in this,
   Should I be blamed by him for whom I acted?

CARLOS. What? Can it be that you do not yet know
   What this man was to me? Oh tell him, help him,
   The question baffles his omniscience;
   This dead man was my friend. And understand,
   I was the cause he gave his life for, I.

KING. Ah, my suspicion!

CARLOS.   Tattered shape, forgive me,   270
   For speaking things like this to men like these,
   But this grey connoisseur of souls must learn
   That his old wisdom has been mesmerized
   By a young man's sharp mind, and sink in shame.
   A higher god than nature made us brothers,
   Sir, we were brothers, love was his vocation,
   And love of me his glorifying death.
   When he received your honours he was mine,
   He mocked your grandeur with his eloquence,
   Your giant spirit was his entertainment.   280
   You thought you could control him, but you were
   As passive as a chisel in his hands.
   It was his friendship's diligence at work
   When I was thrown in here—to save my life
   He wrote a letter to the Prince of Orange,
   It was his first untruth—God! For my sake
   He threw himself upon the death he suffered.
   You honoured him, it was for me he died,
   You forced your friendship and your heart on him,
   Your sceptre was a toy he threw away   290

To die for me!

          [The KING *stands motionless, staring at the*
          ground. All the grandees look at him,
          embarrassed and fearful
          How was it possible
That you could fall for such an easy lie?
How little you impressed him, it would seem,
When he decided that you could be fooled
By such a childish prank. That simple test
Defeated you—you who had thought yourself
Worthy to be his friend. Oh no, oh no,
Not likely, he was not the man for you,
He knew that well when he refused your honours.
Your armoured hand has crushed this instrument,   300
He was too good for you, all you could do
Was murder him.

ALBA [*has not let the* KING *out of his sight until now and has*
    watched his expressions with visible disquiet. Now he
    approaches him fearfully]. Sir, not this death-like stillness,
Look at us, speak to us.

CARLOS.   You were at least
Not insignificant to him. You had
A share in him already. And perhaps
He could have made you happy. He could please you
With just the leavings of the feast he was.
He was so rich, a splinter of his soul
Could have made you a god. It is yourself
That you have robbed. What do you have to offer   310
In place of this?

          [A deep silence. Many of the grandees look away
          or hide their faces in their cloaks
          You who are gathered here,
Oh you who stand here so amazed and pale,
Struck dumb by awe, do not condemn the youth
Who speaks such rage against his King and father.
He died for me! Look there! Have you no tears?
Does blood or molten iron run in your veins?

Look there, and then condemn me if you can.

[*He turns to the* KING *with more control and ease*

Perhaps you wonder how this tale will end,
That is so very strange. Take back my sword.
You are my King again. Do not presume   320
I fear your vengeance. Murder me as well,
And so be rid of all nobility.
My life is forfeit, that I understand,
But what is life to me? I here renounce
Everything I have wished for from the world.
Search among strangers for another heir,
Here lies my inheritance.

> [*He sinks down next to the corpse and takes no
> further part. In the meantime, the confused din
> of voices and crowding people can be heard.
> Around the* KING *there is a deep silence. His
> eyes run through the entire circle but no one
> returns his gaze*

KING.   Does no one answer?
All eyes cast down? All faces turned away?
So then, my verdict is pronounced, my subjects
Judge me with silence.   330

> [*The tumult comes closer and gets louder. A
> murmur runs through the grandees, they
> give each other embarrassed signals.
> Eventually* COUNT LERMA *nudges* DUKE
> ALBA

LERMA. Truly this is a tempest.

ALBA [*quietly*].   So I fear.

LERMA. They are upon us, numberless!

SCENE V

[*An* OFFICER *of the life guards. The former.*]

OFFICER.   Rebellion!
Where is the King?

[*He works his way through the crowds to the*
KING
                    Madrid is up in arms,
Furious soldiers and the common people
Surround the palace in their thousands. Men say
The Prince has been imprisoned, and his life
Hangs in the balance. They must see him free,
Or they will set Madrid alight.

THE GRANDEES [*agitated*]. The King!
Protect the King!

ALBA [*to the* KING, *who stands calm and immobile*]. You
    must escape, your Highness,
We do not know what power has armed the people,   340
There is great danger.

KING [*as if waking, straightens himself and walks among
    them with majesty*]. Am I King no more?
Has my throne fallen? I am King no more.
These craven weaklings whimper, brought to tears
By a boy. You are all waiting for the word
To turn from me. I am betrayed by rebels!

ALBA. Your Highness, these delusions!

KING.   Go to him!
Throw yourself down before the blossoming
Swift-footed King. I am an old man, nothing.

ALBA. What, loyal Spaniards, has it come to this?
            [*Everyone crowds round the* KING *and kneels
            before him with drawn swords. Only*
            CARLOS *stays, alone by the corpse,
            abandoned by everyone*

KING. Dress him in all my royal finery,   350
    Carry him over my trodden corpse to the throne!
            [*Falls unconscious into the arms of* LERMA *and*
            ALBA

LERMA. Help! God!

FERIA.   God! Heaven!

LERMA.   He is overcome!

ALBA [*leaves the* KING *in* LERMA'*s and* FERIA'*s arms*].
Carry him to his chamber. While he rests,
I will control Madrid.

SCENE VI

[CARLOS *stays alone with the corpse. After a few
moments* LUDWIG MERCADO *appears, looks around
shyly and quietly behind the* PRINCE, *who does not
notice him*]

MERCADO.   The Queen has sent me.
Her signet ring is my authority.
                    [*He shows the* PRINCE *a signet ring.* CARLOS
                        remains silent
Her Majesty desires to speak with you,
It is important that you meet today.

CARLOS. There is no more importance on this earth.

MERCADO. Instructions that the Marquis left with her—
She says—

CARLOS.   Then I will come. [*Makes to go*]

MERCADO.   Good Prince, not yet,   360
Wait until nightfall, every door is guarded,
And everywhere the watches have been doubled.
Her Majesty cannot be reached unseen,
You would risk all.

CARLOS.   But—

MERCADO.   There is still a way.
An inspiration of her Majesty's,

Adventurous, and very curious,
Which she presents you to reject or try.

CARLOS. What is it?

MERCADO.   You have heard the famous legend
  That through the cloisters of the royal castle,
  Dressed in the trappings of a monk, at midnight   370
  The Emperor's departed spirit wanders.
  The common folk believe it, and the guards
  Accept that post with very great reluctance.
  If you decide to try it you may pass,
  Dressed as this ghost, unchallenged through the guards,
  And reach the chamber of the Queen unharmed.
  This key will gain you entrance. The disguise,
  And their belief, will shield you from attack.
  But your decision must be made at once.
  Robes and a mask are hidden in your room.   380
  But I must go, the Queen awaits your answer.

CARLOS. When shall my visit be?

MERCADO.   At midnight, Prince.

CARLOS. Tell her that I will come.

                              [*Exit* MERCADO

SCENE VII

[LERMA, PRINCE CARLOS.]

LERMA.   Prince, save yourself!
  The King is raging, you will lose your freedom,
  Perhaps your life, if you remain; escape;
  My Prince, I beg you, question me no further,
  I stole away to warn you.

CARLOS.   God rules all.

LERMA. The Queen has told me that it was your plan
  To leave Madrid for Brussels. Do it now!

Profit from this disturbance to escape,   390
That was the reason why the Queen began it;
No one will dare oppose you for the moment,
The coach is waiting at the monastery,
And here are weapons, should you ever need them—
            [*Gives him a dagger and a pocket pistol*

CARLOS. Thank you, Count Lerma.

LERMA.   What you said today
    Moved me profoundly. Every patriot
    Weeps for you; truly, there are no more friends
    Who love like that. I dare to speak no further.

CARLOS. Him we have lost called you a noble man,
    Count Lerma!

LERMA.   Prince, once more, escape, God guide you;
    Though such as I will not be living then,   401
    A better time will come. Receive my homage.
            [*He gets down on one knee in front of him*

CARLOS [*makes to hold him back, very moved*].
    No, Count, you move me, let me hide my weakness.

LERMA. King of my children! Though their father may not,
    My children will be proud to die for you.
    Reward my children for my services,
    Return in peace to Spain, you who have suffered,
    To seat compassion on King Philip's throne.
    But plan no deed of blood against your father.
    Philip the Second forced the abdication   410
    Of Charles, your grandfather; Prince, plan no murder,
    In turn this Philip fears his son. Think on it!
    And so may all the strength of heaven be yours.
            [*Exits quickly.* CARLOS *is just about to rush off in
            another direction, but suddenly turns round and
            throws himself down next to* POSA's *corpse,
            embracing him once again. Then he leaves the
            room quickly*

SCENE VIII

[DUKE OF ALBA *and* DUKE OF FERIA.]

ALBA. Madrid is calm, how goes it with the King?

FERIA. Badly. He has decided, come what may,
To admit no one. Posa's treachery
Has altered him beyond all recognition
At one terrific stroke.

ALBA.   I have to see him.
We may not leave him to his sorrow now,
We have just made a great discovery.   420

FERIA. A new discovery?

ALBA.   A monk, who stole
Into the Prince's room, inquiring closely
Into the death of Posa, being noted,
Was apprehended by my guards and questioned.
The threat of torture squeezed this secret from him:
That the deceased had given him to bear
Important papers, to present to Carlos
If they should fail to meet again by sunset.

FERIA. What did the letters say?

ALBA.   The letters tell us
That before dawn the Prince shall leave the city.   430

FERIA. What?

ALBA.   That a ship awaits him in Cadiz,*
Ready to carry him to Vlissingen,*
And that the Netherlands, at his arrival,
Will rise as one and break their Spanish chains.

FERIA. Ha! What is this?

ALBA.   Another letter says
That Suleiman has sent a fleet from Rhodes,*

As was agreed, to fight the King of Spain;
It is half-way across the sea by now!

FERIA. Can it be possible?

ALBA.   I understand,
Thanks to these letters, why the Marquis travelled   440
So far and wide from court to court through Europe.
His mission was no less than to assemble
The Northern powers to free the Netherlands,
Through our destruction.

FERIA.   He attempted that!

ALBA. And in those papers there is planned a war
To tear that land for ever from our empire,
With calculations of our will and power,
And figures for the strengths of every region,
Every rebellion to the instant timed.
Pacts are set out, precise in every detail,   450
And their negotiation written down;
The precepts to be followed are foreseen.
The scheme is from the devil but—divine!

FERIA. What a complete, unfathomable traitor!

ALBA. Also these letters tell us of a meeting
To be arranged, the night before he leaves,
Between Don Carlos and the Queen his mother.

FERIA. That is to say, tonight.

ALBA.   Indeed—at midnight.
I have already given special orders
To deal with this eventuality.   460
You see my urgency—time hurries by,
Open the door.

FERIA.   No! No one is to enter.

ALBA. Then I will dare to open it myself,
Weighing the danger.

[*As he walks towards the door it opens and the*
KING comes out

FERIA.   Ha! He comes himself!

SCENE IX

[KING *joins the others; everyone is shocked at his*
appearance, and steps back to let him pass through
the middle. He walks as if in a waking dream, like a
sleepwalker. His clothes and appearance show the
disorder into which his spell of unconsciousness
threw him. He walks past those present with slow
steps, looks at each one blankly without being aware
of any of them. Finally he comes to a stop, pensive,
his eyes cast to the floor, until gradually he gives
vent to his emotions.]

KING. Bring back that dead man. Give him back to me.

DOMINGO [*quietly to* ALBA]. Speak to him.

KING.   He despised me when he died.
   Summon him back, he must think differently.

ALBA [*approaches fearfully*].
   Sir?

KING [*looks around the semicircle for a long time*]
      Who addressed me? Am I not the King?
   Subject, have you forgotten who I am?
   Creature, kneel down, you must submit to me,   470
   I am the King. Because one man despised me,
   Must I be held as nothing by you all?

ALBA. No more of him, another enemy,
   Worse than the one before, defies my King,
   Lodged in your empire's heart.

FERIA.   Your son, Prince Carlos.

KING. He had a friend who died for him. For him!
   I would have shared my empire with my friend.
   How he looked down on me. From a high throne

One does not look so proudly down on men.
Was it not clear, the pride of my Prince Carlos   480
In his great prize? His pain confessed his loss,
Nothing ignoble could provoke such grief.
Oh how I wish and wish he was alive!
The Indies for a sight of him alive!*
There is no comfort in omnipotence,
It cannot even reach into a grave
To mend a little blunder with a life.
The dead do not return. Who calls me happy?
The grave contains a man who held me lightly.
Who cares about the living, they can change,   490
One man stood up in this whole century,
One man was free—he scorned me and he died.

ALBA. So we have lived for nothing! Let us sink,
Spaniards, beneath the earth, this man has won,
Even in death our Monarch's heart is his.

KING [sits *down, his head resting on his arm*].
If he had only died for me. I loved him:
I loved him as a father loves a son.
To me he was a new and cloudless day.
Through him who knows what I might not have done?
He was my first love. Europe, damn me then,   500
But I deserve his thanks.

DOMINGO.   By what enchantment—

KING. Who was he saving with his sacrifice?
The boy, my son? Never. A man like that
Would hardly give his life to save a boy.
I do not think the slender flame of friendship
Is strong enough to fill a heart like that.
The future generations were his calling,
He lived to serve the world, and humankind.
To give them happiness he sought a throne,
And would he give it up, commit high treason   510
Against his own ideals? I knew him better.
Philip shall not be sacrificed to Carlos,
Only, an ancient to a youth of promise.

The father's waning autumn energy
Does not befit the new day's work. The son
Will do it, for his rise is imminent.
Of course! My death is eagerly awaited!

ALBA. What you suspect these letters verify.

KING. But there is something he did not consider.
I am still here. Still here. Thanks be to nature   520
I feel the strength of youth in all my sinews.
And I will make a mockery of him,
Transforming all his dreams to fantasies,
His death into a fool's demise. His fall
Will shame his friend and darken the whole age.
How do men think they would survive without me?
I have the evening still and I will use it
To blight the earth for twenty generations!
He sacrificed me to humanity,
His god—I will avenge that sacrifice!   530
And his beloved puppet shall be first.

                              [*To* DUKE OF ALBA
What did you say about the Prince? Repeat it.
What do these letters tell us?

ALBA.   They contain
The legacy to Carlos of the Marquis.

KING [*skims through the papers, watched closely by all those
     around him. After he has read awhile he puts them away
     and walks silently through the room*].
Bring me the Cardinal Inquisitor,
I ask him for an hour, no more.

               [*One of the grandees goes out. The* KING *takes
                up the papers again, continues to read and
                lays them to one side again*
                              Tonight?

TAXIS. The coach will stop outside the monastery
At two o'clock.

ALBA.   My men have recognized
The Royal Coat of Arms on travel items
Brought to the monastery.

FERIA.   Moorish agents
  Have been instructed to withdraw large sums
  On the Queen's orders, it is said, in Brussels.

KING. Where is the Prince?

ALBA.   Beside the dead Maltese.

KING. Is there still light in the Queen's bedchamber?

ALBA. No, all is still. She sent her maids out early.
  And sleeps, according to the Lady Arcos,
  The last to leave her side.
            [*An* OFFICER *of the guards enters, pulls the* DUKE
            OF FERIA *to one side and speaks to him quietly.*
            He turns, embarrassed, to ALBA, *others gather*
            and murmurings begin

FERIA, TAXIS, DOMINGO [*together*].
                    Incredible!

KING. What is it?

FERIA.   This is strange, and hard to credit.

DOMINGO. Two Switzers, who have hastened from their posts,
  Report—but it is ludicrous and worthless—   550

KING. Continue—

ALBA.   In the left wing of the Palace,
  They say, the spirit of the Emperor
  Appeared, and with a solemn gait walked by them.
  The other guards in the pavilion
  Concur precisely, and they saw the spirit
  Step silently into the Queen's apartments.

KING. What did he wear?

OFFICER.   His trappings of a monk,
  And the same cloak, the last he wore alive.

KING. His trappings of a monk. But tell me, please,
  Did the guards know him when he was alive?   560
  How could they know it was the emperor?

OFFICER. Clearly he had to be the emperor,
  Because he bore the sceptre in his hand.

DOMINGO. Many have seen him walking in this fashion,
  Legend would tell us.

KING.   No one questioned him?

OFFICER. Nobody dared. The guards saluted, trembled,
  Fell to their knees and let the ghost go by.

KING. And so he passed into the Queen's apartments.

OFFICER. Into her antechamber.

KING [*turns round quickly*].   What say you?

ALBA. Sir, we are lost for words.

KING [*after some thought, to the* OFFICER]. Set well-armed
  men   570
  At once at every entrance to that wing.
  I have an urge to ask that ghost some questions.
                          [*Exit* OFFICER, *enter a* PAGE BOY

PAGE. Highness, the Cardinal Inquisitor.

KING. Leave us!
                    [*The* CARDINAL INQUISITOR, *an old man of
                    ninety, blind, leaning on a stick and led by
                    two Dominicans. As he walks through the
                    rows, all the grandees throw themselves
                    down before him and touch the hem of his
                    robe. He gives them his blessing. Exeunt*

SCENE X

          [*The* KING *and the* GRAND INQUISITOR. *A long
                          stillness.*]

INQUISITOR.   Am I before the King?

KING.   You are.

INQUISITOR. I had abandoned hope for such a grace.

KING. I recommence a scene from younger days,
And the Infante Philip seeks advice.

INQUISITOR. Your father never needed my advice,
My pupil Charles.

KING.   All honour be to him.
But Cardinal, I am a murderer,   580
There is no peace.

INQUISITOR.   What did you murder for?

KING. An unexampled, horrible betrayal—

INQUISITOR. I know about it.

KING.   What? How much? From where?

INQUISITOR. For years I knew what you have learned tonight.

KING [alienated]. You knew the nature of this man before?

INQUISITOR. His life began and ended in the records
Of Santa Casa.*

KING.   But you left him free?

INQUISITOR. No, though the rope was long, on which he
floated.

KING. He roamed beyond the borders of my empire.

INQUISITOR. Throughout his Odyssey I shadowed him.   590

KING. If it was known that I was in the hands
Of such a man, why was I not informed?

INQUISITOR. The question is, why did you ask yourself
No questions when you rushed into his arms?
You knew him for a heretic at once,
What urged you to keep back this sacrifice
From our good office? We will not be played with.
Where is our safety when your Majesty
Rejects us for the company of thieves?
When he befriends our bitter enemy?   600
If one can be forgiven in your mind,
Why were a hundred thousand sacrificed?

KING. He *has* been sacrificed.

INQUISITOR.   He has been murdered,
  Impatiently, and privately. His blood,
  That should have poured to glorify us all,
  Has stained the fingers of a hired assassin.
  This man was ours—by whose authority
  Do you impoverish our order, sir?
  His death was necessary to the time,
  The ceremony of his soul's disgrace   610
  Was given to us for a divine parade.
  This was my well considered plan. But now
  Quicklime consumes the work of many years.
  We have been robbed and you are stained with blood.

KING. Forgive me, I could not control myself.

INQUISITOR. It is indeed Infante Philip speaking.
  You lost control! Have I alone grown old?
  Free other minds, and you must walk in chains!

KING. I am a novice in these matters still.
  Have patience with me.

INQUISITOR.   No! You disappoint me!   620
  And you disgrace your years of competence!
  Where was the Philip whose unchanging soul
  Circled his earthly spirit like the stars
  That turn forever brightly round the world?
  Have you dissolved your past, yourself, in tears?
  Where were you when he took your hand, what world?
  Was poison sweet, were good and evil closer?
  What is the use of singleness of purpose
  If in a luke-warm, fickle, girlish moment
  Six decades of self-discipline can perish?   630

KING. I looked into his eyes. Be lenient
  To my relapse into mortality.
  The world has one less path into your heart
  Than into mine—the highway of the light.

INQUISITOR. What could he be to you? What could he say
  That our good words had not prepared you for?

You understand the minds of dreamers, surely?
Was the proud language of reform, the answer
To everything, so novel to your ear?
If your convictions are the kind of fortress   640
Words can destroy, what right had you to send
A hundred thousand to their deaths for doubting?

KING. It was a man I longed for. This Domingo—

INQUISITOR. Why did you need a man? Mankind is numbers,
Nothing but numbers. Must my grey-haired pupil
Learn once again the law of single rule?
The God who rules on earth needs no compassion,
And he must do without the transient.
If you admit that you have need of them,
You have conceded them equality,   650
And over equals what can be your right?

KING [throws himself into an armchair].
I am a man, and nothing but a man,
I feel it now. You ask of the creation
What the creator only can accomplish.

INQUISITOR. No, I am not deceived. I see through you.
You wished to rid yourself of my control.
Our order tired you with its exigency,*
You wanted to be free to rule alone.
                    [He pauses. The KING is silent
We are avenged. And you should thank the Church
That she is pleased to punish as a mother;   660
Now you have learnt, you have come back to us,
I stand before you—but by God tomorrow,
If I had not, you would have stood before me!

KING. You may not speak like this! Control yourself!
I will not tolerate this language, priest.

INQUISITOR. Why do you raise the shade of Samuel?*
I set two kings upon the throne of Spain,*
And hoped to leave a lasting work, but now
The fruit of all my labours has been lost,
Don Philip has himself torn down the vines!   670

So tell me why I have been summoned here,
I will not come in haste a second time.

KING. One final effort, then depart in peace.
We must not quarrel. Are we reconciled?

INQUISITOR. If Philip bows with due humility.

KING [*after a pause*]. The Prince my son is planning a
   rebellion.

INQUISITOR. What is your answer?

KING.   Everything or nothing.

INQUISITOR. And what is everything?

KING.   I let him go
If he may not be killed.

INQUISITOR.   Well sir, go on.

KING. Could you invent a fashion of belief   680
That would condone the murder of a child?

INQUISITOR. To make amends for his eternal justice
The son of God died on the cross.

KING.   Is Europe
Amenable to this interpretation?*

INQUISITOR. Europe, and everywhere the cross is honoured.

KING. How will you fight the mighty voice of nature
That I offend?

INQUISITOR.   There is no voice of nature
If faith denies it.

KING.   I commit to you
My judgement seat, entire, will you receive it?

INQUISITOR. I will.

KING.   It is my only son who dies,   690
For whom then have I laboured?

INQUISITOR.   For decay—
Better inheritor by far than freedom.

KING [*stands up*]. We are agreed then. Come.

INQUISITOR.   Where am I going?

KING. To where you will receive my sacrifice.

SCENE XI

[*One of the* QUEEN's *rooms.* CARLOS, *the* QUEEN,
finally the KING *with his entourage.* CARLOS *is in a
monk's habit, a mask on his face, which he now
takes off, under his arm a bare sword. It is
completely dark. He approaches a door which is
opened. The* QUEEN *comes out, in a night dress, with
a burning candle.*]

CARLOS [*goes down on one knee before her*].
  Elizabeth!

QUEEN [*resting her eyes on him with quiet wistfulness*].
          So this is how we meet.

CARLOS. So this is how we meet again, at last.

QUEEN. Stand up, we must not weaken one another.
  Him we have lost should not be mourned with tears.
  Cry helpless tears for lesser sorrows, Karl,
  He sacrificed his life for you, your life   700
  Was bought with his life, dear and very great.
  Has precious blood been spilt for nothing? Carlos,
  I vouched for you, and when I pledged myself,
  He left me happy. Did I lie to him?

CARLOS [*with passion*]. His tomb shall be more famous than
    the King's.
  His ashes are the seeds of paradise!

QUEEN. You answer as I hoped and knew you would.
  It was belief in this with which he died.
  I am his chosen messenger, the keeper
  Of his last wish. You must fulfil your oath.   710
  I warn you, I will hold you to it, Karl!
  And he has left another legacy—

I gave my word, and in return he gave me,
Oh, why should I be silent?—gave me you.
I will not fear opinion any more,
No matter how I seem, I will be true,
My heart will speak. He called our love a virtue,
Which I believe—my heart will hide no longer.

CARLOS. Queen, do not finish! I have been asleep,
Deep buried in a long oppressive dream.   720
I loved, but am awake. Forget the past.
Here are your letters, take them, burn my own,
Fear no more importunity from me.
I have been hollowed by pure flames, my passion
Lies with the dead beneath the ground, my heart
Has stamped out every flicker of desire.
                    [*After a silence he takes her hand*
I came to take my leave of you, my mother,
There is a higher good, at last I see,
Worthier of desire, than to possess you.
My life's slow pace grew wings and in one night   730
Decades flew by and I became a man;
My work on earth is to remember him,
All that I scattered has been harvested.
          [*He approaches the* QUEEN *who hides her face*
Do you say nothing?

QUEEN.   All I have is tears,
Ignore them, but believe me, I admire you.

CARLOS. You were the only one who knew of us,
You will remain my dearest on this earth.
I cannot give you friendship, any more
Than yesterday I could have loved another.
But if fate crowns me, you, the Royal widow,   740
Will be the sacred image of my worship.
          [*The* KING, *accompanied by the* GRAND INQUISITOR
          and other grandees, appears in the background
Now I leave Spain, and I have seen my father
For the last time on earth, for the last time.
I treasure him no more, deep in my spirit

Nature has perished, he has lost his son.
Resume your duties, be his wife again,
I hurry to relieve my tortured people,
Plagued by oppression. I will not return,
Unless it be in glory as the King.
And now for one last time, farewell!

QUEEN.   Oh Karl!   750
What have you made of me? I understand
I may not share the greatness of a man,
But I can see you, know you and admire you.

CARLOS. How strong I am, Elizabeth, I hold you
But do not weaken. Heaven, yesterday
Death's face could not have chased me from your side,
But that is over. Now mortality
And all its twists of fate are in my hands,
I held you in my arms and did not weaken.
Hush! Did you hear a noise? [*the clock strikes*]

QUEEN.   I only hear   760
The dreadful bell that summons separation.

CARLOS. Mother, goodnight. My first communication
Will be from Ghent, and it will, in effect,*
Make public all our secrets. From now on
I mean to fight Don Philip in the open.
We will do nothing secret from now on,
You have no cause to shelter from the world,
This is my last lie.
          [*He is about to put on the mask. The* KING *steps
          between them*

KING.   Yes, it is your last!
                    [*The* QUEEN *falls, unconscious*

CARLOS [*hurries towards her and catches her in his arms*].
Oh earth and heaven! Is she dead?

KING [*cold and quiet to the* GRAND INQUISITOR].
Cardinal, I have done my part, now do yours.   770

MARY STUART

DRAMATIS PERSONAE

Elizabeth, Queen of England
Mary Stuart, Queen of Scotland
Robert Dudley, Earl of Leicester
George Talbot, Earl of Shrewsbury
William Cecil, Lord Burleigh, Lord Treasurer
Earl of Kent
William Davison, Secretary of State
Amias Paulet, Knight, Mary's warder
Mortimer, his nephew
Lord Aubespine, the French ambassador
Lord Bellievre, Emissary extraordinary from France
O'Kelly, friend of Mortimer
Drugeon Drury, Mary's second warder
Melvil, her steward
Burgoyn, her physician
Hanna Kennedy, her nurse
Margaret Kurl, her maid
The Sheriff of the county
Officer of the Queen's Guard
French and English gentlemen
Trabants
Court servants of the Queen of England
Servants of the Queen of Scotland

ACT ONE

SCENE I

[*A room in Fotheringhay Castle.**]

[HANNA KENNEDY,* *the* QUEEN OF SCOTLAND'*s nurse,
is arguing furiously with* PAULET,* *who is about to
open a cupboard.* DRUGEON DRURY, *his henchman,
with a crowbar.*]

KENNEDY. What are you doing? What is this new outrage?
You shall not touch that cupboard!

PAULET.   Damnable
Feminine cunning! Jewels flung from windows
To bribe the gardeners. Who gave them jewels?
No matter how I search and watch these women,
Infinite secret treasures rise from nowhere.
There will be more to find!

KENNEDY.   Wretch! Keep your distance!
This closet hides the secrets of my Lady.

PAULET. Which are precisely what I mean to find.
                          [*Pulls out some papers*

KENNEDY. These are handwriting exercises, nothing,   10
Written to fill the endless prison hours.

PAULET. Long days are useful to an evil spirit.

KENNEDY. Look, it is French.

PAULET.   And all the worse for that,
It is the language of our enemies.

KENNEDY. These are rough drafts of letters to your Queen.

PAULET. I will convey them to her as they are.
But look, what have we here?
                  [*He has opened a secret compartment and pulls
                  jewellery out*
                          A royal headband,

Bristling with stones, and with the Fleur de Lys!*

> [*He gives it to* DRURY*

Secure it, Drury, put it with the rest.

> [*Exit* DRURY

KENNEDY. Again we suffer the disgrace of force.   20

PAULET. While she still owns things she can still do harm.
And anything is a weapon in her hands.

KENNEDY. Leave these last jewels, sir, for charity,
Their memories of splendour comfort her
And ease the pain of her continual loss.

PAULET. Everything will be safely stored, I promise,
And, when the time comes, faithfully returned.

KENNEDY. Who could detect in these unpainted walls
The dwelling of a queen? Where is the sky
That ought to blaze into my Lady's rooms?*   30
And she is forced to scrape on floors of boards
Feet that are used to carpets soft as air.
Her humble table is disgraced with pewter
That unrespected gentry would not touch.

PAULET. She lived like this in Stirling with her husband,
And drank from gold in secret with her lover.*

KENNEDY. We are denied the slightest things—a mirror—

PAULET. Let her forget the picture that she makes,
It stirs up pride and daring hopes in her.

KENNEDY. She should have books to keep her mind alive.   40

PAULET. She has the Bible to revive her soul.

KENNEDY. Even her zither has been stolen from her.

PAULET. Because the music that she plays is pagan.

KENNEDY. Is this fair treatment for a lady raised
Carefully in the court of the Medici,*
Who was a queen when she was in her cradle,*
And grew up used to plenty and to pleasure?

Enough that she should lose her power, surely,
Why should she lose life's usual comforts also?
When everything is taken suddenly   50
Great hearts find riches in their own existence,
But to be weakened bit by bit is dreadful.

PAULET. You mourn the loss of vanities and pleasures
When you should be repenting your excesses.
To be forgiven for your life of leisure
You must embrace humiliation gladly.

KENNEDY. If her sweet youth was lost at all to waste,
That is a matter for her heart and God,
Not for the conscience of an English court.

PAULET. She will be judged where the disgrace was done.*

KENNEDY. She is too cramped here to do anything.   61

PAULET. And yet she found a hole to reach her arm
Out of these castle walls into the world
To grip the torch of civil war and fling it*
Blazing into the tinder of this kingdom.
She set a swarm of soldiers and assassins
Against our Queen, whom righteous God protected.
How from within these bonds I do not know,
But she inspired infernal regicide
In Babington and Parry; could these bars*   70
Keep her from twisting noble Norfolk's heart?*
No better head existed in this island
But it was lost beneath the headsman's axe,
A sacrifice to the abyss of her.
Yet still undaunted many press to serve,
They crowd the scaffolds, and the steeples toll
Fast as a storm to mark the passing lives.
And there will be no end until this woman
Follows her followers to their guilty graves.
I curse the day our coast hospitably   80
Received this Helen in its open arms.*

KENNEDY. England received her kindly? Oh my Lady.
That is not true. She came here seeking comfort,

A suppliant escaping to her kindred,*
And since that day she has been left in prison,
Wronged and despised, to watch her youth pass by.
She has discovered what a dungeon is,
Every dimension; like a criminal
She has been dragged to stand before accusers,
Who tried her for her life. And yet her body   90
Retains the spirit of a queen unchanged.

PAULET. She came here as a hunted murderer,
She was deposed, and exiled by her people,
Because her deeds had stained their throne with evil.
Plotting to wreck the wealth and pride of England,
She travelled here to make us Catholic,
And take us back to bloody Mary's times;*
To break us and betray us to the French.
Why does she still refuse to sign the treaty
Of Edinburgh, that would release her now,*   100
Renounce her claims to England's throne and go?
She loves the echo of an empty title
Better than freedom, dignity and comfort—
Her choice; which proves that she believes in wrong,
And trusts what her imprisonment can do
By means of plots, will trap us in misfortunes
And bring the country crawling to her dungeon.

KENNEDY. Sir, you heap mockery on our helplessness.
The Lady of this prison trusts no dreams,
Although no voice from her dear home can reach her,   110
And though the only company she sees
Is her cruel guard, and though the only changes
She knows are like the one that recently
Swapped her rough warder for a worse, your nephew.
And though these walls are her unvaried season.

PAULET. No bars on earth can keep her cunning in.
How do I know this iron is not filed through,
The floorstones not prised up and tunnelled under?
The walls look solid but for all I know
They have been hollowed. While I sleep one night   120
You will walk through them. Curse this blasted post;

To keep and watch a bad and clever woman!
I wake afraid, and try the castle bolts,
I take each guard aside and try his conscience,
Dawn finds me shaking, never mind how warm,
For fear of waking to bad dreams come true.
But courage, courage, soon an end may come.
And I would rather guard the damned in hell
Than keep the gates against this Queen of plots.

KENNEDY. She comes herself.

PAULET.   With Jesus in her fist,   130
And a proud world of evil in her heart.

SCENE II

[Enter MARY *in a veil, holding a crucifix.*
Others as before.]

KENNEDY [*rushing towards her*]. Oh Queen, they kick us down
     and give no reason,
  They bury us in scorn and misery,
  And each new day your crowned head bears more wrong.

MARY. Be calm, and tell me what new thing has happened.

KENNEDY. See, here your closet has been broken open.
  The only remnants of your bridal treasure,*
  We took such risks to rescue, and your letters,
  Are in his hands; and you are left with nothing,
  Everything royal has been taken from you.   140

MARY. Nonsense. The tinsel did not make the Queen.
  They can mishandle us but not debase us.
  England has taught me much resilience,
  But I am happy to be tutored further.
  Sir, you have taken forcibly this morning
  A thing I would have given you at noon.
  There is a letter to my royal sister
  The Queen of England somewhere in these papers.
  Give me your word that you will hand it to her,
  Promptly, and not divert it to Lord Burleigh.   150

PAULET. What I will do with it is my decision.

MARY. Sir, let me tell you what the letter says,
Before you read it for yourself. The letter
Asks the great favour of an audience*
With my great sister I have never seen.
I have been stood before a court of men,
None of whom is my equal. In this world
Elizabeth alone is of my rank,
My family and my sex—to her alone,
Woman, Queen, sister, will I freely speak.   160

PAULET. Yet in the past you have consigned your fate
To men less worthy of respect, my Lady.

MARY. I ask a second favour of you, sir.
Only a heart of marble could deny it.
For a long time I have been kept in prison
Without the comfort of the sacrament,
Cheated of any contact with my Church.
The Queen, who has my freedom and my crown,
Whose sentence hovers on my very life,
Will not forbid me the approach to heaven.   170

PAULET. At your request the local deacon—

MARY.   No!
Bring me no deacons! I demand a priest
Of my own Church, and scribes and lawyers also,
That my last will be written. Misery
And prison nights and days like a disease,
Hasten the date of my demise, I fear.
I dress myself in darkness for my death.

PAULET. Considerations fitting to your state.

MARY. Who is to say, a sudden blow from nowhere
May speed what feeble sorrow does too slowly.   180
I want to see my testament spelt out,
And to ordain the fate of what is mine.

PAULET. That you are free to do. The Queen of England
Has no desire to take your realm upon her.

MARY. Where are my servants and my chambermaids?
  Though I can live without their services,
  I wish to know what has been done to them.
  Have they been punished for their loyalty?

PAULET. They are in good hands. [*He moves to leave*]

MARY.   Do you leave me, sir?
  Yes, once again you leave me and, by silence,   190
  Increase the burden of uncertainty
  Upon my frightened heart. I hear no news,
  Your agents stand between me and the world,
  While enemies of mine beyond these walls
  Work out my fate. A painful month has passed*
  Since the commissioners attacked me here,
  Threw up a court of boards and questioned me,
  Forty of them. Deprived of any counsel,*
  I answered as I could from memory
  The calculated cross-examination   200
  Of that unprecedented, rushed proceeding.
  Men came and went like ghosts with accusations,
  Cunningly phrased, which I replied to numbly.
  Since then I have been starved of information,
  And I can only vainly search your eyes
  To learn if truth, the efforts of my friends
  To make my innocence believed, prevails,
  Or evil and my enemies' desires.
  I beg you, break your silence, let me know
  What I may dare to hope, what I must fear.   210

PAULET [*after a pause*]. Make peace with heaven.

MARY.   God will show me mercy,
  I hope for justice on this earth no less.

PAULET. You will get justice, have no fear of that.

MARY. But has my sentence been decided, sir?

PAULET. I do not know.

MARY.   Am I condemned to die?

PAULET. My Lady, I know nothing, as I say.

MARY. They like to get things over quick in England.
　Will I be taken by surprise again,
　But by assassins, not commissioners?

PAULET. Compose yourself for such a sudden end,　　　　220
　And it will find you if and when it comes,
　Better prepared than you appear at present.

MARY. There is no judgement that through Burleigh's hatred
　And Hatton's zeal, a court at Westminster*
　Could make, that would astonish me, but would
　The Queen of England dare to act on it?

PAULET. Only their conscience and their Parliament
　Rule England's rulers. When all three decide,
　Justice is done for all the world to see.

SCENE III

[MORTIMER,* PAULET's *nephew, enters and, without
paying any attention to the* QUEEN, *addresses* PAULET.]

MORTIMER. Uncle, they look for you.　　　　　　　　230
　　　[*He leaves in the same way. The* QUEEN *notices it
　　　with displeasure and turns to* PAULET, *who
　　　makes to follow* MORTIMER

MARY. I have another wish to ask you, sir.
　I can accept the scorn of one so old,
　But insults from a youth I will not stand.
　Spare me the sight of his dismissive manner.

PAULET. His rudeness is his usefulness to me.
　You will not find in him the tender fool,
　Liable to be melted by a tear,
　No, he is travelled, he has been to Paris
　And Reims and come back not a whit less English.
　Try all your arts, you will not change him, Lady!　　240
　　　　　　　　　　　　　　　　　　　　　[*Exit*

SCENE IV

[MARY, KENNEDY.]

KENNEDY. The wretched man can say this to your face!

MARY. When we were mighty we were too attentive
  To flattery, and that we should be forced
  To listen to a harsher tune, is fitting.

KENNEDY. My Lady, have they crushed you, do you bow?
  You used to be the oak and I the reed,
  I used to have to scold you for your blitheness,
  Not for your melancholy.

MARY.   Yes, I see.
  It is the bloodstained shade of Darnley rising,
  Raging, from under stone, and I will never,   250
  Until my ransom of disgrace is paid,
  Have peace with him.

KENNEDY.   What fears are haunting you?

MARY. You can forget, my memory is faithful.
  That evil action's anniversary
  Has come again today—it is this date*
  I celebrate with such austerity.

KENNEDY. Banish the evil spirit to its rest.
  It has been paid with years of suffering,
  And with continual regret. The Church,
  Which has the cure for every ill of conscience,   260
  And heaven, have forgiven you.

MARY.   Guilt rises
  Bleeding again like a reopened wound,
  Out of its shallow grave! No altar boy
  Can send it to the vault again with bells,
  Nor cross nor candle in a reverend hand.
  My husband's ghost will have revenge.

KENNEDY.   My lady,
  You did not kill him—others did that murder.

MARY. I knew it was to happen. I allowed it.
I flattered him and lured him to the ambush.

KENNEDY. You are excused by immaturity,   270
You were still tender.

MARY.   And that tenderness
Loaded itself with guilt.

KENNEDY.   You were provoked,
You suffered blood and insults from the man
Whom you had raised with love, like God, from nothing.
You led him from your chamber to the throne,
Graced him with your hereditary crown
And let him use your beauty. Could it be
That he forgot that love had made him King?
Yet he forgot, and so became unworthy,
He shadowed your good nature with suspicions,   280
And turned your sweetness bitter with blunt manners,
Transforming your enchantment to repugnance.
You fled in rage from the embrace of shame,
And let him dwindle in contempt. What efforts
Did he then make at reconciliation?
Was he repentant, did he kneel and beg you,
Promising to be kinder, for forgiveness?
The horrifying man, who was your creature,
Offered defiance, acting like your King.
He had your friend, sweet Rizzio the singer,*   290
Slaughtered before your very eyes. My Lady,
What you did then was just revenge for murder.

MARY. And my revenge will be avenged on me.
Your speech of comfort is my death sentence.

KENNEDY. It was not you—when you allowed that deed,
You had the conscience of another person.
You were delirious with love like fever,
The terrible seducer had you chained,
Unlucky Bothwell overpowered you,
Ruled you with male will, rousing you with potions,   300
Distorting you with hellish arts.*

MARY.   His magic
  Was his male power and my female weakness.

KENNEDY. That is not true. To weave his subtle circle
  Around your senses, he was forced to summon
  Every ungodly spirit from hell's fires.
  You could no longer hear the voice of warning,
  Your eyes, once clear, were blind to right behaviour,
  Becoming human shyness fled from you,
  And the soft glow of blushes was replaced
  By the high angry colour of desire.   310
  And you threw off the cloak of secrecy,
  Arrogance took the place of innocence,
  You honoured and displayed your shame with pride.
  Oh, you allowed that man to bear before you,
  Triumphantly, the royal sword of Scotland,*
  The murderer the people's curses hunted
  Through every vane and wynd in Edinburgh.
  You walled the Parliament around with swords,
  And forced your judges, in a farce of justice,*
  There in the temple sacred to your rule,   320
  To clear the murderer—and you went further,
  And, God!

MARY.   No need for more. And at the altar
  Gave him my hand.

KENNEDY.   Oh, let eternal silence
  Swallow that act. It was a horror worthy
  Of a soul subject to abomination.
  But you, I know you, and you are not fallen.
  I love you as I love myself, I raised you,
  Your heart is not of steel to keep out shame,
  Your only vice is recklessness. I swear,
  As I have sworn before, that there are spirits   330
  That make their dwellings in unguarded minds,
  Commit all kinds of vileness, and return
  To hell, at which the stained heart wakes, aghast.
  Since that misdeed, that blackened all your days,
  As I can witness, you have done no wrong.

You are another person. So take courage,
And be at peace. Whatever your regrets,
Your guilt is not for England to decide,
Neither Elizabeth nor Parliament
Can be your judge. The power is unrighteous   340
That threatens you—and to the court's presumption
You may reply with innocence as mighty.

MARY. Who comes?

[MORTIMER *shows himself at the door*

KENNEDY.   It is the nephew. Enter then.

SCENE V

[*The others as before.* MORTIMER *enters shyly.*]

MORTIMER [*to* KENNEDY]. Stand guard outside. I must speak
   with the Queen.

MARY. Hanna, you stay.

MORTIMER.   My Lady, do not fear me.
   This is my introduction.

[*Gives her a letter*

MARY.   Ha! What's this?

MORTIMER. Go, Lady Kennedy, and guard the door.
   Watch that my uncle does not spring on us!

MARY [*to* KENNEDY]. Do as he says. Go! Go!

SCENE VI

[MORTIMER, MARY.]

MARY.   From France, my uncle
   The Cardinal of Lotharingia.*   350
   'Trust without fear the bearer of this letter.
   Sir Mortimer is faithful, in all England

You have no better friend.' Can this be so?
Or is it an illusion mocking me?
When I believed that I had been abandoned
By the wide world, I find a friend beside me,
And find him in the nephew of my jailer.

MORTIMER [*throwing himself at her feet*]. My Queen, forgive
    the hideous disguise
Which I must thank for bringing me to you
With help and rescue.

MARY.   You astonish me,   360
    Stand up, sir. I cannot uplift myself
From deepest sorrow in a single bound.
Explain my change of fortune in clear terms,
So that I can believe it.

MORTIMER.   Time slips by,
    And it will bring my uncle soon, and with him
A man of hate. But I have news of rescue
From heaven that will eclipse the shock he brings.

MARY. God is unbounded in his miracles!

MORTIMER. Allow me first to tell you of myself.

MARY. Tell, sir!

MORTIMER.   When I had lived for twenty years,   370
    Darkened by hatred for the Holy Father,
Strict in my duties, I was suddenly
Ravished by an unkillable desire
To tread upon the Continent. I left
The sermon dungeons of the Puritans,
My home, and journeyed at a restless pace,
Burning, through France and precious Italy,
Searching for something. It was at the time
Of a great festival, and everywhere
The roads and paths were thronged with streams of pilgrims,
And every wooden saviour wore a crown.   381
It was as if the human race was moving
Together towards the everlasting kingdom.

And I was torn by the believing river
Helplessly through the open gates of Rome.
Oh Queen, my feelings then! The colonnades*
And the triumphal arches drank me in;
Magnificent, the colosseum swallowed
My awe. A wing-borne spirit of creation
Carried me to a world of miracles,   390
The arts, whose raptures I had never felt,
The goddess of the arts, redeemed my mind.
My home religion cursed all images,
Exiled the senses and adored abstractions;
But now each church I entered greeted me
With music drifting down from paradise,
And figures gestured from the walls and ceilings,
Extravagantly given. The sublime
Wavered before my senses and remained; .
For one ecstatic moment my own eyes   400
Were shown the creatures that abide with God,
I saw the salutations of the angels.
I saw the Virgin, and the birth of Jesus.
I saw the Holy Trinity descending,
And the Transfiguration's brightness lit me.
And when I saw the Pope in all this splendour,
Blessing the faithful celebrating people,
I understood that Kings and Emperors,
Who blaze with precious stones and gold, are nothing
Compared to him divinity adorns.   410
His house is not a dwelling of this world,
Because its form reflects the deathless kingdom.

MARY. Oh mercy, torture my imagination
With the bright tapestry of life no longer
I am both weak with sickness and imprisoned.

MORTIMER. Queen, so was I, but suddenly my prison
Burst its own bonds, and my unshadowed spirit
Entered the beauty of the day forever.
I swore to hate the dark and narrow book,
And to adorn my brows with a new crown,   420
To rally to the flag of happiness.

And there were many noble Scotsmen there,
And merry companies of Frenchmen too
Surrounded me and led me to your uncle
The great and noble Cardinal of Guise.
Ah, what a self-assured and lucid man!
To be so strong and yet to be so wise.
How wise of fate that he was born to rule.
The very model of a royal priest,
A ruler such as I had never seen.   430

MARY. You have beheld the face of one much loved.
When I was young he was my guardian,
That noble man is very dear to me.
Does he still think of me? Oh speak of him!
Is fortune still a constant summer to him?
And is he still the rock the Church relies on?*

MORTIMER. His excellency very graciously
Took it upon himself to clear my thinking,
And to interpret for my benefit
The highest teachings of our faith. I learnt   440
That reason is a wild misleading mood,
And that the truth must be for eyes to see,
A solid, real and earthly Church, descended
From the deliberations of the fathers.
And so the childhood of my soul was over.
His understanding, fighting in his words,
Conquered, and I surrendered to the truth,
And gave my erring soul into his hands.

MARY. So you are one among the many thousands
He, like the blessed Preacher on the Mount,*   450
Has caught by speaking in the net of heaven.

MORTIMER. Soon afterwards the duties of his office
Called him to France, and me he sent to Reims,
Where the steel-souled Society of Jesus*
Is training priests to save the Church in England.
I met the noble Scotsman Morgan there,*
And faithful Lesley, the illustrious
Bishop of Ross, both living without joy,

Exiled to French soil. For my faith's defence
I bound myself in friendship to these men.   460
And then one day my eyes, in straying round
The pictures in the bishop's residence,
Were halted by the portrait of a woman,
That struck my spirit with its charm to wonder,
And held me still with an extreme emotion.
And the good bishop said, 'It is with reason
That you are forced to linger by this picture,
For the most lovely woman in the world
Suffers the ugliest disgrace, enduring
For our faith's sake, and in your native country.'   470

MARY. Oh righteous man! Misfortune has not robbed me
Of all my wealth when such a friend remembers!

MORTIMER. And then he started to recount to me,
With words that sank into my soul like arrows,
Your martyrdom, and how your enemies
Lust for your blood, and how your lineage
Connects you to the royal house of Tudor.*
I was convinced that you should be our Queen,
And not this fake rejected by her father,
This bastard daughter of adultery.   480
Unwilling to believe the bishop's tale
Without corroboration, I consulted
Lawyers, and antique books of heraldry,
And every learned source confirmed your claim.
You suffer wrong because your right is known.
You are imprisoned in your property,
You are the victim of your own lost kingdom.

MARY. Oh this unlucky right of mine to suffer!

MORTIMER. And then I learnt that you had been transferred
From Talbot's castle to my uncle's keeping.   490
And I perceived in this coincidence
A rescue planned by heaven with my hand,
Destiny calling me to set you free.
My friends agreed with me, the Cardinal
Gave me his blessing, and instructed me

In the arcane intricacies of plotting;
With his advice a plan was swiftly made,
And so I journeyed to my home again,
And, as you know, arrived ten days ago. [*He pauses*]
Oh Queen, my eyes saw you—not just your portrait,   500
But you yourself. Oh what a hoard of treasure
This castle covers. It is not a prison,
It is a hall more brilliant than the court!
How blessed is the man who is allowed
To breathe this sainted air. How wise the woman
Who keeps you hidden from your people here.
The youth of England would arise, and tumult
Would riot up and down this peaceful island,
With swords unbaited, if the British nation*
Should glimpse the beauty of the Queen denied it!   510

MARY. I would be happy if the British nation
Saw with your eyes.

MORTIMER.   If every British man
Could see your gentleness in misery,
Your gracious strength beneath a rain of insults,
They would observe as I do that your beauty,
Your calm in suffering, proclaims you Queen.
Your soul disdains to be humiliated;
You have been robbed of the supports of life,
Yet life itself adorns you with its light,
And I can never step into your cell   520
Without a spear of pity piercing me,
But then my heart is healed by seeing you.
But the decision is approaching fast,
And every minute brings disaster nearer.
I must delay no longer, I must say
What fills my speech with dread I cannot hide.

MARY. My sentence? Has it been pronounced? Reveal it.
It will not break me.

MORTIMER.   It has been pronounced.
The forty-two commissioners, your judges,
Pronounce you guilty, and the House of Lords   530

Insists with both the Commons and the City
Of London very strongly, that the sentence
Be carried out at once. Elizabeth
Alone holds back, but this is a pretence,
To make it seem that she was forced to sign.
Her Majesty is not inclined to mercy.

MARY. Sir Mortimer, your news does not surprise me,
Nor am I frightened. I have been expecting
Just such a message, and my heart is ready.
I know my judges—having made me suffer   540
They will be loath to set me free to hurt them.
Therefore they plan to keep me here forever
To shield themselves from vengeance with this castle,
And hide the justice of my cause in darkness.

MORTIMER. No, Queen! Their purpose reaches even further,
The tyranny is not content with prison,
There is no dungeon deep enough on earth
To fix the Queen of England on her throne.
While you are living, even in a cell,
You keep her fears alive. You have to die.   550

MARY. Is she prepared to see a crowned head bowed
Basely before an executioner?

MORTIMER. She is, my Lady, oh do not doubt that.

MARY. To cast into the dust the dignity
That she and I and every monarch share?
France would avenge me, does she not fear that?

MORTIMER. She has contracted endless peace with France,
She is about to give the Duke d'Anjou*
Her hand and throne.

MARY.   But will the King of Spain
Not arm his race against her?

MORTIMER.   With her people   560
Content, she is prepared to fight all nations.

MARY. And will this entertainment please the people?

MORTIMER. My Lady, in its recent history
This land has witnessed other royal women
Descending from the throne to climb a scaffold.
The mother of the Queen was executed,
Catherine Howard also, Lady Grey.*
Both were crowned heads.

MARY.   No! You are blind with terror!
Your heart is sick with its concern and lost
In terrors that can never be. The block   570
Is not the end I fear. There is a world
Of ways to rid herself of me forever,
Secretly, for the Queen. Far easier
For her to hire a killer, than for me
To come by a defence. Sir, this I fear,
And when I set the goblet to my lips,
I shudder at the thought that it may bring me
My sister's love.

MORTIMER.   You never will be murdered.
Neither by stealth nor in a public place.
My Queen, be fearless, everything is ready,   580
Twelve noble English youths have joined with me.
We pledged this morning on the sacrament
To lead you out by fighting from this cell.
The French Ambassador, Count Aubespine,
Helps us—his palace is our meeting-place.

MARY. I tremble, sir, but it is not for joy.
Black wings of evil omen beat inside me.
Are you aware of what you undertake?
Do you not fear the horror set on high,
The bloody heads of Babington and Tichburn,*   590
Impaled on London Bridge to stare their warning?
Do you not fear the fates of countless others,
Shipwrecked in this impossible endeavour,
Whose failures only added to my bonds?
Unlucky youth, misled to me, fly, fly!
Burleigh already knows your plans in detail,

One of your comrades will be his paid traitor,
Flee from this country, only luckless men
Rally to Mary Stuart.

MORTIMER.   No, my Lady.
I do not fear the horror set on high,   600
Nor do I dread the fates of countless others.
They died for you, and it will be remembered,
And everlasting fame is their good fortune.

MARY. They died in vain! The enemy is cunning,
And has the power of this island. Paulet
And all his pikemen do not watch alone,
The whole of England guards my prison door,
And neither guile nor violence can save me,
Only the will of Queen Elizabeth
Can set me free.

MORTIMER.   Then you are lost for ever!   610

MARY. There is a man who can subvert that will.

MORTIMER. Oh say his name.

MARY.   It is the Earl of Leicester.*

MORTIMER. Leicester! Lord Leicester, your chief persecutor,
Favourite of the Queen!

MARY.   That is the man.
Go to him. Only he can rescue me.
Reveal your wishes freely to that man,
And take this letter, which contains my picture,
As an assurance that I sent you to him.
        [*She pulls a paper from her bosom.* MORTIMER
          steps back and hesitates to take it
Take it. I had to hide it from your uncle,
I could not send it, every route was blocked.   620
Now a good angel has provided you.

MORTIMER. This is a riddle, Queen, explain it to me.

MARY. Leicester will tell you what it means. Believe him.
Trust him and he will speak the truth to you.
Who comes?

KENNEDY [*entering hastily*].
     Sir Paulet and a gentleman from court.

MORTIMER. It is Lord Burleigh. Queen, prepare yourself!*
 Hear calmly what he has to tell you!

SCENE VII

[MARY, LORD BURLEIGH, *Lord Treasurer of England,*
and PAULET.]

PAULET. Today you asked to know your fate for certain.
 Lord Burleigh brings you certainty. Accept it
 With resignation.

MARY.   It will be received   630
 By innocence, and so with dignity.

BURLEIGH. I come as emissary from the court.

MARY. My Lord is quick to lend the court his mind—
 Now it must thank him for his tongue as well.

BURLEIGH. You sound as though you have foreseen our
  verdict.

MARY. Lord Burleigh brings it, thus I see its colour.
 But to the point, sir.

BURLEIGH.   You submitted to
 The judgement of the court of forty-two.

MARY. My Lord, forgive my sudden interruption,
 However, that is not the way things happened. 640
 How could I let my standing sink so low?
 Surely you see it never could have been?
 I know my duty to the dignity
 Of princes, to myself, and to my child.
 It is the law of England—the accused
 Must stand before a jury of his peers.
 There were no kings on that committee, sir.

BURLEIGH. Yet you attended to their accusations,
    And spoke about them to the court.

MARY.   Indeed,
    I let myself be led by Hatton's cunning   650
    Into attending to those accusations,
    And when they had been said I made my answer,
    Out of respect for the nobility
    Of the mistaken lords, and just for honour,
    Not bowing to their court, which I reject.

BURLEIGH. Whether you recognize that court or not
    Is now a point of etiquette, my Lady.
    You are in England, breathing English air,
    England protects you, England comforts you,
    And you are therefore under English law.   660

MARY. Do I enjoy its comfort and protection,
    Breathing in prison? Is this prison England?
    Sir, I am not an English citizen,
    I do not know your laws, I have not seen them,
    I am a foreign Queen and not your subject.

BURLEIGH. And is the title of a queen a licence
    To nurture tumult in another country?
    How would it be for our security
    If the impartial blade that Themis wields*
    Could touch a beggar but not reach a queen?   670

MARY. I am prepared to answer to a court.
    It is your choice of judges I reject.

BURLEIGH. The judges! What, my Lady, are they outcasts,
    Renegades chosen by the common people?
    What, are they shameless gossips, swapping stories,
    Buying and selling law and truth, contented
    To be oppression's mercenaries, are they?
    They are the highest persons in the land,
    They have no fear of Lords, no need of bribes.
    Suspicion withers when their names are said;   680
    Their leaders are the people's goodly shepherd,

The pious and beneficent Archbishop
Of Canterbury, next, the wise Lord Talbot,
The greatly trusted keeper of the seals,
Next, the brave Howard, Lord High Admiral.*
The monarchy contains no men more fitting
To act as judges in this royal case.
Who better could her Majesty have chosen?
And even if a partisan emotion
Bewitched one man, as could be possible,   690
I do not think that forty-one would join him!

MARY [*after a silence*]. Your eloquence has always brought
   me trouble.
But I am startled by its storm-like strength.
And how can I, a woman and no scholar,
Hope to reply to such an education?
Yes, it is true that if these lords you speak of
Were as you say, my cause would be in tatters.
If such as they were to declare me guilty
I would lose hope and shame would seal my silence.
But are they so? These names with which you conjure,   700
Who are to crush me with their court of virtues,
When I recall the annals of this country,
Their actions seem to wear another colour.
I see the high nobility of England,
The lofty senate of the Kingdom, bowing,
Rather like eunuchs in a sultan's harem,
To the erratic lusts of my great-uncle,
Henry the Eighth! I see the House of Lords,
As vile as their poor cousins in the Commons,
Making and changing laws and marriages   710
To fit the figure of the man of power.
Today a daughter is declared a bastard,
Disgraced and disinherited—tomorrow,
She is crowned Queen. I see these pious peers
Tailoring the religion to demand,
Four times in four reigns tacking to the wind.*

BURLEIGH. You say you are a stranger to our laws,
   But you are well acquainted with our troubles.

MARY. And they judge me! Hardworking Treasurer,
  I give you credit, pay me back in kind;   720
  Men say that you are incorruptible,
  Unwearying and ever-vigilant,
  That you want good for England and the Queen.
  Well I believe it—not your own enrichment
  Drives you but the advantage of your sovereign,
  Of Queen and country. For this very reason
  You should be anxious to prevent advantage
  From picking out injustice as its method.
  I do not doubt that there are men of honour
  Besides yourself among my band of judges,   730
  But they are faithful English Protestants,
  Put into power over me, a papist,
  And Queen of Scotland. You have heard the saying—
  No Scot is ever innocent in England.
  And this has hardened into common custom,
  And since the ages of our forefathers,
  No Englishman has ever been permitted
  To testify against a Scot in court,
  No Scot against an Englishman, in England.
  Necessity established this strange ruling,   740
  But there is wisdom in the old traditions,
  And we are fools if we ignore them. Nature
  Cast our two peoples, struggling in the ocean,
  One plank, and disproportioned its division,
  Necessitating fight. The Tweed alone
  Parts our fierce spirits with its narrow bed;
  Swords ready, we have threatened one another
  Across its waters for a thousand years.
  No enemy has ever turned on England
  Without the Scotsman rushing to abet him,   750
  No civil war has ever blazed in Scotland
  That England did not set the match to. Hatred
  Will not die out until one Parliament
  Unites us, and until one sceptre rules us,
  We cannot live as brothers on this island.

BURLEIGH. And shall a Stuart unify the Kingdoms?*

MARY. Yes, I confess it, why should I deny it?
　It was my hope to bring these famous nations
　Under the shadow of one olive branch,
　Free and at ease. I did not prophesy   760
　That I would suffer their united hate.
　I longed to smother the ancestral envy
　And to dig out the fires of primal discord.
　As my forefather Richmond once entwined
　Two roses to untangle bloodstained armies,*
　So I desired to bind by peaceful marriage
　England and Scotland in a sacred union.

BURLEIGH. Yet you pursued the way of devastation,
　Seeking to wreathe the throne you craved in flames,
　And pluck it from the smoke of civil war.   770

MARY. Show me the proof. Almighty God in heaven,
　I did not want that. When did I attempt it?

BURLEIGH. It is no longer open to debate.
　The voices of the forty have established,
　As against two, that you have contravened
　The Act of last year, and have placed yourself*
　In breach of law. That Act proclaimed as follows:
　'If treason be occasioned in the Kingdom
　On the behalf or for the benefit
　Of any claimant to the throne, that person   780
　Must be pursued as guilty of that crime,
　Through the procedures of the courts to death.'
　And since it has been proved that—

MARY.   Ah, Lord Burleigh!
　This law was passed to justify my murder,
　To furnish me with crimes in retrospect.
　Pity the victim if the sentencer
　Invented the offence for which he damns her!

BURLEIGH. This law was made to warn you. You yourself
　Have used it as a noose. A chasm opened,
　You saw it clearly, others told you of it,   790
　But you strode blithely onwards. You colluded

With Babington, the traitor, and his comrades,
You hunted with that band from start to finish,
Leading them from this cell by influence.

MARY. When did I do this? Show me documents.

BURLEIGH. You saw them recently in court.

MARY.   Those copies,
Written by God knows who? Bring me your proof
Both that those letters were my own dictation
And that the writer copied what I uttered.

BURLEIGH. They are the letters Babington received,   800
As he confessed to us.

MARY.   But not to me.
Why was he hurried from the world, my Lord,
And never made to say this to my face?

BURLEIGH. Also your secretaries, Kurl and Nau,*
Attest that you dictated what they wrote,
Which are the letters Babington received.

MARY. Can I be sentenced by my servants, then?
And is the testimony credible
Of those who give condemning evidence
Against the Queen to whom they swore allegiance?   810

BURLEIGH. You have described before this time the Scotsman
Kurl, as a man of conscience and of virtue.

MARY. And so he was. But in the hour of danger
Virtue can disappear. No doubt the fellow
Invented a confession under torture,
Likely enough to save his life, but false,
And so unlikely not to be disproved.

BURLEIGH. He testified without the need of torture.

MARY. Not before me! Oh did he really, Sir?
Then there are still two witnesses alive,   820
Let him repeat his statements to my face,
A favour, though the right of murderers.

I know because Lord Talbot told me it,
That there has been a royal ordinance
Under the present Government, ordaining
That the accuser faces the accused.
Did I mishear him? Is this not the case?
Sir Paulet, you are honest, are you not?
You say you are—now prove it, tell me truly,
Is this or is this not the law of England?   830

PAULET. It is the law here, that is true, my Lady,
And I may not deny it.

MARY.   Well, my Lord,
Shackle me to the letter of the law,
And serve it to my benefit yourself
No less than when it bends to my oppression.
Why was not Babington produced to me,
According to the law? I will be answered!
Why are my secretaries not brought forward?

BURLEIGH. Lady, do not excite yourself. Your plot
With Babington is not the only charge.   840

MARY. But only that can legalize my death,
And so it will be answered. Come, my Lord,
Do not avoid the subject.

BURLEIGH.   Proof exists
That you have entered into secret dealings
With the ambassador from Spain, Mendoza.*

MARY. Do not avoid the subject!

BURLEIGH.   Proof exists
That you have brooded on the overthrow
Of the religion of this country, calling
Every crowned head in Europe to the contest.

MARY. And if I did? In truth I have not done this,   850
But if I did? Consider this, my Lord,
I am imprisoned. Yet I came to England
Not with a sword but as a suppliant,
Owed by the duty of the Queen my cousin

The sacred right of hospitality.
I sought protection; my imprisonment
Is contrary to every kind of law.
I have been seized with violence and chained,
But am I bound in conscience to this kingdom?
What is my duty? It is to be free.   860
Freedom is sacred and the law is holy
That makes me struggle to escape, to answer
Power with power, calling for the pressure
Of every Christian nation on the earth
To add its weight to my demand for freedom.
Justice and chivalry alone dictate
What methods I may use in this just war,
I only shrink from secret bloody murder,
My conscience and my pride forbid that practice,
Murder would stain me with disgrace—you hear me,   870
Disgrace, for fighting basely, not damnation
Or legal guilt. For in this war of ours
The issue is not law but human power.

BURLEIGH [with deliberation]. You should be wary of that
     word, my Lady.
   Power is not the god of prisoners.

MARY. Yes, I am weak and she is powerful,
   And she can strengthen her position further
   With ease through my destruction. But she should
   Confess to that, and not describe as justice
   Pure murder. It is not the sword of law   880
   The Queen unsheathes to hush her opposition,
   Nor can she hide the passion of this deed
   In sacred robes—the world will not be fooled!
   My death cannot be buried in the law!
   There is no law that will support my death,
   No matter what she does, Elizabeth
   And she must end this pitiful attempt
   To win the praise of angels for a crime.
   Will lose her shine, the world will censure her,
   She will appear in her true character!   890

                                                              [Exit

SCENE VIII

[BURLEIGH, PAULET.]

BURLEIGH. Thus she defies us, and she will defy us
Upon the very scaffold steps, Sir Paulet.
This pride-hard heart cannot, I think, be broken.
Was she the least dismayed by what I told her?
Did her cold eyes let slip a single tear?
She not so much as sighed to rouse our pity.
The Queen of England, by her hesitation,
Terrifies us, and makes this Queen the braver.

PAULET. Chancellor, her defiance will soon fade.
It will decline when we remove its cause.   900
Procedure has been skirted. Babington
And Tichburn should have been produced to her,
As should her secretaries.

BURLEIGH.   No, Sir Paulet!
We cannot let her blur and blank their minds,
With the great female power of her tears.
Her secretary Kurl, if brought before her,
Would, when the moment came to say the sentence
On which her life depends, withdraw, struck dumb,
And cancel his confession.

PAULET.   And thereafter
Rumours would run among our enemies,   910
To make the graceful showing of the court
Seem but a decoration of disgrace.

BURLEIGH. This is our Queen's concern. Oh if that worry
Had only died before it trod our land!

PAULET. I say amen to that!

BURLEIGH.   Or in this dungeon,
Removed by a discreet disease.

PAULET.   This country
Would have been spared much trouble.

BURLEIGH.   Ah, but still,
Even if nature had obeyed our wish,
We would have won the name of murderers.

PAULET. People will think what people like to think,   920
They do not change.

BURLEIGH.   Yet it could not be proved,
And that would blunt the uproar.

PAULET.   Let them rage,
It cannot hurt if it is only loud,
Justified blame alone can do us harm.

BURLEIGH. Oh, spotless justice suffers blame no less!
Opinion always justifies the fallen,
And fastens on the fortunate with envy.
The sword of law, that men are loath to wield,
Is hated by them in a woman's hand.
And when a woman suffers by a woman,   930
The world will not believe that law was honoured.
We judges searched our consciences for nothing!
Our Queen must exercise her right of pardon,
It will be too stern, and too horrible,
If she allows the sentence to be acted.

PAULET. And so—

BURLEIGH [interrupting him quickly]. This Queen shall be
    left living? No!
She may not live! No longer! It is this,
Precisely this, that wakes our Queen with nightmares,
Ridding her bed of sleep. Her troubled lips
Dare not express the longings of her heart,   940
That struggles in her, speaking through her eyes.
Her silence brims with meanings such as this:
Is there not one among my servants faithful,
Who is prepared to spare his Queen the horror
Of choosing endless terror on my throne
Or the beheading of the Queen my cousin?

PAULET. It is unchangeable necessity.

BURLEIGH. It could be changed with ease, the Queen believes,
  If she were only more acutely served.

PAULET. Acutely?

BURLEIGH.   With an ear and hand so loyal   950
  That they can hear and do unspoken orders.

PAULET. Unspoken orders!

BURLEIGH.   What the Queen desires
  Is servants who, when set to guard a serpent,
  Do not protect it like a priceless diamond.

PAULET [*deliberately*]. The reputation of our Queen is priceless,
  That, sir, cannot be guarded too acutely!

BURLEIGH. The Lady was removed from Shrewsbury
  And given to your care with the intention
  Or hope that you—*

PAULET.   I hope with the intention
  That I would undertake this worst of tasks   960
  In the best manner. If I had suspected
  That I was picked for any other reason
  Than my unstained and unmatched reputation,
  I would have spurned this post. But I perceived
  That it requires the finest man in England.

BURLEIGH. Your reputation will remain. The rumour
  That she is sick will be disseminated,
  And she will weaken slowly in our story,
  Departing from the people's memory
  Before she dies in fact, without a murmur.   970

PAULET. My conscience would fall sick and die with her.

BURLEIGH. You do not wish to lend a hand yourself,
  But you will not refuse a stranger—

PAULET.   No!
  There will be no assassins in this place,
  Her life is sacred, while my household gods*

Prop up the roof that shelters her, to me
The Queen of England's life is not more sacred.
You are the judges, for the love of Christ,
Judge! Make the right time come, and I will welcome
The carpenter who comes with axe and saw   980
To build the scaffold, through my open gates;
The Sheriff and the executioner
Will not be barred. But for the present moment
Her life has been entrusted to my strength,
And rest assured that she will do no evil,
But nor will any wrong be done to her!

                                      [*Exeunt*

ACT TWO

SCENE I

[*The palace at Westminster.**]

[*Enter the* EARL OF KENT *and* SIR WILLIAM DAVISON.*
To each other.]

DAVISON. My Lord of Kent! And is the jousting over,
  Are you returning from the sport already?

KENT. What? Did you not attend the spectacle?

DAVISON. My post restrained me.

KENT.   Sir, it has denied you
  The most amazing blessing to the eyes
  That dream could dare or art perform—imagine,
  The fortress of chaste beauty is presented,
  Endangered by the armies of desire.
  Fighting for her we see the Lord High Marshal,
  Besides the Seneschal, the Lord Chief Justice,*   10
  And the Queen's ten best knights—and the besiegers
  Are France's finest horsemen. At their head
  A herald challenges the graceful castle
  With a sweet madrigal, and from a rampart
  The Chancellor replies. And then the archers
  Begin to bow soft music from their weapons,
  And charming little culverins explode
  With cannonades of perfumes and of blossoms;
  In vain! The walls resisted these advances,
  And the dejected French, rebuffed, retreated.   20

DAVISON. Not a good omen for those men, my Lord,
  In their endeavour to annex a bride.

KENT. It was a lover's game! In earnestness,
  I think the fortress is about to fall.

DAVISON. In my opinion it cannot be taken.

KENT. But France has levelled to a settlement,
And every conflict has been overwhelmed.
Monsieur is happy for his services
To be conducted in a private chapel,
While he will honour and protect in public   30
The sovereign religion of this kingdom.
And the delirium of everyone
When this ecstatic news was spread! The people
Have always feared that she would fail to give them
An heir of her blood, and that once again
England would suffer in the womb of Rome,
Under the Stuart.

DAVISON.   They need fear no more.
While she is playing in her bridal chamber,
The Stuart will be in a coffin, sleeping.

KENT. Here comes the Queen!

SCENE II

[*As before.* ELIZABETH, *led by* LEICESTER. *The* EARL
OF AUBESPINE, BELLIEVRE,* *the* EARL OF SHREWSBURY,
LORD BURLEIGH, *enter with French and English
gentlemen.*]

ELIZABETH.   Count, I commiserate   40
These nobles who have shipped a gallant cargo
Of zeal with them across the sea; the splendour
Of St Germain is absent from my gardens,*
I cannot conjure up such holy days
Or heap such endless feasts up to my God
As does the mother of the King of France.
My pride is in a good and happy people,
That crowds about me when I show myself,
And blesses me. That is the spectacle
This country offers to amaze the stranger.   50

The blazing of those suns, the noble ladies
Who bloom in Catherine's unfading garden*
Would instantly eclipse my own dim moonbeams.

AUBESPINE. The stranger at the court of Westminster
Wonders, that there is just one woman here,
Yet one adorned with every kind of wonder
That one can find in woman anywhere.

BELLIEVRE. Grant us, exalted Majesty of England,
That we might take our leave and seek our master,
Monsieur, to soothe his passion with the answer   60
He burns to hear. He has removed from Paris
To Amiens—the former was too far.
From where he is, his posts can reach to Calais,
To speed like birds the Yes your royal lips
May deign to whisper to his waiting heart.

ELIZABETH. Lord Bellievre, do not scratch my surface,
The present shines, as I have said already,
Blackly on marriage plans. This Kingdom frowns
Under bleak weather, and a flower of mourning
Would better suit me now than wedding garlands.   70
There is a dagger pointed at my heart,
And at my house, and it will strike me soon.

BELLIEVRE. Nevertheless, give us your promise, Queen,
For better days than these to realize.

ELIZABETH. The hearts of princes must obey their station,
We may not do our will. From the beginning
It was my wish to go to God unmarried.
I could have been content beneath a tombstone
On which, 'Here lies the virgin Queen,' was written,*
That would have been sufficient fame. However,   80
My fearful subjects peer across my shoulder,
Into the time when I shall be no more.
No matter how the kingdom flourishes,
I must be married off to guard their future.
I must surrender my virginity,
All of myself, my freedom and my treasure,

To those I rule—I must accept a master.
This seems to tell me that I am a woman,
Yet I have ruled this Kingdom like a man,
Or so it seems to me, yes, like a King.   90
I know that to disfavour nature's laws
Is to slight God, and those who ruled before me
Were right to break the power of the cloisters;
Thankfully all those houses have returned
To serving nature, crumbled into earth.*
You see that queens cannot be contemplatives,
But one who tirelessly and endlessly
Attends the gravest of all human duties,
Ought to be kept apart from nature's use,
Whose purposes make half the human race   100
A helpless service to the other half.

AUBESPINE. Since your accession there is not a virtue
That has not found expression in your person.
What task remains for you but to example
The special female excellence, your Highness?
On earth of course there is no living man
Worthy to wear the favour of your freedom,
But if nobility of birth and bearing,
Masculine beauty and heroic courage,
Could fit a man to try to win that honour,   110
Then—

ELIZABETH.
          Yes, Ambassador, it is an honour
To promise marriage to a prince of France!
Let us be frank—what has to be will be,
Fate cannot change, and if my people's wishes
Are stronger, as I fear they are, than I,
Then there could be no other man in Europe
To whom I would resign with less reluctance
My precious freedom and my greatest treasure.
You must refine content from this confession.

BELLIEVRE. It is a hope more beautiful than day,   120
Yet it is less than what my Lord desires.

ELIZABETH. What will he have?
> [*She pulls a ring from her finger and
> contemplates it*

And so the common woman
Is equal to the Queen. Both wear this duty,
Whose meaning is subjection. Marriages
Are made of chains, for chains are made of rings.
Carry this present to his Majesty.
It has not yet been bound into a chain,
But it could be, and so in time could I.

BELLIEVRE [*kneels and receives the ring*].
Queen, I receive this token in his name,
And kiss the hand of my Princess in homage.   130

ELIZABETH [*to* LORD LEICESTER, *whom she has watched stead-
fastly throughout this last speech*].
My Lord, permit me!
> [*She takes the blue band off him and hangs it
> round* BELLIEVRE*'s neck*

Dress his Majesty,
Just as I dress you and receive you here
Into my order, with this decoration.
Remember, *Honi soit qui mal y pense*!*
May the suspicion that divides our nations
Be drowned, and may the knot of truth and trust
Bind our two crowns together for all time.

AUBESPINE. Exalted Queen, this is a day of joy!
Today may no one mourn in all this island!
Mercy is shining from your face like light,   140
Oh that a portion of its rays might fall
Blithely on an unfortunate Princess,
A question of concern to both our nations.

ELIZABETH. That is a matter for another mood.
Leave it, my Lord, it will not mix with this one.
If France desires a serious alliance
Then she must share my burdens, and deflect
Her favour from my open enemies.

AUBESPINE. Yet you yourself would think it base of France
Were she to spurn her co-religionist,   150
This luckless woman, widow of her King,
And make no stir to aid her through this union.
Common humanity alone demands—

ELIZABETH. I know what it requires you to demand.
And I respect the warmth of your attempt.
France has fulfilled her duty as a friend.
Permit me to proceed with mine as Queen.
              [*She bows to the French delegates, who retire
              respectfully with the other gentlemen*

SCENE III

[ELIZABETH, LEICESTER, BURLEIGH, SHREWSBURY.
The QUEEN *sits down.*]

BURLEIGH. Glorious Queen! Today your will has raised
The yearnings of your people to the throne!
You have transformed the future's frowns to laughter,   160
And at long last the blessed days are on us.
Only one fear still walks about the land,
All voices cry for one last sacrifice,
Grant it, and the foundation of this day
Will be for fortune infinite indeed.

ELIZABETH. What does my country still require of me?
Say it, be plain.

BURLEIGH.   The head of Mary Stuart.
To make your people certain of their freedom,
And to perpetuate the light of truth,
Hard-won for us, she may not be let live.   170
Unless we are to fear for you forever,
Your enemy must die! Idolatry
Still keeps its secret legions in this island,
Loyal to Rome and hostile to your crown;
In their belief the Stuart is their monarch;

As you know well, this land is many-minded.
This creed is in collusion with the Guises,*
Invariable enemies of ours,
It is a rabid party and has sworn
A war whose aim is our extermination,   180
Whose weapons are the heresies of hell.
Reims is the city of the cardinal,
And that is where they have their armoury,
Where shining lies and lightning bolts are forged,
And where they learn to murder Kings. From there
They shoot forth zealous missions to this island,
Disguised as every kind of innocence.
Driven by visions from the mind of hell,
Replacing one another tirelessly,
They come to die. Two of their murderers   190
Have trod that road, and now a third is here;
And the creator of this endless war,
Their bitter Ate, sits in Fotheringhay,*
Feeding it at her bosom like a child,
Stirring this realm by love into a furnace.
For she encourages her flatterers,
And the enamoured youths, dazed by her eyes,
To prove their ardour hurry to destruction.
Their battle-cry is her release, their purpose
To set her in your place. The Guises believe   200
That heaven did not present you with this throne,
But that a stroke of fortune made it yours;
They have persuaded, by their plots, a fool
To take the title of the Queen of England.*
No peace with her, or any of her tribe,
It is not possible! You must pre-empt,
Or you will be surrounded. If she lives,
My Queen, you fall, and if she dies you stand.

ELIZABETH. It is not relish for the undertaking
    That feeds your diligence, my Lord, I know.   210
    The source from which your guidance flows is stainless.
    And yet when wisdom speaks of blood, my soul
    Loathes it throughout. My dear Lord Shrewsbury,

Mint me a milder picture if you may—
Tell us your thinking.

SHREWSBURY.   You are well advised
  To praise the care that runs in Burleigh's veins.
  It beats in my heart no less fervently,
  Although my lips may speak it with less strength.
  Queen, for your people's peace and happiness,
  May you live long. Since kings have ruled this island,   220
  It has not known such days of splendid increase.
  But let them not be at the cost of glory!
  Or when they are, may Talbot's day be over.

ELIZABETH. Heaven prevent that we should lose our honour!

SHREWSBURY. Then you must save it by a course of honour,
  And not the execution of the Stuart.
  You may not judge her, she is not your subject.

ELIZABETH. My privy council and my parliament,
  And every court of justice in the country,
  Have ceded me that right, without division,   230
  My Lord, are they misguided, to a man?

SHREWSBURY. For all her courts, this land is not the world.*
  Your Parliament is not the human race,
  And a misguided verdict can be given
  By a majority. Things are never equal—
  The England that has been was not this kingdom,
  Nor will the future kingdoms be this England.
  And as the nation changes like a wave,
  So does the verdict likely to be given
  In any question, trough and crest and break.   240
  You may not claim that the necessity
  Of popular opinion rules your actions,
  Whenever you desire to, try your freedom,
  One outburst of your will can break that pressure.
  Test it! Proclaim that you will not shed blood,
  And that it is your will to save your sister,
  Show those whose council is against your will

That truth is not their prudence but your anger.
And then necessity will fade away,
And you will see injustice change to grace.   250
But you must be the judge, and you alone,
Do not depend on everchanging councils,
But trust the constant weather of your kindness.
A woman's heart was not created hard,
And they who built this kingdom, by decreeing
That female rule is lawful, signified
That government in England should be tender.

ELIZABETH. Shrewsbury is an able advocate
    For England's enemies and mine. My favour
    Leans more towards advice that seeks my safety.   260

SHREWSBURY. She has no other advocate but me.
    There is no argument to her advantage
    But that invites your rage against its speaker.
    And no one dares. But I, whose nearest neighbour
    Is now my grave, may speak without suspicion
    That my defence of the already conquered
    Proceeds from hopes of gain. Shall it be said
    Self-interest was loudest in your council
    And mercy silent? Let it not be so—
    Evil and good have made a league against her,   270
    And you have never even seen her face,
    She is a stranger, nowhere in your heart.
    I do not judge her innocent or guilty,
    Men say she had her husband killed. For certain
    She took her husband's killer as her husband—
    Horrible crime! But one that was committed
    In the confusion of a civil war,
    A dark oppressive time when she, the weakest,
    Surrounded by rebellion pressing hard,
    Fled for protection to the strongest man,   280
    Bewitched by who knows what infernal skill?
    For woman is a creature made of weakness.

ELIZABETH. Woman is not. There are strong souls among us.
    Do not announce that error here, good Talbot.

SHREWSBURY. You had misfortune for an education,
  Life did not turn its kinder face towards you.
  Your eyes were lifted to no distant throne,
  But lowered to your shadow, saw a grave.
  In Woodstock, and benighted in the tower,*
  The tender father of creation brought you   290
  Through sorrow to the knowledge of your duty.
  No flatterers attached themselves like flies
  To make your mind an emptiness of noise,
  But you learnt early how to shrink your spirit,
  Spiral by spiral, into its own thought.
  And so you treasured your inheritance.
  But that poor soul has not been thus preserved.
  Delicate when a child, she was transplanted
  To France, where at the court of endless pleasure
  The festival of recklessness makes false   300
  The voice of truth. And blinded in the dazzling
  River of vice, she was borne down to ruin.
  The useless blessing of her outward grace
  Outshone the beauty of all other women,
  Competing with her greatness to exalt her—

ELIZABETH. Lord Shrewsbury, remember where you are!
  We are assembled here in sober council.
  Her surface grace must be a sight indeed
  To catalyse such transports in the ancient.
  My Lord of Leicester—you alone are silent.   310
  Does what excites him, make you dumb with shyness?

LEICESTER. My Queen, it is surprise that keeps me quiet.
  It is amazing that these tales of terror,
  That thrill the rabble in the London streets,
  Should find their way into your highest council,
  And that wise men should brood on fairy stories.
  It staggers me completely, I confess,
  That this unwanted, outcast Queen of nothing,
  Who could not even keep the throne of Scotland,
  Who was the laughing stock of her own subjects,   320
  Should, God almighty, while she sits in prison,
  Terrify you. Why do you fear her so?

Is it because she claims the throne of England?
Is it because the Guises oppose your reign?
How can the disagreement of the Guises
Ever take from you what is yours by birth,
As Parliament confirms? Did Henry's will*
Not cast her off without a word? Shall England,
Ecstatic in its new enlightenment,
Surrender to the Papist and desert you,   330
Its goddess, for the murderess of Darnley?
Who are these people whose continual cries
Torment you with the question of an heir,
Who put themselves about to get you married,
To claim the rescue of the Church and state?
Do you not stand before us young and strong,
Does she not wilt with every passing day?
By God—I see you dancing on her grave
For years to come, no need to push her down.

BURLEIGH. This has not always been Lord Leicester's mind.

LEICESTER. True, in the court I voted for her death.   341
    But in this Council I speak differently.
    It is advantage that concerns us here,
    Not justice. How is she a danger now,
    Cut off from France, her only friend, now ours,
    Since you have pledged your hand to its King's son?
    And there is hope in England for new heirs.
    Why execute her? She is dead already,
    Powerlessness is death. But if you kill her,
    Pity and rage will raise her name to power.   350
    I counsel therefore that her sentence stay,
    But that the execution is not done.
    So she will live beneath the headsman's axe,
    And if one traitor stirs for her, it falls.

ELIZABETH. My Lords, I thank you for your careful thoughts.
    I will submit your reasons to my mind,
    And, with the help of God, who counsels kings,
    Promote the most adroit of them to action.

SCENE IV

[*As before.* PAULET *and* MORTIMER.]

ELIZABETH. Sir Paulet. Noble friend, whom do you bring?

PAULET. Glorious Majesty! I present my nephew,   360
  Who has returned from travelling afar,
  And, pledging to you all his youthful strength,
  Throws himself at your feet. Receive his service,
  And mercifully shine with life on him.

MORTIMER [*kneels*]. Long live my royal Lady, may your brow
  Be crowned with glory and the best of fortunes.

ELIZABETH. Stand up, young man. I welcome you to England.
  You have been far indeed, through France, to Rome,
  And you have spent some time in Reims. So tell me,
  How goes the malice of my enemies?   370

MORTIMER. May God perplex their aims, and fling their
      arrows,
  Shot at the Queen, back in the archers' faces.

ELIZABETH. Did you see Morgan there, or the unholy
  Bishop of Ross?

MORTIMER.   Yes, I met all the Scotsmen
  Who plot against this realm in Reims in exile.
  Indeed, I stepped into their confidence,
  To learn about them from within their ranks.

PAULET. Letters intended for the Queen of Scotland,
  Written in cipher, were entrusted to him,
  Which he has passed to us, for he is loyal.   380

ELIZABETH. What is their latest drift of strategy?

MORTIMER. It was a terrifying lightning storm
  For them to learn that France has cleaved to England,
  Turning from them. Now they have turned to Spain.

ELIZABETH. The same that Walsingham communicates.*

MORTIMER. Pope Sixtus has pronounced a bull against you,*
  Which was received by Reims as I was leaving.
  With the next ship it will arrive in England.

LEICESTER. England no longer shakes before such weapons.

BURLEIGH. But they can kill when wielded by believers.   390

ELIZABETH. What is your answer if I say you studied
  Another faith in Reims, renouncing this one?

MORTIMER. It was my hope that this would be believed.
  My wish to serve you sunk me to such depths
  Of self-distortion.

ELIZABETH.   What is this you give me?

PAULET [*presenting her with a letter*]. A letter that the Queen
    of Scotland sends.

BURLEIGH. Give me that letter!

PAULET.   Chancellor, forgive me,
  She ordered me to hand this to the Queen.
  She tells me that I am her enemy,
  And I am hateful to her vice indeed,
  But when a service such as this, by chance,   400
  Marches with duty, then I must obey.
        [*The* QUEEN *has taken the letter. While she reads
        it,* MORTIMER *and* LEICESTER *exchange a few
        words secretly with one another*

BURLEIGH [*to* PAULET]. What will the contents of the letter
    be
  But stubborn rage, against which common duty
  Should keep the target of the Queen's heart guarded?

PAULET. She told me frankly what the letter says.
  It begs the favour of a meeting.

BURLEIGH.   No!

SHREWSBURY. Why, is that not the least that she deserves?

BURLEIGH. The Queen of murderers has forfeited
The right to gaze serenely on the eyes   410
Of her whose life she lusted to destroy!
He who advises to the contrary
Cannot be loyal to the Queen he serves.

SHREWSBURY. But if the Queen desires to grant this wish,
Will you oppose such gentleness in power?

BURLEIGH. She is condemned to death! The axe is raised!
To speak to someone under such a sentence
Would compromise the standing of the monarch!
The implication of the royal presence
Is mercy—once the interview has happened   420
The sentence will be inapplicable.

ELIZABETH [once she has read the letter, drying her eyes].
The joy of man's life dies before the life.
How far this Queen has travelled from her pride.
Called to the oldest throne in Christendom,*
By now she hoped she would have worn three crowns,*
But she has learned to bear less fine attire
Since she was dressed in England's coat of arms,
And smiled to hear her court of flatterers
Title her Queen of all the British Isles.
My Lords, forgive me, but it wounds my heart,   430
And melancholy lacerates my spirit,
Making my soul weep blood, when I consider
That what we build on earth has no foundation;
And when I see fate's shadow fall so near me.

SHREWSBURY. The hand of God is on your heart! Oh Queen!
Claim and obey the calling of this moment!
Surely her years of penance should be ended?
Her guilt was grave but she has suffered deeply.
Stoop, and extend to her an angel's hand,
Reaching from light into her death-dark prison.   440

BURLEIGH. Great Queen, be steadfast, do not be misguided
By an emotion, never mind how worthy.

Permit yourself to choose necessity.
You cannot pardon her. You cannot save her.
Therefore do not invite the self-reproach
That you rejoiced to mock her to her face.

LEICESTER. Let us not overreach ourselves, my Lords;
The Queen is wise and needs no help from us
To find the way of greatest dignity.
A meeting of the Queens would not displace   450
The court of law. It is the law of England,
Not the Queen's wish, that calls for Mary's death.
Elizabeth is worthy of herself
If she behaves with generosity.
Meantime the law can follow its straight road.

ELIZABETH. Leave me, my Lords. The path is yet to find
That will combine the mercy we desire
With the necessity we comprehend.
Now—leave!
            [*Exeunt. At the door she calls* MORTIMER *back*
            Sir Mortimer, a word with you.

SCENE V

[ELIZABETH, MORTIMER.]

ELIZABETH [*after she has measured him searchingly with her
    eyes*]. You have behaved with an audacity   460
And self-control not common in the young.
One who can practise such deceits so early
May cancel years from his apprenticeship
And claim to be of age before his time.
Fate calls you to be great—I prophesy it,
And happily for you I have the power
To make my prophecies come true.

MORTIMER.   Great mistress!
All that I am is yours to set in motion.

ELIZABETH. You have observed the enemies of England.
   Their hatred of me is unchangeable,   470
   Their spring of murders inexhaustible.
   Though the Almighty has protected me,
   My crown is not secure while she is living,
   The aim and pretext of the visionaries.

MORTIMER. But say the order and she is no more.

ELIZABETH. Oh sir! The end is only the beginning.
   I thought the law could undertake this matter,
   So that my hands would not be stained with blood.
   The sentence has been said, but am I saved?
   I have to give the order, Mortimer!   480
   The horror of the deed oppresses me,
   It must be done, its face cannot be changed.
   What could be worse?

MORTIMER.   If in appearance, Queen,
   The act seems evil, in reality
   The cause is just.

ELIZABETH.   But listen to the truth:
   We will be judged for what we seem to be,
   No one is ever tried for what they are.
   My right to rule this kingdom is in doubt,
   So must my part in her destruction be.
   A fog best hides these good and evil acts,   490
   The worst mistake is that which comes to light.
   One cannot lose if one does not concede.

MORTIMER. Therefore the safest course to steer would be—

ELIZABETH. Of course it would! Ah, my good angel's voice!
   Oh worthy sir, speak on to the conclusion.
   Your understanding clarifies and pierces,
   You see that this is something serious,
   Your uncle is another kind of man!

MORTIMER [*taken aback*]. Did you reveal your purpose to
   that Knight?

ELIZABETH. Mistakenly I did.

MORTIMER.   Forgive his years.   500
  He has become a waverer. Such actions
  Require the courage of the young.

ELIZABETH.   Perhaps—

MORTIMER. My hand is yours to use. As best you can
  You must preserve your reputation.

ELIZABETH.   Sir!
  If you should wake me with this news one day—
  'Last midnight your opponent Mary Stuart
  Passed from this life!'

MORTIMER.   You may depend upon it!

ELIZABETH. When will my slumber be returned to me?

MORTIMER. Before the next new moon you will be happy.

ELIZABETH. All power to you—do not be insulted   510
  If I must cloak my gratitude in silence.
  Sweet silence is the god of happiness,
  Our most true allies are the ones we hide.
                          [MORTIMER *bows. Exit* ELIZABETH

SCENE VI

[MORTIMER.]

MORTIMER. Go then, arch-hypocrite, deceiving Queen!
  I am the vengeance of the cheated world,
  It is a virtue to be false to you.
  Am I the picture of a murderer?
  Do I suggest base practice by my manner?
  Depend on me, and let your own hand rest,
  Preserve the pious lie of your appearance,   520
  Secretly hoping that the deed is done,
  So you will give us time to steal her freedom!
  You want to make me great, you smile and point

To a bright prize that glitters in the distance,
But there is nothing you can give to me,
The luxury of fame is not my dream.
Only she tempts me, to embrace this life,
An everlasting song of happiness
Sung by the gods of youth and grace floats from her,
And she contains the ecstasy of the sky.   530
But you can only weight me with dead metal.
The one reward acceptable to life
Is when two hearts bewitched by one another
Surrender self-awareness to delight.
But you have never worn the secret crown
A woman wins through passion from a man!
Now I must hand her letter to my Lord.
A hateful duty this, to trust a courtier.
I need no help, the prize is mine to claim,
So mine be both the danger and the fame!   540
      [*As he makes to leave,* PAULET *meets him*

SCENE VII

[MORTIMER, PAULET.]

PAULET. What did her highness have to say to you?

MORTIMER. Nothing important, sir.

PAULET.   Ah, Mortimer,
  It is uncertain ground where you are treading,
  Youth, eager for the honours princes give,
  Can easily be tempted. Fear ambition!

MORTIMER. Was it not you that brought me to this place?

PAULET. I wish I had not done so. Here at court
  The honour of our house has never prospered.
  Nephew, stand firm, do not buy fame too dear.
  Do not destroy your soul.

MORTIMER.   What troubles you?   550
  What are you thinking of?

PAULET.   The Queen may promise
  To make you great, but she will never do it.
  Once you have done her will, to clear her name,
  She will avenge on you what she commanded.

MORTIMER. What deed is this you mean?

PAULET.   Enough pretence!
  I know what act of blood the Queen requires.
  She hopes that youth, desiring fame, will bend
  More easily than age. Will you comply?
  How did you leave it?

MORTIMER.   Uncle!

PAULET.   If you do,
  I damn you and discard you evermore.   560
                              [*Enter* LEICESTER

LEICESTER. Good sir, a moment with your nephew, please.
  Her Majesty is well disposed towards him,
  And wishes that he should without restriction
  Have access to the person of the Stuart.
  The Queen depends upon his honesty.

PAULET. His honesty? Well I am glad to hear it.

LEICESTER. What did you say, sir?

PAULET.   Let the Queen trust him,
  My Lord. Myself I trust my own two eyes.
                              [*Exit* PAULET

SCENE VIII

[LEICESTER, MORTIMER.]

LEICESTER [*astonished*]. What has possessed the Knight?

MORTIMER.   I do not know.
  Perhaps the unexpected confidence   570
  Her Highness granted me bewilders him.

LEICESTER [*looks at him searchingly*]. And are you worthy of
  that confidence?

MORTIMER [*in the same manner*]. I must return the question,
  my Lord Leicester.

LEICESTER. You had a secret to confide to me.

MORTIMER. I must be sure that you are worthy first.

LEICESTER. Who pledges that I may be sure of you?
  Do not be hurt that I am slow to trust.
  You have displayed two faces at this court,
  One of them must be counterfeit—but which?

MORTIMER. The same is true of you for me, my Lord.   580

LEICESTER. How shall we instigate our confidence?

MORTIMER. Let he who has the least to lose trust first.

LEICESTER. Well that is you!

MORTIMER.   No, it is you, my Lord.
  Your testimony would demolish me,
  You have the rank, the favour and the power.

LEICESTER. You are mistaken. Yes I do have power,
  In everything but this unbalanced matter.
  I am the weakest man at court in this,
  And a suspicious word could topple me.

MORTIMER. If the almighty Leicester can confess   590
  Such weakness to me, I may think myself
  Greater perhaps than I have done hereto,
  And be magnanimous in my new status.

LEICESTER. Confide your secret and my own will follow.

MORTIMER [*pulling the letter out quickly*]. These words are
  sent you by the Queen of Scotland.

LEICESTER [*starts in surprise and grabs it quickly*]. Speak that
  name softly! Sir, what do I see?
  Oh it is her!
          [*Kisses the picture and looks at it in silent delight*

MORTIMER.   My Lord, I trust you now.

LEICESTER [*after he has scanned the letter quickly*].
Sir, do you know the contents of this letter?

MORTIMER. No I do not.

LEICESTER.   She trusts you absolutely.

MORTIMER. Yet she refused to answer me this riddle,   600
Telling me it was yours to clarify:
It mystifies me that the Earl of Leicester,
The favourite of Queen Elizabeth,
The open enemy and judge of Mary,
Should be the man from whom she hopes for rescue.
Yet I see clearly that it must be so,
Because your eyes express your hopes for her.

LEICESTER. First tell me why you wish so fervently
To fight for her, and how you won her trust.

MORTIMER. Few words are needed. I renounced my faith   610
In Rome, and am an ally of the Guises.
A letter from the Cardinal of Reims
Vouched for my honour to the Queen of Scotland.

LEICESTER. I heard that you had joined the Church of Rome.
It was that news that woke my trust in you.
Give me your hand. Forgive me my suspicion,
I cannot be too cautious. Walsingham
And Burleigh hate me and set traps for me,
You could have been their creature and their snare.

MORTIMER. What fearful steps the great must take at court.
I pity you, my Lord!

LEICESTER.   With unstrained joy   621
I throw myself into a true friend's arms,
Where I may set my burden down at last
Of long imprisonment. You wonder, sir,
How I could turn so suddenly to Mary.
But truly I have never turned against her,
Only the time constrained me to pretend.

You know that she was promised to me once,
Before she gave her hand and throne to Darnley,
When glory played around her still like laughter.   630
I coldly pushed that happiness away,
But now that she is at the gates of death,
Waiting in prison, I am drawn to her,
And I will risk my life for her.

MORTIMER.   That action
Would be the peak of honour and of courage.

LEICESTER. The state of play has changed immeasurably.
It was ambition that set by my feelings
Towards her youth and beauty. Mary's hand
Seemed an unprizable possession then,
When I had hopes to win the Queen of England.   640

MORTIMER. Who loved you more than any, it is known.

LEICESTER. It seemed so, noble sir. But ten lost years*
Of constant courtship and devout restraint
Have left me—ah, my heart is breaking open!
I must be eased of this long-standing grief.
I am an enviable man. But envy
Would perish if it knew what chains it covets.
After ten years of bitter sacrifice
To the pale idol of her vanity,
Prostrated like a slave beneath her temper,   650
That changing Empress, or that pendulum
Of proud inconstancy, that dandled me,
A toy to drain of its delight and break,
Tortured alike by favour and disgrace,
Imprisoned in a cage of jealous eyes,
More numerous in her than those of Argus,*
Brought to account like an unruly boy,
Raged at like a forgetful servant—words,
You are too weak to bear my memories!

MORTIMER. My Lord, I pity you.

LEICESTER.   And after all,   660
The prize retreats beyond my reach forever.

Another suitor comes, and, at the end,
Steals the reward for which a fortune tried.
My long-established rights have been transmitted
To a fresh bridegroom, and I must descend
From the great stage where I so long outshone.
The new arrival looks to take her favour,
Not just her hand, and I am left with nothing.
He is desirable, she is a woman.

MORTIMER. He is the son of Catherine Medici,   670
  The best of tutors taught him how to flatter.

LEICESTER. So my barque founders—and among the wreckage,
  I search for something able to preserve me.
  And I look back into another time,
  And see my first fair hope still shining there—
  Mary, adorned with glory like the day,
  Stands once again before me in my mind,
  Beauty and youth have repossessed their right,
  And cold ambition melts into the ground.
  My heart compares what is with what is lost,   680
  And knows at last that it forsook the best.
  Aghast, I see her fallen in the pit,
  Precipitated by my guilt. But hope
  That I might save her yet and have her, lives.
  And I succeeded in revealing to her,
  By loyal messenger, my secret feelings,
  And the reply that you have brought assures me
  That she forgives me and will, if I save her,
  Give herself to me.

MORTIMER.   Yet you set in motion
  No steps towards her rescue—you permitted   690
  The death sentence to be pronounced, you helped it!
  It took a miracle, the light of heaven
  Had to be sent into her jailer's nephew,
  God had to save her life by an unlooked-for
  Conversion in the Vatican in Rome!
  Or you would never have received that letter.

LEICESTER. Sir, this has earned me misery enough.
When she was taken into Fotheringhay,
From Talbot, and entrusted to your uncle—
He is too strict, and she could not be reached,   700
And still before the world I had to curse her.
But you must never think that I would leave her
To pass through suffering to death. I hope
And hope that that extreme will not be faced,
And that a way to rescue her exists.

MORTIMER. Your noble trust deserves a like response.
Leicester, a way to free her has been found.
I came to you because I mean to do it,
And your support assures us of success.   709

LEICESTER. What do you say? This is a shock. You want to—

MORTIMER. Open her prison gates by force and take her.
I have companions, everything is ready.

LEICESTER. Several know of this? Oh God in heaven!
Into what chaos are you thrusting me?
And your companions know my secrets too?

MORTIMER. Take heart, this plot was born without your
    knowledge,
And would have risen thus to its success,
If it was not for her insistent will
That her salvation should be won by you.

LEICESTER. Then you can give me a complete assurance   720
That I have not been named among your number?

MORTIMER. Depend on it, my Lord! But why so frightened
By news that brings you certainty of glory?
You long to rescue and possess the Stuart,
Suddenly means and friends fall from the sky,
And yet you seem more cornered than inspired.

LEICESTER. Force is too dangerous a means for this.

MORTIMER. So is delay!

LEICESTER.   I tell you plainly, sir,
Action cannot be risked.

MORTIMER.   By you perhaps,
  Who want her, we who merely wish to save her   730
  Feel no such fear.

LEICESTER.   Young man, you are too sudden,
  And would rush headlong through a wood of thorn.

MORTIMER. You are too cautious in a heavenly cause!

LEICESTER. You cannot see the nets stretched out for us.

MORTIMER. But I can feel the strength to shake them off.

LEICESTER. Such courage is a form of lunacy.

MORTIMER. Such wisdom is a form of cowardice.

LEICESTER. And so you long to follow Babington?

MORTIMER. And are you loath to share great Norfolk's fame?

LEICESTER. I never heard that Norfolk took the bride.   740

MORTIMER. But it is rumoured that he proved his worth.

LEICESTER. If we should fall, we pull her down with us.

MORTIMER. But she will fall, if we preserve ourselves.

LEICESTER. You neither think nor listen, you are blind,
  And you will trample, root up and devour
  Schemes that slow skill has carefully arranged.

MORTIMER. Your skilful care, no doubt? What have you done?
  If, as Elizabeth supposed, my Lord,
  I had been eager to obey her order,
  To do the murder she is waiting for,   750
  What preparations for your love's defence
  Are now in place to save her from me, tell!

LEICESTER. Did the Queen order you to do that evil?

MORTIMER. She thought me base, as Mary thought you brave.

LEICESTER. And did you promise to obey?

MORTIMER.   I did,
  To keep the Queen from hiring other blades.

LEICESTER. You have done well. This gives us space to move.
  While she is waiting for your secret blow,
  She will postpone the open execution,
  And time is ours.

MORTIMER.   Yes, it is ours to use!   760

LEICESTER. Counting on you, she will be more content
  To make a show of mercy to the world.
  Perhaps I can mislead her and persuade her
  To speak with her opponent. It would bind her.
  An execution after such a meeting,
  As Burleigh says, would be against tradition.
  Yes, I will try it, risking everything.

MORTIMER. And what will it achieve? Elizabeth
  Discovers that she was deceived in me,
  Because the Queen of Scots is still alive—   770
  Nothing will change; imprisonment for ever
  Will be the mildest consequence for us,
  And Mary will be safer in her cell.
  Why not begin as you must end, with valour?
  You have the power, you could raise an army,
  Muster the nobles sleeping in your castles.
  She still has many secret friends. The houses
  Of Howard and of Percy bristle still*
  With heroes, though their fathers' heads have fallen.
  All they require is some great Lord to lead them.   780
  Declare yourself! Refuse to be deceitful,
  Defend your lover like a knight of old,
  Fight for her name and yours. The Queen of England
  Will follow you wherever you invite her,
  Lure her within your castle walls, and there
  Speak to her like a man of strength and hold her
  To ransom for the freedom of the Stuart!

LEICESTER. I am astonished. This is horrible,
  Where is your howling madness dragging you?
  Do you know where you are? Have you not seen   790
  How close the spirit of this court is bound,
  And how a woman's spirit binds this land?

Where are your heroes? Once they shook the kingdom,
Now they attend the turning of a key,
Which she has buried. Follow my advice,
Begin no ventures that depend on daring!

MORTIMER. But Mary hopes! Must I return with nothing?

LEICESTER. Take her my promise of eternal love.

MORTIMER. Take it yourself. Or keep your messages
Of absent love and I will bring her rescue!   800

                                                    [*exit*

SCENE IX

[ELIZABETH, LEICESTER.]

ELIZABETH. Who left you then? I heard a conversation.

LEICESTER [*turning round quickly as she speaks, startled*].
It was Sir Mortimer.

ELIZABETH.   My Lord, so flustered.
What is the matter?

LEICESTER.   You. You startle me.
I never saw you so immaculate.
I stand here blinded by the sight. Oh God!

ELIZABETH. What makes you sigh?

LEICESTER.   Who has more cause to sigh?
The nameless ache that had begun to fade,
Renews itself beneath your beauty's light,
And loss to come grows greater than before.

ELIZABETH. What will you lose?

LEICESTER.   Your heart, and my desire.
You will be happy in your husband's arms,   811
The heart you give him will be his alone,
For he is youthful, passionate and royal.
The first and last I lack, I must confess,

But for the second, let the world be summoned
To witness that of all on earth who love you,
No one alive adores you more than Leicester.
The Duc d'Anjou has never seen your face,
He loves you for the sunshine of your fame,
But I love *you*. Were you a shepherdess,   820
And I the foremost monarch of the earth,
I would descend, surrendering my state,
And cast away my crown to win your hand.

ELIZABETH. Dudley, accuse me but do not upbraid me.
I may not serve my heart like other women.
And how I envy those who use their powers
To raise their loves, a luxury denied me.
But not the Stuart—she was fortunate,
And gave herself to him she loved the best.
And she allowed herself the best of life,   830
She drained a cup of strange and varied raptures.

LEICESTER. Now she must taste the bitter cup of sorrows.

ELIZABETH. She would not listen to the world's opinion,
She made life easy for herself, would never
Submit to such a yoke as I have carried.
I wish I could have ordered my existence
To pleasure me, and earth to make me happy,
But I was drawn to sober royal labour.
Yet she, by being simply woman, captured
The simple adoration of all men,   840
And young and old alike seek her affection.
Men are just like that, vain, undisciplined,
They run to joys like rivers to the sea,
Frivolity and pleasure's butterflies.
They cannot honour anything of worth.
Why, when he spoke of her deliciousness
Even old Talbot rambled like a youth!

LEICESTER. Forgive him that. He was her warder once,
She has bewildered him with flattery.

ELIZABETH. Shall I believe in truth that she is lovely?   850
    I have to hear her beauty praised so often,
    I would delight to know the truth about it.
    Portraits can lie, descriptions can imagine,
    But my own eyes would tell me in a moment.
    What has amazed you?

LEICESTER.   My imagination
    Suddenly showed me Mary next to you.
    Oh I confess I covet that delight!
    If it could be effected secretly—
    To set your beauty opposite the Stuart.
    Then victory unbounded would be yours!   860
    I could not blame you if you shamed her so,
    For she would see, with envy's razor eyes,
    How she is crushed to nothing by your grace
    No less than by your more important gifts.

ELIZABETH. She is the younger woman.*

LEICESTER.   Is she younger?
    Not in appearance. That is suffering.
    Pain is her posture, her expression prison.
    Ah! It would deepen even that defeat
    If you appeared before her as a bride.
    To her, life's hopes are figments of the past,   870
    To see you striding on to happiness,
    And promised to the King of France's son—
    France, where her power and her knowledge were,
    Whose might she boasts is still at her command,
    Where her own marriage so exalted her!

ELIZABETH [carelessly throwing down the comment].
    Why am I always being pressed to see her?

LEICESTER. It is a favour that would punish her.
    To step on to the scaffold will appal her
    Less than it will to fade before your beauty.
    So you will kill her spirit secretly,   880

Just as she planned by stealth to murder you.
When she sees beauty that is truth's reflection,
And strengthened by the golden name of virtue,
Beauty that she so carelessly discarded,
Uplifted by the brilliance of the crown,
And by the April bravery of a bride,
Then she will know that she outstays her time.
Yes, when I turn my eyes upon you now,
I see that you were never better armed
To win the fight for beauty in your life.   890
You entered like the sun, surrounding me
With summer when you came into this place.
Ah! If you could appear before her now,
As you are now—no better time will come—

ELIZABETH. Now? No, I must discuss this first with Burleigh.

LEICESTER. Burleigh thinks only of the state's advantage,
You must obey your woman-wishes also.
This is an issue for your court of one,
For you to bring before yourself, not him,
Though statesmanship itself would counsel it,   900
Because it would display kindheartedness,
And win you popular opinion. After,
Shake off the nuisance in your chosen fashion.

ELIZABETH. To see my cousin fallen so profoundly*
Would not seem fitting. It has been reported
That she is not attended like a Queen.
Her poverty would be an accusation.

LEICESTER. No need to peer into her rooms. Hear me—
Coincidence has planned for our desires.
Today the great hunt passes Fotheringhay,   910
And there the Stuart could be loosed, perhaps,
To walk about the park. You happen by,
And then, as if by accident, you see her.
If it upsets you, ride away in silence.

ELIZABETH. If I should venture on this folly, Leicester,
The recklessness is yours, not mine. Today,
Of all my subjects I have hurt you most,
And I cannot deny you anything,
Though it be foolish notions. After all,
This is how Queens embrace their favourites,   920
By granting them what wisdom would deny.

      [LEICESTER *falls at her feet. The curtain falls*

ACT THREE

SCENE I

[*In a park, with trees. A wide view in the distance.*]

[MARY, KENNEDY.]

KENNEDY. You have grown wings but I am still a woman,
  I am too old to follow. Wait for me!

MARY. Run with my limbs into the sun
  Burn away years and make us one!
  The land is flying like a carpet,
  Close eyes, step light, and fly upon it!
  How have I climbed from day to night?
  Where is the vault that blocked out daylight?
  Oh I have parched in deserts, dry
  Not of water but of sky.   10

KENNEDY. Oh my dear Lady, you are not yet free,
  Only, your cell has been a little widened.
  We cannot see the walls that seal us in
  Only because the branches cover them.

MARY. Oh praises, praises, bright kindhearted green,
  For conquering the vision of a dungeon.
  Leave me to dream my soul into the world,
  Why wake me up from such a sweet escape?
  Can you not see me half-way up the sky?
  My eyes are not in prison, they can travel   20
  Along the skyroads, measured by no miles.
  Those wind-uplifted mountains far away
  Are in my kingdom. Even these close clouds,
  Charioteering through the afternoon,
  Can see their shadows on the face of France.
  Storm-driven vikings of the sky!
  What hearts are in your company?
  I have no messengers but you,
  Carry my kisses to my country!

Your road is open through the blue,   30
The Queen who keeps me here in chains
Cannot command the voyaging rains!

KENNEDY. Oh my dear Lady, your captivity
Has altered you—it tortures you with visions.

MARY. See where that man puts out his fishing boat.
That shape of nails and pitch and planks
On which his starving life depends
Could float me to a world of friends!
And I would pay him more than thanks!
How he would row if he could know   40
What wealth his resting nets had won,
Giving their place to my salvation!

KENNEDY. You wish in vain. Have you not clearly seen
How the spy's footsteps follow where we go?
How a dark prohibition terrifies
All sympathetic creatures from our way?

MARY. It is not so, good Hanna! I believe,
And so should you, that it was not in vain
My dungeon door creaked open. This concession
Heralds a greater, more secure good fortune.
I am not dreaming, strong-willed love has done this,   50
I recognize the might of my Lord Leicester.
Slowly my dungeon's limits will retreat,
Small mercies will prepare my heart for more,
Until the face of freedom finally
Takes off its devil mask of stones and chains!

KENNEDY. And yet these contradictions will not rhyme.
Yesterday you were waiting for the end—
Today you are unfettered to the air.
Those who are soon to leave all cells forever   60
Have their chains somewhat loosened, I have heard.

MARY. Can you hear the huntsman's cry
Rising brightly from a glade
To the riders in the sky?
Oh to join that wild parade,

Swinging to my hunter's back
To shatter down the pockmarked track!
Echoing memory returns,
Oh I have ridden where that cry
Burst through thundering mountain burns.   70
Now I hear it through a sigh.

SCENE II

[PAULET. *Others as before.*]

PAULET. Now then, my Lady! Does this suit you better?
 Do my attentions merit thanks for once?

MARY. What, sir? Can it be you who gained this favour?

PAULET. Who should it be but me? I was at court,
 I gave the Queen your letter, as requested.

MARY. You gave it to her—really? And this freedom
 Is the reply?

PAULET.   And there is more to follow.
 Prepare yourself for something even stranger.   79

MARY. What do you mean by that, sir—something stranger?

PAULET. You hear the huntsman's horn?

MARY [*stepping back, with an inkling*]. What does it mean?

PAULET. The Queen is hunting in this countryside.

MARY. What?

PAULET.   In a moment she will stand before you.

KENNEDY [*rushing up to* MARY, *who is trembling and about
 to fall*]. What is the matter, you grow pale, my Lady!

PAULET. Your wish is granted sooner than you thought.
 Is it no longer your desire, my Lady?
 Well? Is your freedom not so welcome now?

You always had hard words to fire before,
But they were wasted—speech is needed now.

MARY. Why must this come when I am unprepared?   90
Oh, I am not prepared at all, not now!
What I requested as a grand concession
Now seems a chasm I implored to open.
Come, Hanna, lead me back into the house,
There I will breathe a little and recover.

PAULET. No, you must stay here. Well may I believe
That it dismays you to await your judge.

SCENE III

[*The* EARL OF SHREWSBURY *joins the others.*]

MARY. Ah, it is not that, God knows, not quite that!
Most noble man, you have been sent by heaven,
An interposing angel. Shrewsbury,   100
I must not see her, save me from my hatred.

SHREWSBURY. Queen, be yourself in this decisive hour,
Summon your courage!

MARY.   I have spoken to her
Over and over again, year after year,
In my imagination, stirring words,
Etching them on my mind in preparation.
Now everything is on a sudden empty,
And I remember only agony,
The death of every echo but its own.
My conscience is a mad-eyed animal,   110
And gentle thoughts escaping for their lives
Are changed to hailstones by my Gorgon hair!*

SHREWSBURY. Calm your enraged blood, sweeten your sick
     heart!
Hate sowed in hate produces bitter fruit.
Though it appals your spirit to the core,

Obey the face of things, that rules the time.
She has the power, you must kneel to her.

MARY. No, it cannot be done.

SHREWSBURY.   It must be done!
Be easy with her, but be deferent,
Try to attract her magnanimity,   120
Do not defy her, it is not the time,
Do not insist upon your right to her.

MARY. Damnation is the answer to my prayers,
And I have pleaded for my own destruction.
We two should never see each other, never!
No good can come of it. Rather let fire
Kiss water or the lamb embrace the tiger.
I am too deeply injured to revive,
Her insults are too grievous for redress,
No reconciliation can be made!   130

SHREWSBURY. First see her face before you swear such nevers.
See her as I did when I watched her eyes,
Reading your letter, fill with tears—and trust her.
Her heart is warm, which is precisely why
I came to you before her to prepare you,
Hoping to smooth the ridges of your passion.

MARY [takes his hand]. Oh Talbot, you have always been my
    friend.
If only I was still your prisoner!
I have been badly treated, Shrewsbury.

SHREWSBURY. But let that vanish, and begin to plan   140
How you will meet her peaceably and meekly.

MARY. Is the malignant spirit Burleigh with her?

SHREWSBURY. Only the Earl of Leicester rides beside her.

MARY. My Lord of Leicester!

SHREWSBURY.   You need not fear him.
He does not seek your fall—it was his efforts
That brought the Queen to meet you.

MARY.   Oh I knew it!

SHREWSBURY. What did you say?

PAULET.   The Queen! The Queen is coming!
[*Everybody steps to the side, except* MARY, *who
stays, leaning on* KENNEDY

SCENE IV

[*As before.* ELIZABETH, LORD LEICESTER,
their retinue.]

ELIZABETH [*to* LEICESTER]. What is this place?

LEICESTER.   The name of the estate
Is Fotheringhay Castle.

ELIZABETH.   Send the hunt
On into London. In the narrow streets   150
The people press too closely. We will shelter
In the fresh space of this still park.
            [SHREWSBURY *removes the retinue. She fixes her
            gaze on* MARY, *while she addresses herself to*
            PAULET
                                My subjects
Love me too much, as if I was an idol,
Their transports have the character of worship.

MARY [*has all this time been leaning on her nurse, almost
fainting, but now straightens up, and her eyes meet*
ELIZABETH's *unswerving gaze. She shivers and throws
herself back at her nurse's breast*]. Oh God, these words
were spoken by no soul.

ELIZABETH. Who is this Lady? [*universal silence*]

LEICESTER.   This is Fotheringhay,
Therefore, your Highness—

ELIZABETH [*acts surprised and astonished, directing a dark
look at* LEICESTER].   Who has done this thing?
Lord Leicester?

LEICESTER.   Queen, you have been led by grace,
Heaven has let this happen, let the outcome
Be an amazing victory for pity!   160

SHREWSBURY. Allow it to be begged, your Majesty,
That you direct the sunshine of your eyes
Towards this woman wasting in the frost.

> [MARY *pulls herself together and tries to walk*
> *towards* ELIZABETH, *but stops half-way there*
> *and stands shaking, her gestures expressing*
> *the strongest inner conflict*

ELIZABETH. What, Lords? Who was it that prefigured me
A woman bent in two by her misfortunes?
I see before me one whom pride has steeled,
Not one unstiffened by her miseries.

MARY. I will conform to their description then,
And bow to this as to each former blast.
I shed my pride, my soul's unchosen skin,   170
Unconscious colour of nobility,
And strengthen the oppression I endure,
Furthering it by falling at its feet.

> [*She turns towards the* QUEEN

The scales of heaven find for you, my sister!
Victory glitters on your head like gold.
Whichever god has lifted you I'll follow.

> [*She falls at* ELIZABETH's *feet*

But you must meet surrender with a gesture,
Do not permit me to lie graceless here,
Stretch down the right hand of your Majesty,
To lessen my immeasurable fall.   180

ELIZABETH [*steps back*]. This is your proper station, Lady
    Mary.
And I will always praise the grace of heaven
That it has not required me so to lie.

MARY. But think how change unravels humankind.
Remember, there are gods that hate vainglory!
Honour whatever flings me at your feet,
But do not shame me, raise yourself in me,

Before these men of lesser families,
Honour the Tudor blood that runs in us.
Sanctify that, and, by Almighty God,   190
Do not remain as faceless as a cliff.
My whole existence and abilities
Are crowded on the weak raft of these words,
Clinging for life to timbers made of tears.
Set free my heart that it may fly to you,
When you oppress me with a winter stare,
Terror draws back the tears into my eyes,
And shrinks my heart, and traps my speech in it.

ELIZABETH [*coldly and sternly*]. What was it that you wished
    to say to me?
You mentioned a desire to speak with me.   200
I have forgotten the insulted Queen,
In order to be tender to a sister,
To whom I lend the comfort of my presence,
Which generosity exposes me
To reprimand, because you planned my murder.

MARY. Where to begin, oh how to learn the cunning
    To shape my words to win and not to harm?
Oh God exalt my speech and make it giant,
But tame its rage and take away its weapons,
Because I may not tell you of myself   210
Without attacking and accusing you,
And that I do not wish to do. Your actions
Have not been just, I am a Queen like you,
And you have held me as a prisoner.
I came to you a suppliant: you, mocking
The sacredness of hospitality,
The common rights of nations, shut me up
In dungeon walls. My servants and my friends
Were mercilessly stolen from my side,
And I am left to suffer infamies,   220
Stood like a child before a so-called court!
No more of this. Let me forget that horror.
Look! I can call my sorrows Providence,
You are no more to blame for them than I.

A spirit of destruction rose from nothing
To set hate in our hearts, which had already,
Unconsciously in youth, suffered division.
Discord grew up with us, and evil men
Fed the annihilating flame. Mad zealots
Set daggers in assassins' hands unbidden.   230
This is the cursed, inverted gift of kings,
That with a quarrel they can burn the world,
And that their sins can damn the human race.
But now our talk does not depend on liars.
    [*Approaches her confidingly, and with an intimate
        tone of voice*
Now we can speak by clearer means than rumours,
Facing each other. Sister, state my crime,
And I will answer to your satisfaction.
If you had only come to me before,
We never would have ended in this place,
Where this sad meeting magnifies our pain.   240

ELIZABETH. The stellar fortune that preserves my life
Prevented me from clutching to my breast
Death's poison fangs. It is not destiny*
That your black spirit rightly should accuse,
But the unsafe ambitions of your house.
There had been no unfriendliness between us
Until your uncle, the proud tyrant priest,
Crown-covetous, began his feud with me,
By tempting you to take my coat of arms,
Which you accepted, with my royal title,   250
So cursing us to struggle for our lives.
And since that time, in his continuing war,
Whom has he not incited? Pious madness
Makes priest's words and the people's swords good weapons;
Even where peace sleeps deep, here in my kingdom,
He has stirred civil war. But God is with me,
The cleric stumbles bleeding from the field,
My head was aimed at but your head will fall.

MARY. God holds me in his hand. You will not step
So far beyond the powers he ordains.   260

ELIZABETH. Who tells me so? Your uncle showed the way,
Teaching all kings how to placate their foes.
And I will follow St Bartholomew!*
What are these sacred rights? They are too subtle,
Like ties of blood, too frail to bridle me.
The Church of Rome cuts through all human duties,
Makes regicide a blest and saintly action,
Disloyalty sublime—I only practise
What your priests preach. Suppose I let you go,
What surety will you exchange for freedom?   270
What padlock could secure your loyalty
Against St Peter's key? None. Peace is force.
There can be no diplomacy with evil.

MARY. It is the sad deceit of your suspicion
That has created me your enemy.
If you had only, out of honesty,
Proclaimed me your successor, in return
You would have gained a relative and friend.

ELIZABETH. Your friendship shines on other countries, Mary,
The house you spring from is the Vatican,   280
Monks are your brothers. Name you as my heiress!
Bottomless pit! And see you, in my lifetime,
Another Armida, bewitch my people,*
Stealing the kingdom's noble youths with lewdness,
Turning all eyes towards your dawn, while I—

MARY. Reign strongly and serenely. All my claims
I here renounce. Your Kingdom is your own.
My spirit's strings, by which I sung, are broken,
And all my claims to greatness die to silence.
You are the victor, this is Mary's shadow,   290
The dungeon shame wore out the noblewoman.
You have achieved the uttermost in me,
The image of a woman in her prime
Contains a dead self. Sister, finish now,
Say what you came to say, for that you came
Simply to mock me, I will not believe.
Speak the word, tell me, 'Mary, you are free,
You felt my strength, now learn to praise my mercy,'

Say it, and I will take my life and freedom
Not as a right, but as a gift from you.   300
One word from you and I have never suffered,
Oh do not let me wait in hope too long!
Pronounce the ending of my agonies,
Say it before you leave me, or be cursed,
For if you do, you will depart a goddess,
Leaving behind a lesser paradise,
Otherwise, sister, not for all these islands,
Nor everything that shines beneath the sun,
Would I desire to stand above you now,
Shadow your life as now you shadow mine.   310

ELIZABETH. Do you at last concede an utmost end?
Have all your intrigues withered secretly?
Are no more killers creeping in your cause,
Is there no errant melancholy Knight
Keeping your eager hopes alive with crimes?
Yes, Mary, I can see that it is over,
No more light souls will fly from me to you,
Another moon has risen, yours has waned.
No one is lusting to become your fourth
Consort—for it is known to be as deadly   320
To be your lover as to wed you!

MARY [*flaring up*].   Sister!
Sister! God, God, remember moderation!

ELIZABETH [*looks at her for a long time with an expression
     of proud disdain*]. Is this the power that rules men
     through their eyes
Without the need of any other force?
Is this the image near to which no woman,
Fearful of fading, dares to stand, Lord Leicester?
That reputation was not hard to earn.
Beauty, to purchase common approbation,
Needs only to be common property.

MARY. That is too much!

ELIZABETH [*laughing mockingly*]. Now the true face appears,
Cracking the mask!

MARY [*glowing with rage, and yet with noble dignity*].
                    I failed, but openly,   331
I was too human in my youthful power.
But I would not pervert myself to fictions,
Or shrink my royal frankness for appearance.
The worst of me is open to the world,
My highest virtue is as yet unknown.
But you, God help you if the canopy
Is ever snatched away, that hides the passion
And the wild instincts that command your actions.
Your blood preserves the virtues of your mother.   340
It is well known for what crime Anne Boleyn
Went to the scaffold!*

SHREWSBURY [*stepping between the two queens*]. Blessed God
    in heaven!
How has it come to this? My Lady Mary,
Is this submission, is this moderation?

MARY. I have endured all that can be endured.
Let moderation fly for help to heaven,
Lamb-hearted self-restraint descend to flames,
Trapped patience, breathe, and break your steel-bound
    prison
Of long-held-in resentment—you who gave
The basilisk the eyes of death, give me*   350
A wounding tongue to linger out death-torture.

SHREWSBURY. She is delirious with rage, forgive her,
It is not her.
            [ELIZABETH, *speechless with rage, darts furious
            looks at* MARY

LEICESTER [*in the utmost disquiet, tries to lead* ELIZABETH
    away].   Be deaf to these attacks!
Forsake at once this inauspicious place!

MARY. England has raised a bastard to the throne!
Arch-cunning mocks the noble British people!
If justice was the ruler in this country,
You would be lying in the dust, not I—

For I am your King.
                    [ELIZABETH *exits quickly, lords follow in great*
                    consternation

SCENE V

[MARY, KENNEDY.]

KENNEDY.   Oh, what have you done?
  She parts from you enraged, and hope with her.   360
  Now it is finished.

MARY [*still beside herself*]. Yes, she leaves enraged,
  Death in her heart! Oh God, at last, at last,
                    [*Falls about* KENNEDY's *neck*
  Hanna, the joy, the joy! A single instant
  Transfigures by revenge years of subjection
  To triumph! And the blade that splits her heart
  Casts off a leaden mountain from my own!

KENNEDY. Unhappy woman, madness drags you on,
  You have insulted the implacable.
  She is the Queen, she grips the thunderbolts,
  You mocked her in the presence of her lover!   370

MARY. Oh I have made her small in Leicester's eyes!
  He was a witness of my victory!
  When I destroyed her he was standing there,
  Sending me strength to push her from the height!

SCENE VI

[MORTIMER *joins* MARY, KENNEDY.]

KENNEDY. Oh, sir! Disaster!

MORTIMER.   Yes, I heard it all.
                    [*Gives* KENNEDY *a sign to return to her look-out*
                    post, and then steps closer. His entire demean-
                    our expresses a passionate mood

She kissed the ground! The victory is yours!
You are the Queen, she is the criminal.
Your bravery amazes and exalts me,
I worship you, you are magnificent,
You are my goddess, I see nothing else!   380

MARY. And did you give my present to Lord Leicester?
The letter and the picture, did you sir?

MORTIMER [gazing at her with an ardent expression].
Ah, how your beauty in the royal fire
Of your high anger caught new clarity!
To teach me plainly what I all but knew,
That you alone on earth are beautiful!

MARY. I beg you, answer my impatience, sir,
What did my Lord say? Is there hope for me?

MORTIMER. Who? He? He is a coward and a wretch,
Foster no hopes of any help from him,   390
Despise him and forget him utterly.

MARY. What do you say?

MORTIMER.   He rescue, he possess you?
He you! Do not imagine he will dare,
First he would have to fight me to the death!

MARY. You did not hand the Lord my letter then?
Oh then my hope is gone.

MORTIMER.   He wants long life,
As do all cowards. He who sets himself
To rescue you and have you for his own,
Must serve another lady in your cause,
Death, and be always fit for her embrace.   400

MARY. He will not help me then?

MORTIMER.   Forget his name!
What can he do that is beyond our powers?
I mean to rescue you myself alone!

MARY. And what can you do?

MORTIMER.   Undeceive yourself,
  See that it is no longer yesterday.
  The manner of the Queen's departure now,
  And the direction of your argument,
  Everything shouts that everything is lost,
  There is no road to mercy any more.
  We must transcend this dead debate to action.   410
  Before tomorrow rises from the sea,
  Everything must be risked—you must be free.

MARY. Tonight, you say? How is that possible?

MORTIMER. Hear what has been begun. I have assembled
  My band of comrades in a secret chapel.
  A priest has heard perhaps our last confessions,
  And has absolved us of our former sins,
  And of our sins to come. We can go down,
  We have received the last rites, extreme unction.

MARY. Terrible preparations!

MORTIMER.   We will climb   420
  The castle walls in darkness. We will murder
  Your guards and take you from your room by force.
  I have the key—in order that the rescue
  Shall not be told to any living soul,
  Our hands will end them all.

MARY.   What, Drury, Paulet,
  My prison masters? They would rather perish
  In a great fight.

MORTIMER.   My knife will be their battle.

MARY. Your uncle will be killed, your second father?

MORTIMER. He dies by me, his nephew murderer.

MARY. Horrible crime!

MORTIMER.   Our sins have been forgiven.   430
  I can commit the worst that I desire.

MARY. Oh how terrible, how terrible!

MORTIMER. Even if I should stab Elizabeth,
  I am protected by the sacrament.

MARY. No, Mortimer, before such blood for me—

MORTIMER. What is my life beside my love and you?
  Ah, let the chain from which the world hangs break,
  And let a second deluge flood our lungs,
  Creation is your shadow, nothing more.
  Before I stand between myself and you,   440
  Let the last midnight chime the world to bed!

MARY [*steps back*]. God, sir, what speech, what looks, you
    terrify me,
  You frighten me away!

MORTIMER [*with disconcerted glances and an expression of
    quiet madness*]. It is one moment,
  Life, death. So let them drag this death to Tyburn,*
  And tear off limb by limb with red hot iron—
                  [*As he walks up to her forcefully, with
                    outstretched arms*
  When I am in the fire of you, my love—

MARY [*steps back*]. Madman, step back.

MORTIMER.   Flames kissing at my mouth,
  Love breathing heat into my lungs—

MARY.   God, sir!
  Let me go in!

MORTIMER.   He is a lunatic
  Who fails to clasp in an embrace like mountains   450
  Whatever bliss God shines into his life.
  Ah, if it takes a thousand screaming deaths,
  You must be saved, I have to rescue you.
  And as God lives, so truthfully I swear,
  I also must possess you and I will.

MARY. Oh will no angel nor my God protect me?
  My fate is to be like a bird of flame,
  Rushing from burning boughs to burning air.
  Was I conceived to be the womb of rage?
  Is hatred in a mask of love my life?   460

MORTIMER. They hate—I love you with an equal heat.
  They want this shining milk-white skin to break
  Around the grey blade sinking through this neck.
  Oh you must sacrifice to bliss-great life
  What is already consecrate to death.
  This beauty has already been devoured,
  Use it to raise your lover into beauty.
  This curling unimaginable silk,
  Death has already scattered on the ground,
  Weave it around your slave, for him to wander   470
  Enraptured through the maze of you forever.

MARY. Oh what must I endure? My suffering
  And my misfortune should prevent you, sir,
  Even if due respect does not!

MORTIMER.   The crown
  Has tumbled from your head. You are no longer
  A ruler in this world. Try, give an order,
  See if the strength remains to be obeyed.
  Nothing remains to rule me but your beauty,
  A power sent by heaven that commands me
  To risk and win all, rushing in attack   480
  Against the blade of the beheading axe!

MARY. Oh who will save me from this rage?

MORTIMER.   Brave service
  Bravely rewarded, is the proper manner.
  What does the hero run with blood to win?
  Life is the only prize for which life dies.
  Only the mad expend themselves for nothing!
  First I must rest where life is warmest, strongest.
                [*He presses her forcefully against himself**

MARY. Oh must I cry for rescue from the man
  Who claims to be my saviour?

MORTIMER.   You can feel.
  The world has never called you stern or cold.   490
  You can be touched by love's sincerest prayer,
  You raised the singer Rizzio to bliss,
  And Bothwell found the conquest not too hard.

MARY. Insolence!

MORTIMER.   He was like a king to you,
  You trembled when he touched you. Well, if terror
  Alone can win you, by the god of hell—

MARY. Leave, you are mad!

MORTIMER.   I too shall see you tremble!

KENNEDY [*rushes in*]. People are coming! They are in the
    garden,
  Armed men are everywhere!

MORTIMER [*starts, and reaches for his dagger*]. I will protect
    you!

MARY. Oh Hanna, save me from him! Where can I,   500
  Weakest of women, find a hiding place?
  What saint can help me? Murder waits within,
  But open force and madness drive me there.
              [*She flees towards the house, followed by*
              KENNEDY

SCENE VII

[PAULET, MORTIMER.]

PAULET. Fasten the gates, and raise the drawbridges!

MORTIMER. Dear uncle, what is the matter?

PAULET. Drag down the murderess to a deeper dungeon.

MORTIMER. What is the matter? What is happening?

PAULET. The Queen! Cursed enterprise! The hands of demons!

MORTIMER. The Queen, you say? Which Queen?

PAULET.   The Queen of England!
She has been murdered on the London road!   510
                         [*Rushes into the house*

SCENE VIII

[MORTIMER, *and then* O'KELLY.]

MORTIMER. Have I gone mad, or did a man just now
    Run by me calling that the Queen is dead?
    No, no, it cannot be, it was a dream,
    Delirious hallucination sets
    Before my eyes the creatures of my fear.
    Who comes? It is O'Kelly, terrified.

O'KELLY [*bursting in*]. Mortimer, we are broken, fly this place!

MORTIMER. What has undone us?

O'KELLY.   Do not question me,
    Think of a swift escape.

MORTIMER.   Say what has happened.

O'KELLY. Sauvage attacked, the madman, he began.*   520

MORTIMER. So it is true.

O'KELLY.   True? True? Oh save your life!

MORTIMER. She has been killed, and Mary is the Queen.

O'KELLY. Who says so?

MORTIMER.   You yourself.

O'KELLY.   She lives! She lives!
    Death chooses us.

MORTIMER.   She lives!

O'KELLY.   The thrust was false,
   Her cloak wrenched wide the blade, and Shrewsbury
   Struck down the swordsman's arm.

MORTIMER.   She is alive.

O'KELLY. Alive to bury us, unless we fly.
   They will surround the park.

MORTIMER.   Who did this thing?

O'KELLY. The Toulon Barnabit who was consumed
   By brooding while the monk explained to us   530
   The reason for the Queen's anathema.*
   Impatient passion for the martyr's crown
   And for the freedom of the Church of God,
   Drove him to take the harebrained, headlong way,
   A bold assault—he told the priest alone,
   And, on the open road to London, struck.

MORTIMER [*after a long silence*]. O woman of misfortunes,
      you are wed
   To a blackbrowed and foul fate. Now I see,
   Now you will die; I understand, your angel
   Itself has planned your downfall.

O'KELLY.   Tell me, friend,   540
   Where will you fly to? I intend to hide
   In the deep forests of the north.

MORTIMER.   Go there,
   And may God's mercy hurry you away.
   I will remain behind alone, to save
   My Lady or attend her to her grave.

ACT FOUR

SCENE I

[*Antechamber.*]

[*The* EARLS OF AUBESPINE, KENT, *and* LEICESTER.]

AUBESPINE. How is the Queen? My Lords, you see me still
  Lost in a chaos of distress myself.
  How did it happen? How could it have happened
  There in the midst of her true-hearted people?

LEICESTER. The blow was struck by no one of our people.
  It was a subject of your King, a Frenchman.

AUBESPINE. A lunatic!

KENT.   A papist, Aubespine!

SCENE II

[*Others as before.* BURLEIGH *in conversation with*
DAVISON.]

BURLEIGH. Draw up the orders for the execution,
  And have them sealed—as soon as they are ready,
  Convey them to the Queen for her to sign.   10
  Go! Waste no time.

DAVISON.   It shall be as you say.
                             [*Exit*

AUBESPINE. My Lord, my heart rejoices with this land,
  Rightfully; let our praises rise to God
  For helmeting the royal head today.

BURLEIGH. He should be praised because he has allowed
  Our enemies to blunder and be shamed.

AUBESPINE. May heaven damn whoever tried this action.

BURLEIGH. Whoever set him on is damned with him.

AUBESPINE [*to* KENT]. Is it your pleasure to present me now,
　Your Highness my Lord Marshal, to her Highness,　　　　20
　That I might proffer to her great desert
　The gratulate expressions of my monarch?

BURLEIGH. Do not explode with effort, Aubespine.

AUBESPINE [*officiously*]. Lord Burleigh, I am conscious of my
　duties.

BURLEIGH. Your only duty is to leave this country.
　At once.

AUBESPINE [*steps back, astonished*]. What? How so?

BURLEIGH.　　　　　　　　　　You are safe from harm
　By virtue of your office—till tomorrow.

AUBESPINE. And what might my transgression be?

BURLEIGH.　　　　　　　　　　　　Once named,
　It cannot be forgiven.

AUBESPINE.　　　　　But my Lord,
　The rights of diplomats—

BURLEIGH.　　　　　　　Do not protect　　　　30
　Traitors.

　　　　　　　　　[LEICESTER *and* KENT *murmur*

AUBESPINE. My Lord, express yourself with caution.

BURLEIGH. There was a passport written by your hand
　In the assassin's pocket.

KENT.　　　　　Can it be?

AUBESPINE. This hand has issued many documents,
　I cannot fathom each receiver's heart.

BURLEIGH. The killer said confession in your house.

AUBESPINE. My house is open.

BURLEIGH.　　　　　To our enemies.

AUBESPINE. I call for an investigation!

BURLEIGH.   Fear it!

AUBESPINE. An insult to the King's ambassador
Insults the King—he will discard the treaty.   40

BURLEIGH. The Queen has torn it into shreds already.
England will not speak France the vows of marriage.
My Lord of Kent, the Queen commissions you
To speed the earl in safety to the sea.
The citizens have wrecked his house, enraged,
And there they found a mighty arsenal.
They shout that they will tear him when he comes.
Hide him until the tempest has moved on.
Your life for his.

AUBESPINE.   Yes, I will leave this island
Where right is stamped and trampled in the dirt,   50
And solemn treaties are a game of cards.
But hear me well, my monarch will demand
Blood for this insult.

BURLEIGH.   Let him come and get it.
                    [*Exeunt* KENT *and* AUBESPINE

SCENE III

[LEICESTER *and* BURLEIGH.]

LEICESTER. So you yourself are the unraveller
Of what you, self-urged, took such pains to tie.
And you will get but little thanks from England.
My Lord, you could have saved yourself the trouble.

BURLEIGH. My course was right. God willed a different end.
Blest be all those unstained by secret wishes.

LEICESTER. Cecil's hard-burdened words, when he is hunting
For roots and seeds of treason, are well known.   61
My Lord, once more your reaping time has come,
A horrifying murder has been tried,
And many secret paths lead from the doer.

A court of inquisition will begin,
Looks will be questioned, statements, even thoughts,
Will strive on scales to make a feather stay.
And while this lasts, you are the central stone,
The rock of state, an Atlas of importance.*

BURLEIGH. Yet I must bow to you in much, my Lord.   70
My words could never hope to win for me
Such an amazing prize as yours have earned.

LEICESTER. What prize, my Lord?

BURLEIGH.   Who else's eloquence
Could have conveyed the Queen to Fotheringhay
Unknown to me?

LEICESTER.   Unknown? Not by design.

BURLEIGH. She did not go with you to Fotheringhay,
You went with her—it was her gift to you.

LEICESTER. What do you mean, my Lord?

BURLEIGH.   Or did you make her
A shining and triumphant figure there?
And was her unsuspecting Majesty   80
Justly presented, in a kindly light?
Oh Queen, your trust was mercilessly taken,
Shamelessly mocked! It was greatheartedness,
Was it, that overcame you in the council,
A sudden storm of mildness, and the Stuart,
She is contemptible, an enemy,
Of course, not worth the mess of execution.
A good sharp scheme, but sadly just too fine—
The point broke off on contact.

LEICESTER.   Worthless wretch!
Follow me now, come with me to the Queen,   90
Accuse me to her!

BURLEIGH.   I will meet you there,
And when I do, my Lord, speak well, speak well.
                                        [*Exit*

SCENE IV

[LEICESTER *alone, then* MORTIMER.]

LEICESTER. I am discovered, nothing shelters me.
How did the evil huntsman find my trail?
I am a ghost, if he has proof. The Queen!
If she believes there was an understanding
Between myself and Mary, I am guilty
Beyond reprieve. All my advice was lies,
Everything leading up to Fotheringhay,
When she was given to her loathed opponent;   100
Never, oh never can it be forgiven.
What she regrets will seem to have been planned,
Even to where their conversation blazed
And ruined her with laughter, as she bore
The triumph of her enemy's delight.
Yes, and the fearful, forceful intervention,
Horrible shock of fate, the murderer,
He too will seem to have been armed by me.
I see no gleam of safety anywhere!
Ha! Who is coming?

MORTIMER [*enters in the most agitated state and looks round
      fearfully*].   Leicester, is it you?   110
Can we be heard here?

LEICESTER.   Wretch, run from this place!
Why have you come here?

MORTIMER.   They are hunting me—
And you. Be very careful.

LEICESTER.   Leave me now!

MORTIMER. They know about the secret gatherings
At Aubespine's.

LEICESTER.   Why should that trouble me?

MORTIMER. That the assassin—

LEICESTER.   He is your affair!
  How dare you try to weave your guilt round me?
  Insolent wretch! Your evil is your own!

MORTIMER. Just listen to me please—

LEICESTER.   Damn you to hell!
  Why do you fasten like a vampire to me?   120
  I am no friend of murderers, leave me,
  I do not know you!

MORTIMER.   I have come to warn you,
  If you would only hear me—all your schemes,
  Like mine, have come to light.

LEICESTER.   Ha! We shall see!

MORTIMER. The Chancellor appeared at Fotheringhay,
  After the sad attempt. A brutal search
  Of the Queen's rooms discovered—

LEICESTER.   What?

MORTIMER.   A letter,
  Unfinished, from the Queen to you.

LEICESTER.   Madwoman!

MORTIMER. In which she begs you not to break your vows,
  Renews the promise of her hand to you,   130
  Asks you to kiss her picture—

LEICESTER.   Death and hell!

MORTIMER. Lord Burleigh has the letter.

LEICESTER.   I am lost.
    [During the next speech he paces up and down in
      desperation

MORTIMER. No! Take control and save yourself—save her.
  Accuse, deflect, swear; I can do no more.
  The allies have been scattered, the alliance
  Will not recover—I am bound for Scotland,

There to create new friends. You must remain.
Fight for and with your reputation, strive,
See what a front of arrogance can do—

LEICESTER [*suddenly comes to himself*]. That I can do—
                    [*Goes to the door, opens it and calls*
                                    Ho there, Trabant!
            [*To the officer, who enters with armed men*
                                    This traitor
Is to be taken into custody,   141
And guarded closely. So a plot is broken.
I will inform her Majesty myself.

MORTIMER [*initially stands still in astonishment, but soon composes himself and looks at* LEICESTER *with an expression of deepest contempt*]. Ha! Man of shame! And yet the
    blame is mine!
What made me trust this pool of apathy?
My neck must stretch to make his bridge to safety,
He walks away across my fall to honour!
So save yourself! No words of mine will widen
My doom to make a space in it for you.
Even in death I do not want you near me,   150
Keep life, it is a curse to such as you.
        [*To the* OFFICER *of the guard, who steps forward
        to take him prisoner*
Tyrant's paid slave, what do you want from me?
I am not crushed, I spit such creatures out!
                                    [*Draws dagger*

OFFICER. He has a dagger—strike him on the arm.
            [*They fall upon him, he fights them off*

MORTIMER. Free to the last, my heart shall speak, its truth
My tongue untie. Fall to eternal fire,
    You traitors to your God and to your Queen,
Who turned like cut-throats from your earthly Mary,
As from your heavenly, and to a bastard
    Sold your inheritance.

OFFICER.   To him! Silence him!   160

MORTIMER. My love! My courage could not set you free,
  But I will show you what my strength can do.
  Holy Mary, pray for me, and take me
  Into the heaven of yourself for ever.
        [*He stabs himself and falls into the guard's arms*

SCENE V

[*One of the* QUEEN'*s rooms. Enter* ELIZABETH *with a
        letter in her hand.* BURLEIGH.]

ELIZABETH. To lead me to his mistress like a monkey
  Dressed up to dance forth laughter from a whore!
  Treason! Oh Burleigh, never was a woman
  Betrayed so hard.

BURLEIGH.   As yet I cannot see
  By what occult subversions he was able
  So to amaze the reason of my Queen.   170

ELIZABETH. Oh I am sinking in a storm of shame.
  How he was laughing inwardly at me.
  When I believed that I could bring her low,
  I was to fall beneath her chariot wheels.

BURLEIGH. The loyalty of my advice appears.

ELIZABETH. Yes, I have been immeasurably punished
  By a minute digression from your help.
  But how could I have crushed my best belief?
  Are we not fools to fear the ones we love?
  Where could I place my trust if he proved false,   180
  Whom I created foremost of you all,
  Only to bring him nearest to myself,
  Permitting him an air of majesty,
  As if he was a king here at my court!

BURLEIGH. And for all that, his faithless heart pertained
  To the false Queen of Scotland.

ELIZABETH.   She will pay.
The price of his devotion is her life.
Have you drawn up the warrant?

BURLEIGH.   As you said.

ELIZABETH. She will fall first, and he shall see her die,
Then he shall follow her. My love has flown,   190
My heart is vacant of his face and name,
But crammed with vengeance in anticipation.
As high in light as once he climbed, so low
Into the black of shame shall be his fall,
And as he showed my weakness to the world,
So shall he be a monument of horror
To my severity. Set him in the Tower;
Pick out forthwith the peers who are to judge him.
I give him to the fury of the law.

BURLEIGH. He will fight through thick walls to you to plead.

ELIZABETH. What can he plead? Is not the letter clear?   201
Glittering with his guilt?

BURLEIGH.   But you are kind,
And merciful, the power of his presence—

ELIZABETH. When will I ever see his face again?
The order to refuse him has been given,
If he should dare to come?

BURLEIGH.   It has been given.

PAGE [enters]. My Lord of Leicester.

ELIZABETH.   A detested title.
I do not wish to see him. Tell him so.
He is not favoured here.

PAGE.   I would not dare,
And he would not believe me anyway.   210

ELIZABETH. He has become so great by my design,
That my own servants fear him more than me.

BURLEIGH [to PAGE]. The Queen forbids him to appear.
                              [Exit PAGE tentatively

ELIZABETH.   And yet—
  If he could answer even this near charge—
  Tell me, my Lord, could it be possible
  That Mary meant this letter to be found,
  So as to tear my dearest from my heart?
  No pirate is her equal in deceit,
  Perhaps the words she wrote are seeds of evil
  Sown by her wicked skill in me, to flourish,   220
  And part the loving subjects of her hate.

BURLEIGH. But think, my Queen—

SCENE VI

[As before. LEICESTER.*]*

LEICESTER [*bursting in*].   I wish to see the person
  Who claims the right to keep me from my ruler.

ELIZABETH. Ha! The bold man!

LEICESTER.   They spurn me from her doors,
  But she will see me if she sees Lord Burleigh!

BURLEIGH. You are too brash, to break in unpermitted,
  My Lord.

LEICESTER. You are too insolent, my Lord,
  To answer for your betters uninvited!
  What, there is no one, no one at this court
  From whom the Earl of Leicester will permit   230
  Permission, or denial.
                    [*He approaches* ELIZABETH *humbly*
                    But my Queen.

ELIZABETH [*without looking at him*].
  Despicable, be gone.

LEICESTER.   This coldness swears
  Against the nature of Elizabeth.
  Burleigh is speaking in these words, not her,
  A hostile accent. But I step past that;

His voice is in you, my Elizabeth,
Open your mind to mine.

ELIZABETH.   Speak then, betrayer,
Increase your evil by denying it.

LEICESTER. First bid this too insulting person leave.
My Lord, depart, what she and I must share   240
Is better said unwitnessed. Go.

ELIZABETH.   Remain.
It is an order.

LEICESTER.   Do we need a third?
My business is with her whom I adore.
Let the lord go, the place he takes is mine,
And I demand it as my sacred right!

ELIZABETH. Proud words!

LEICESTER.   I speak the language of the proud
Because I am the happy-fortuned man
Raised by your love above my crowding peers.
Your heart and mine reciprocated pride.
And what love gave my life, by God Almighty,   250
I will defend till life and love's destruction.
Let him depart, and in a moment's space,
If I may speak, we will be one again.

ELIZABETH. Your words have lost their power to deceive.

LEICESTER. A gossip might perhaps thus waste the time,
But I intend to use it to speak true.
And what I dared believing in your love,
I mean to justify by proving mine.
Your favour is my only court of law.

ELIZABETH. It is exactly where you are most damned,   260
Disgraced man. Burleigh, he may read the letter.

BURLEIGH. Take it!

LEICESTER [*skims through the letter without altering his expression*].   This is the hand of Mary Stuart!

ELIZABETH. Read and be silent!

LEICESTER [*once he has read it, calmly*].
                              Though appearances
  Condemn me, I may hope that you suspect them.

ELIZABETH. Can you deny that a corrupt connection
  Exists between the Stuart and yourself?
  That you received her portrait secretly,
  And in return, sustained her hopes of freedom?

LEICESTER. It is the witness of an enemy.
  If I were guilty I might cling to that.   270
  But as it is I feel at ease to say
  That what she writes is true.

ELIZABETH.   Well then, poor man!

BURLEIGH. His own mouth damns him.

ELIZABETH.   Traitor, to the Tower,
  Out of my sight!

LEICESTER.   A traitor I am not.
  My only sin has been to hide my plans,
  For they were honest, and the steps I took
  I took to undermine your enemy.

ELIZABETH. Pitiful cry.

BURLEIGH.   Too late, my Lord, too late.

LEICESTER. I played a daring game, and in a fashion
  None but the Earl of Leicester would have dared.   280
  That I detest the Stuart is well known,
  My rank, your trust, must counter any rumours
  That I am prone to criminal intentions.
  And surely your defender, granted favour
  In a far greater measure than all others,
  May cut a bolder path than them to duty?

BURLEIGH. If what you did was good, why keep it quiet?

LEICESTER. You like to talk before you act, my Lord,
  You loudly prophesy your own affairs.
  So much for you. I speak when deeds have prospered.   290

BURLEIGH. But now you speak because you must.

LEICESTER [*measures him proudly and contemptuously with his eyes*].   Your pride
    Depends on thinking that you have provided
    A treason drawn, the safety of the Queen;
    That this stupendous triumph stems from you.
    Nothing evades the sunbeams of your eyes,
    All knowledge streams into your ocean brain,
    So you believe—absurd self-flatterer,
    For all your cobweb-watching, Mary Stuart
    Would have been free this instant but for me.

BURLEIGH. You—

LEICESTER.   I, my Lord. The Queen believed a man,
    Mortimer, and unwrapped her thoughts to him,   301
    Going so far as to commission him
    To visit Mary with a deed of blood,
    Because his uncle had rejected it.
    Is this not so?
          [*The* QUEEN *and* BURLEIGH *look at each other, embarrassed*

BURLEIGH.   How did you learn of that?

LEICESTER. Is it not so, my Lord? And oh, my Lord,
    Where were you gazing with your thousand eyes
    When he stepped by beneath your nose unknown?
    He was a papist, henchman of the Guises,
    A devil-mad creation of the Stuart,   310
    Whose purpose in these islands was to free
    The false pretender and destroy the Queen.

ELIZABETH [*with the utmost surprise*]. Mortimer!

LEICESTER.   Was the conduit of the Stuart,
    Through which she reached her secret arts to me.
    And so I came to know him. By tonight
    She was to have been ushered from her dungeon,
    His own mouth told me when the time would be,
    I had him seized, but in his desperation,

Discovered, and his slowly built glass palace
Shattering, mirrors crashing all around him,   320
He took his life.

ELIZABETH.   Oh, I have been deceived
Horribly—Mortimer!

BURLEIGH.   This happened now?
After I left you now?

LEICESTER.   For my own ease
I must regret that he is thus removed.
His testimony, could he give it now,
Would cleanse me of my seeming evil straight.
It was that thought that timed my taking him
To give him up to justice. Sharpest justice
Was to have sealed me guiltless to the world.

BURLEIGH. He turned assassin of himself, you say?   330
Or did you help him?

LEICESTER.   Insolent suspicion!
Question the guards he robbed of their arrest.
        [*He goes to the door and calls out. The* OFFICER
        of the guard enters
You will report the death of Mortimer.

OFFICER. I was positioned in the antechamber.
My Lord came running to the door and shouted
That we were to arrest the Knight for treason.
The Knight became enraged, and drew his dagger,
Whilst shouting insults at the Queen. He plunged it
Into his chest before we could prevent him,
Collapsed, and perished from the blow soon after.   340

LEICESTER. Good. You may go now, sir, the Queen knows
    all.

        [*Exit* OFFICER

ELIZABETH. Infinite dark abyss!

LEICESTER.   Who saved you now?
Was it my Lord of Burleigh? Did he see

Dangers around you like a ring of fire,
Dancing? Did he disperse them? No, your angel
Was Leicester!

BURLEIGH.   Lord, the death of Mortimer
Was fortunate for you.

ELIZABETH.   What can I say?
I half believe that I do not believe you,
Yet how can I be sure that you are guilty?
Damnable woman, thus to knot my sorrows!   350

LEICESTER. Kill her. My stand has shifted. My advice
Was that the sentence should be left unacted
Until another arm was raised for her.
This has now happened and my new demand
Is that she be despatched immediately.

BURLEIGH. You say this, you!

LEICESTER.   Though it appals my nature
To step to an extreme, it is now clear
That the well-being of her Majesty
Can be increased by a blood sacrifice.
Therefore I want the execution order   360
Written at once.

BURLEIGH.   Since he advises it
With such sincerity, in my opinion
The final execution of the sentence
Should be my Lord's commission.

LEICESTER.   Mine?

BURLEIGH.   Exactly.
What better way to cleanse your reputation
Of present stains than this one could be found?
Behead the woman you are said to love.

ELIZABETH [*fixes her gaze on* LEICESTER].
So it shall be. My Lord advises well.
This is your fixed commission.

LEICESTER.   My great name
  Should spare me such a melancholy duty,   370
  Far more germane to Burleigh's rank and nature.
  An inauspicious task is unbefitting
  To the support of England's royal spirit.
  However, for her ever satisfaction,
  And to make plain my zealous lust for service,
  I will subdue my dignity to duty,
  Hateful though it may be.

ELIZABETH [*to* BURLEIGH]. It shall be borne
  By Burleigh also. See the writ prepared
  Instantly.
          [*Exit* BURLEIGH. *Outside, fighting is heard*

SCENE VII

[*The* EARL OF KENT *joins the others.*]

ELIZABETH. Kent, what is this crying out?

KENT. The citizens are at the palace gates,   380
  Queen, they demand to see you.

ELIZABETH.   For what cause?

KENT. Terror spreads rumours that your life is threatened,
  That killers sent by Rome are all around you.
  The Catholics are said to have declared
  That they will haul the Stuart from her cell,
  And throw you down, and set her up as Queen.
  The crowd believes it, and they are enraged,
  Only the Stuart's death will send them home,
  They say her head must fall before tonight.

ELIZABETH. What, would they be my Queen?

KENT.   They have determined
  Not to disperse till you have signed the order.   391

SCENE VIII

[BURLEIGH *and* DAVISON *enter with a piece of
writing. The others as before.*]

ELIZABETH. What do you bring me, Davison?

DAVISON.   O Queen,
According to your order—

ELIZABETH.   What is this?
          [*as she is about to take the piece of paper, she
            shudders and starts back*
Oh God—

BURLEIGH.   The people's voice is God. Obey it.

ELIZABETH [*fighting with herself*].
How may I know, my Lords, if what I hear
Is the great voice that speaks for all the people?
What if I should concede it mastery,
And then too late a second voice is heard,
The mouths that will me to this action now,
Cursing me for it when the time has gone?   400

SCENE IX

[*The* EARL OF SHREWSBURY *joins the others.*]

SHREWSBURY [*enters in great agitation*].
Queen, do not bend, they want to push you—stand!
                    [*As he notices* DAVISON *and the order*
Or is it done? What is this apparition?
There is a dreadful paper in his fingers,
That should not come before my Queen today!

ELIZABETH. Great Shrewsbury! They force me!

SHREWSBURY.   Who can force you?
You are their ruler, demonstrate your might
In this for all, and frighten into silence
The barks and growls that try to rule your will,

To brutalize your reason. Mad blind fear
Lashes the people, you yourself are angry,   410
Not wise at present, human, void of judgement.

BURLEIGH. This has been judged a good long time ago.
We do not wait for judgement to be passed,
But to be done.

KENT [*who left when* SHREWSBURY *entered, now re-enters*].
                    The crowd is growing greater,
We can no longer keep the people back.

ELIZABETH. You see—my will is dead.

SHREWSBURY.   But give me time,
Fortune is now a motion of your pen.
For half a life you have considered this,
Should now an instant's disarray decide?
Give me a short time, gather soul to mind,   420
Await a wiser moment.

BURLEIGH.   Doubt, delay,
Dither until the Kingdom turns to flame,
Until the efforts of the enemy
Succeed at last. Three times Almighty God
Has turned their ambush, and today they touched you.
It would be blasphemy to test him further.

SHREWSBURY. Our maker, by his ever-present power,
Has saved you three times. By a miracle
Today he gave an old man's arm young vigour
To overcome a man possessed. This God   430
Merits our faith. I do not raise my voice
To plead for justice, it is not the time,
Men cannot hear a sermon in a storm,
But think of this—you fear the living Mary,
But you should feel more terror for another—
Tremble before the dead one, she will rise,
Beheaded goddess of disharmony,
To rush about your Kingdom as a ghost,
Sliding cruel steel into your subject's hearts,
Turning them from you, whispering revenge.   440

The English hate to name that woman now,
But they will sing her when she is no more.
Though she once threatened death to their belief,
She will become the daughter of their kings,
And they will pity her, and see her fall
As worthiness destroyed by jealousy.
Winter will come upon you suddenly,
After her death, ride through the streets of London,
Among the people who rejoiced in you,
And you will see another English race.   450
Justice, whose sunshine won their love for you,
Will dance around your head no longer. Fear,
Echoing from the tread of tyranny,
Will clear the streets before you as you go,
And give you back your city stone by stone.
You will have carried strength to its extreme,
And when a sacred life is yours to use,
Whose humble head is safe?

ELIZABETH.   Oh Shrewsbury!
Why did you save me from the murderer?
Why did you stop my death from finding me?   460
If you had not, my storm would now be calm,
And in my grave, an uncontested field,
Doubt would no longer beat, guilt would be silent.
Ah Talbot, I am very tired of ruling,
And if in order for a Queen to stand
A Queen must fall—and, as I see the case,
No other way exists—then may not I?
I will return the sceptre to the people,
Let them decide—I have not stayed alive,
God is my witness, for my own delight,   470
But to fulfil the wishes of my people.
And if it sees a hope of better times
Under the easy Stuart's younger days,
Then I will give my throne to her and go
To solitude with gladness, where I passed
In Woodstock's parks my youth without demands;
I was the sovereign of myself alone,

Far from the world-proud spectacle of might.
I am unfit to make men's destinies,
I cannot turn my gentle heart unkind.   480
To rule these islands was a strange delight
When all they asked of me was happiness.
The first hard, bitter deed of sorrow finds me
Too used to mercy.

BURLEIGH.   By the rage of God!*
Hearing such folly, not to speak is treason!
You say you love your people more than life,
Show it! Do not take shelter in yourself,
And leave your kingdom arkless to the flood.
Should superstition, which her reign would bring,
Shatter our Church? Shall monks be ministers,   490
Shall legates sent from Rome uncrown our kings,*
And tear down our cathedrals? For the souls
Of all your subjects I demand salvation,
Heaven and hell depend on your next words.
This is no time for feminine compassion,
The safety of your people is your duty.
Shrewsbury's swiftness saved your life. My wisdom
Will save your country, which is even greater.

ELIZABETH. Leave me alone with God. No human thought
Can comfort me or aid me in this fight.   500
You must give place to the immortal judge.
Whatever he commands me will be done.
Withdraw, my Lords. [*To* DAVISON] You sir, do not go far.
            [*Exit the lords. Only* SHREWSBURY *remains
            standing in front of the* QUEEN *for a few
            moments with an earnest expression.
            Then he exits slowly with an expression
            of deepest pain*

SCENE X

ELIZABETH [*alone*]. Oh, that a Queen should be the slave of
    slaves!

Ah how I tire of singing to this idol,
Which my deep soul despises, endless praises.
Unterrifying Queen, when will you stand,
Free of your people's weight, tall and alone?
Can I move awe, who must obey opinion,
And bargain, swindle honour from the rabble,   510
Cutting my figure to the taste of crowds
Who would prefer the magic of a clown?
Oh he is not yet king, who lives to charm,
A king is he who scorns the world's applause.
Why was I just? Why did I bind my hands
Against the act of blood that had to come,
Opposing wantonness and loving law?
I am my own impossible example,
Slave to myself. If I had been a tyrant,
As Spanish Mary was, my predecessor,*   520
I could dispose of royalty untroubled!
But did I choose to walk the road of justice,
Or was I forced? The god necessity,
Prison of free will, overlord of kings,
Force-fed me with that virtue. Tempest-tossed
By antichrists, to keep my reign from sinking,
I am dependent on my subjects' love.
The Continent is reaching for my throat,*
The Pope spits endless excommunications,
Brotherly France betrays me with a kiss,   530
While Spain caulks, victuals, and fits out attack.*
I am besieged, an undefended woman,
By the whole world! With unexampled virtue
I seek to veil the weakness of my right,
To paint the blemish of my birthbed clean,
My father's firm decree of shame. In vain!
My enemies expose me happily,
Placing the Stuart like a skeleton
Ever before me. But this fear shall die.
Her head shall fall and years of peace shall rise!   540
She is the Fury always following,
No matter what I plant, a serpent grows,
And it is her. She swallows up my husband

While he is still a groom, and steals my lover;
Every misfortune I have ever known
Was Mary Stuart by another name.
Once free of her I shall be mountain air! [*silence*]
With what contempt she cast her eyes on me,
As if her look could knock me to my grave.
Impotent female! I need no such eyes,   550
My weapons kill for real and evermore.
      [*Walking up to the table she quickly picks up a
        pen*
Am I a bastard in your eyes? Well then,
The eyes shall die, and bastard be erased.
The question of my birth will not arise
When you are sleeping, answered by a blade.
When there are no more queens than I, the bed
Where I began will be an honoured one!
      [*She signs with a swift and firm stroke of the pen
       and then lets the pen fall and steps back with
       an expression of horror. After a pause she rings
       the bell*

SCENE XI

[ELIZABETH, DAVISON.]

ELIZABETH. Where are their Lordships?

DAVISON.   Gone to calm the crowds.
When Shrewsbury approached, the uproar died.
A hundred voices cried, 'He saved the Queen,   560
This is the man, the bravest blade in England,
To him we listen!' Then the noble Talbot
In gentle tones upbraided the assembly
For their uncouth commencement. And such firm,
Convincing words continued from his lips,
The crowd dispersed in silent reverence.

ELIZABETH. A fickle field, that bends to every wind.
Woe betide him who tries to build on them.

However, it is good, Sir Davison.
Now you may go.
                              [*As he turns towards the door*
                    And take this paper back.   570
I place it in your hands.

DAVISON [*casts his eyes on to the document and starts*].
                         My Queen, your name.
You have decided.

ELIZABETH.   I was asked to sign,
And I have signed. But paper cannot kill,
Nor is my name death.

DAVISON.   But your name on this
Is like a lightning bolt precisely flung.
This paper orders the commissioners
To speed on having read it to the Sheriff
Of Fotheringhay Castle and the Queen
Of Scotland, to announce her sentence to her,
And the next sunrise to enact the sentence.   580
There is no mention of delay. Her life
Is over when this paper leaves my hand.

ELIZABETH. Indeed, sir, God has placed into your grip,
Too weak, the engine of his destiny.
Pray for illumination. I am going,
I leave you to your duty.
                              [*She makes to leave*

DAVISON [*steps into her path*]. No, my Queen!
Do not forsake me with your will unclear.
Interpretation is beyond my wisdom.
You set this deadly paper in my hand,
That I might shoot it onwards to its mark?   590

ELIZABETH. The aim is for your spirit to decide.

DAVISON [*interrupting quickly and shocked*].
No! Not for mine! God keep it from my mind.
All I have learnt in life is to obey.
The merest tremble here is regicide,

Never to be forgiven gross misfortune.
Grant that I may, in this tremendous business,
Be your unthinking, witless instrument.
Express your will transparently to me.
What is to be the fate of this death warrant?

ELIZABETH. Its name should tell you.

DAVISON.   Then its swift completion
Is your desire?

ELIZABETH.   I did not say those words.   601
I hate to think them.

DAVISON.   Then your wish is rather
That I should keep it for a time?

ELIZABETH.   You dare!
My will is your responsibility.

DAVISON. Mine! God above! What is your will? Speak, Queen!

ELIZABETH [*impatiently*]. My will is that this business should
    relinquish
My days and nights, and die to me forever.

DAVISON A single word of yours can buy that quiet.
Declare the future of this document.

ELIZABETH. I have declared it. Cease to torture me!   610

DAVISON. You have? But not perhaps to me. O Queen,
Feel able to repeat—

ELIZABETH [*stamps the ground*]. Intolerable!

DAVISON. I only took this office recently,
I am still foreign to the courtly tongue.
Pity your servant, who was raised to plainness
In a tradition of simplicity.
Forbear, and let explaining patience nurture
Blooms in the wasteland of my ignorance.
        [*He approaches her pleadingly, she turns her back
        on him, he stands in despair, then speaks in a
        determined tone*

Take back this dreadful paper! Take it back!
It burns me like an ember! Choose another   620
To do your will in this horrific business!

ELIZABETH. Do your job.

[*Exit*

SCENE XII

[DAVISON, *followed shortly by* BURLEIGH.]

DAVISON.   And so she leaves me unadvised,
Holding the poison of this document.
What should I do? Keep it, or pass it on?
                    [*To* BURLEIGH, *who enters then*
Oh my good Lord, thank heaven you have come.
It was from you that I received this office,
Expel me from it! When I took it on
I did not know what weight it would entail.
Return me to invisibility,
From which I came, the court is not my place.   630

BURLEIGH. Compose yourself. What has possessed you, sir?
The Queen has seen you. Did she give the word?

DAVISON. She left in a heroic rage! Oh help me!
Advise me, pluck me from the fire of doubting.
Here is the order, signed.

BURLEIGH.   Signed? Give it me.

DAVISON. I cannot do that.

BURLEIGH.   What?

DAVISON.   On her desire
She cast a mist that is as yet uncleared.

BURLEIGH. But she has signed. Give me the document.

DAVISON. Shall I permit her name to be obeyed?
Oh God! Can I allow it not to be?   640
I do not know what I am not to do!

BURLEIGH [*urging him forcefully*].
  Hesitate and be damned. Give me the order.
  This very instant must begin its flight.

DAVISON. But I am damned if I proceed too quickly.

BURLEIGH. You are a fool, or mad! Give me the paper!
      [*Tears the document out of his hands, and rushes
      away with it*

DAVISON [*hurrying after*]. What are you doing? Stop! You
  have undone me!

ACT FIVE

SCENE I

[*The scene is the room in which the first act took place.*]

[HANNA KENNEDY, *dressed in deep mourning, with red eyes from crying and a great, but silent pain, busies herself sealing letters and packages. Often she is interrupted in this by her sorrow, and she is seen praying intermittently.* PAULET *and* DRURY, *also in black, enter; they are followed by many servants carrying gold and silver vessels, which they are heaping at the back of the room.* PAULET *hands a jewellery box to the nurse, as well as a piece of paper. He gestures to her that the paper is an inventory of all the things being brought into the room. At the sight of these riches the nurse's grief is renewed; she sinks into deep mourning whilst the others withdraw quietly.* MELVIL* *enters.*]

KENNEDY [*cries out, as soon as she sees him*]. Melvil! And so
    I see your face again!

MELVIL. Yes, Kennedy, we were to meet again.

KENNEDY. Our separation is an aged wound.

MELVIL. Healed by a luckless, melancholy meeting.

KENNEDY. God, you have come—

MELVIL.   To say a last farewell
    To my eternal Queen.

KENNEDY.   Thus finally,
    On her last morning, your long-wished-for presence
    Is given for an hour. I will not ask you
    To say your fate since you were reft from us,
    Or tell you ours—the time for that will come.   10

Oh Melvil, Melvil, why are we alive
To see the dread beginning of this day?

MELVIL. Let us not summon one another's tears.
    While I have life, its reason will be weeping,
    My face will never weaken to a smile,
    Nor will my mourning change to suit the time,
    So I may stare through marble eyes today.
    Promise me to resist surrender too,
    And when the others, as they may, concede
    To unconcealed despair, let us encase   20
    Our tender sorrow in a shell of strength,
    And be her pillars on the path to death.

KENNEDY. Melvil! You are mistaken utterly
    If you believe that she needs strength from us.
    The opposite is true, she strengthens us.
    You may believe that Mary Stuart's death
    Will show her as a heroine and Queen.

MELVIL. But how did she receive the news? I heard
    That she was ill prepared when it was said.

KENNEDY. She was. Another terror at that time   30
    Oppressed my Lady. It was not the shadow
    Of death, that fear, but of the rescuer.
    We had been promised freedom. Mortimer
    Swore that tonight would free us from this place.
    And in a state half-way to hope from fear,
    Doubtful if honour could commit its name
    Into the vessel of that reckless person,
    My Lady waited for the morning. Then—
    A pounding like a storm of many doors
    Hammered our ears—an uproar in the castle;   40
    Hope wakes and shouts, it is our rescuers!
    Life, like the sun, begins to rise unsummoned,
    Infant, rejoicing—then the prison door
    Opens, and it is Paulet, who announces
    That carpenters are building in the hall
    Beneath our feet, the scaffold.
                    [*She turns away, seized by great sorrow*

MELVIL.   God, oh God.
  Oh tell me, how could she withstand this change?

KENNEDY [*after a pause, during which she has composed her-
      self a little*].
  It is not flowers turning to the sun,
  Nor the slow steering round of ships or swans,
  When we abandon life it must be sudden,   50
  A leap of lightning. And in such an instant,
  God sent my Lady the unwishful spirit
  To give away the world and take on heaven.
  There was no room in her for fear, faith filled her,
  Whose face is not pale. Not one sound of pain
  Disgraced my Lady. Only when she heard
  Of her hell-black betrayal by Lord Leicester,
  And of the deep misfortune of the youth
  Who worthily forsook his life for her;
  When the vast grief of the old knight appeared,   60
  Whose only hope had perished in her cause,
  Then her tears gushed in torrents, forced to fall
  Not by her fate but by the pain of others.

MELVIL. Where is she now?

KENNEDY.   What night remained she spent
  Praying, and writing farewell to her friends.
  And with her own hand she wrote out her will.
  Now she is passing her last moments resting,
  In final sleep refreshing.

MELVIL.   Who is with her?

KENNEDY. Her ladies, and Burgoyn, her own physician.

SCENE II

[MARGARET KURL* *joins the others.*]

KENNEDY. What message, mistress? Is the lady waking?   70

KURL. She is already dressed, and asks for you.

KENNEDY. I come. [*To* MELVIL, *who makes to accompany her*]
    Wait here until I have prepared her.

                              [*Goes into* MARY's *room*

KURL. Melvil! Our steward!

MELVIL.   It is still my name.

KURL. Oh but this house has no more need of stewards!
    You come from London, Melvil, can you tell me
    Anything of my husband?

MELVIL.   It is said
    That he will be released the minute that—

KURL. The Queen is dead! The wretch, the bloody traitor!
    He is my Lady's murderer, I know,
    His was the witness that decided it.   80

MELVIL. Indeed.

KURL.   So may he burn in hell for ever!
    He gave false witness!

MELVIL.   Mistress Kurl, take care!

KURL. I want to swear it to his face in court!
    I want to hear it shouted through the world!
    She did not do the crime for which she dies.

MELVIL. God grant your wish!

SCENE III

[BURGOYN *joins the others. Thereafter* HANNA
KENNEDY.]

BURGOYN.   Oh Melvil!

MELVIL.   Good Burgoyn!

BURGOYN [*to* KURL]. Bring to the Queen a cup of wine at
    once.

                              [*Exit* KURL

MELVIL. What, does my Queen fare ill?

BURGOYN.   Her courage grows,
And she displays a hero's resolution,
Maintaining that her strength needs no supplies,   90
Which is an error. If her enemies
Are not to boast that death's approach undid her,
Nature must be sustained until the end.

MELVIL [to KENNEDY, who enters]. Am I to see her now?

KENNEDY.   She comes to you.
You gaze in wonder and your glances ask,
Why so much splendour in a place of death?
Oh sir! We suffered poverty in life,
Dying provides a brevity of wealth.

SCENE IV

[As before. Two other maids of MARY's, also in
mourning. They break out into loud sobbing at the
sight of MELVIL.]

MELVIL. Oh what a meeting! Gertrude! Rosamund!
Joy of my grief!

SECOND CHAMBERMAID.
                         She sent us from her side.   100
She wants to speak with God for the last time
Alone on earth.
                         [Two other female servants enter, in mourning
                         like the others, showing their sorrow in silent
                         expressions

SCENE V

[MARGARET KURL joins the others. She carries a
golden cup full of wine and puts it on the table,
at the same time, pale and trembling, holding on to
a chair.]

MELVIL. Mistress, what makes you shudder so? What horror?

KURL. Oh God!

BURGOYN.   What ails you?

KURL.   What my eyes have seen!

MELVIL. Come to your senses, tell us what it was.

KURL. As I ascended with my Lady's wine
The staircase that descends to the great hall,
A door was opened and I looked inside,
And saw—oh God!

MELVIL.   Be calm! What did you see?

KENNEDY. The walls are hung with black, and from the ground
A scaffold rises, also draped in black,   111
And in the centre sits a block, pitch black,
And next to it a stole. And not far off
Leans the bright smiling blade. The hall was full
Of people pressed around the dreadful structure,
Awaiting, eyes alive with lust, the victim.

CHAMBERMAIDS. Oh God show mercy on our Lady!

MELVIL.   Hush!
Compose yourselves! She comes!

SCENE VI

[*The same characters as before.* MARY *enters dressed
in white,* as if for a feast. Around her neck she
wears an agnus dei on a chain of small beads, a
rosary hangs from her belt, she holds a crucifix in her
hand and wears a tiara in her hair. Her large black
veil is turned back. As she enters, all present step
back to either side and express their deepest pain.*
MELVIL *has without thinking fallen to his knees.*]

MARY.   Why are you crying?
Who are you mourning? Celebrate with me

The coming of the end of all my shames.   120
Soon my last chains will fall, my cell's walls open,
And my bright soul dart up on angel's wings,
Happy in everlasting liberty.
The time to weep was when my enemy
Held me alive in her insulting power,
Forcing me to endure indignities
Unworthy of a Queen once great and free.
My death, with black wings veiling my disgrace,
Approaches like the end of a disease,
A friend at last. Fate visits all of us,   130
Even the worst, with the same grace at last.
It is as if I feel my crown again,
Because I have recovered dignity.
                    [As she steps forward a few more paces
What? Melvil here? Stand up, beloved sir.
It is my triumph you have come to see,
And not my death. And you will glorify it.
And I salute my fate, that has provided
A better record than my enemies
Would give the future of my character.
By fortune a confessor of my faith,   140
And a true friend, shall witness my last instant.
Tell me, good knight, in this unfriendly country,
How have you fared since you were reft from me?
Concern for you has often seared my spirit.

MELVIL. I have endured no hardship or oppression
    Other than grief to be denied the power
    To serve my Lady in her suffering.

MARY. And what of Didier, my Chamberlain?
    But he was old, and I suppose by now
    Is in the service of eternal sleep.   150

MELVIL. God has withheld that bliss from him, my Lady,
    His age survives to dig your youth a grave.

MARY. If I could but have won the grace to kiss
    The much-loved head of a blood relative.
    But as it is, the tears that will attend me

Will fall from strangers' newly loving eyes.
I set my wishes for my own in you,
Melvil, my strongest and most precious casket.
My blessing to the royal house of France,
And its most Christian King, my husband's brother.   160
My blessings to the Cardinal, my uncle;
To Henri Guise, my noble cousin, blessings.
Further, I bless the pope, Christ's great vice-regent,
And the Most Catholic King, who, strong in honour,
Swore first to save and after to avenge.
These gifts of love are written in my will,
And are to be received in place of wealth.
                              [*Turning to her servants*
All you are recommended there to France,
My royal brother. He will treat you well,
And plant you in a second motherland.   170
Now, if my final wish has any weight,
You will not stay in England, for this people
To glut their hatred on your suffering.
Let not my servants serve my enemies!
Swear on the image of Christ crucified
To leave this land when I have left this world!

MELVIL [*touches crucifix*]. I swear it on behalf of all those
     present.

MARY What I, the poorest woman, still possessed
When they had robbed me, what I still command,
I have divided equally among you.   180
My final orders will, I hope, be honoured.
Also the things I wear to death are yours.
Earth's beauty briefly once again, then heaven!
                              [*To the young ladies*
To you I leave my dresses and my pearls,
To you, my Alix, Rosamund, and Gertrude,
Because your youth still yearns to be adorned.
Margaret, foremost in unhappiness
Of those I leave behind, you merit next.
That I do not seek vengeance on your husband
In you, my legacy to you will show.   190

For you to whom bright stones are not temptations,
Nor gold a virtue, oh my loyal Hanna,
My only gift can be my memory.
So take my scarf, that I embroidered for you
With my own hands in sorrow's hours. Hot tears
Are in the weave. It is from you my Hanna,
That I desire this service at the last,
When the time comes, to bind my eyes with this.

KENNEDY. Melvil, I break!

MARY.   Come to me, everyone!
Receive my last farewell!
            [*She holds out her hands and one after another
            they fall at her feet and kiss the offered hands
            amid much sobbing*
                              Farewell to you,   200
Margaret, farewell Alix; ah, Burgoyn,
I thank you for your loyal services.
Gertrude, your mouth burns hot. I have been hated,
But I have been much loved! Love needs such hearts,
So may a noble man give Gertrude love.
Berta! You choose the straighter way to heaven,
It is your wish to be a bride of God!
Oh, be impatient to fulfil your vows,
Earth's glory is a trick, your mistress proves.
Enough! Farewell! Farewell! Farewell! Farewell!   210
            [*She turns away quickly. All but* MELVIL *withdraw*

SCENE VII

[MARY, MELVIL.]

MARY. All my affairs on earth are set in order,
And I expect to leave in no one's debt.
Only one shadow still oppresses me,
From rising into brightness like the sun.

MELVIL. Reveal it to me. Throw your burden down,
Commit what haunts you to your loyal friend.

MARY. Though I am pressed against eternity,
   And must soon hear the judgement of my God,
   I have not yet made peace with my own soul.
   I am denied a priest of my religion,   220
   The sacrament, the manna of the spirit,
   Becomes an insult in a false priest's hands,
   My only bliss is in my own belief,
   I wish to die respectful to my Church.

MELVIL. Peace be upon you. A disabled faith
   Is no less faithful in the eyes of God.
   And though oppression binds the lips and hands,
   Worship can rise to heaven unimpaired.
   Form is the body, faith its heart and spirit.*

MARY. Ah Melvil, but the heart is insufficient!   230
   Weak in belief, it needs an earthly pledge
   That is why God descended as a man,
   Blessings from heaven hidden in his form,
   But visible through mystery. The Church
   Sets up a ladder to the infinite,
   We call it universal, catholic,
   Because the faith of everyone increases
   The faith of one. When thousands pray together,
   Faith turns to flames of love that leap to heaven.
   Oh happy people, gathered by a creed,   240
   Their church a single cry of joy to God!
   The altar is adorned, the candles shine,
   Censers shake fragrance, gentle bells resound,
   There stands the bishop in his stainless robe—
   He takes the chalice and he blesses it,
   And he announces the high mystery
   Of transubstantiation, and the faithful,*
   Convinced, undoubting, sense their God among them.
   Oh I alone am exiled, and the blessing
   Of heaven cannot find me in my dungeon!   250

MELVIL. Trust the Almighty. He is never far.
   The staff grows green in a believer's hands,
   And he who drew the water from the stone

Can conjure up an altar in a dungeon,
Can, in an instant, make this earthly wine,
And this unsacred chalice, heavenly!
>   [*He seizes the goblet, which is standing on the
>   table*

MARY. What? Do I understand you? Yes I do!
There is no priest, there are no relics here,
This is no church, and yet our saviour says,
'Where two or three are gathered in my name,   260
There am I also.' Who ordains this priest*
To speak the gospel? A believing heart!
So you can be the messenger from heaven,
A priest to me, and you can bring me peace,
Though you are unordained. My last confession
Shall be to you, and so I find salvation.

MELVIL. As you have grasped this truth, so may you know
That God is with you by a miracle.
This is no church, there is no host, you say,*
There is no priest here—but you are misled,   270
There is a priest here, and your God is here.
>   [*He uncovers his head and at the same time
>   shows her the host in a golden bowl*
I am a priest. To hear your last confession,*
And to pronounce atonement over you,
I have received the seven consecrations,*
And this I bring you from the Holy Father,
Blessed by himself, the Holy Sacrament.*

MARY. Even at death's gate bliss awaits me,
Prepared by heaven! Just as an immortal
Descends on golden clouds, just as the angel
Led the apostle from a broken dungeon,*   280
So heaven's messenger could find me here,
When every mortal help had died. And you,
My servant once, are now the voice of God,
And servant of the highest! As your knees
Bend before me in everything but this,
Now before you I sink into the dust.
>   [*She kneels in front of him*

MELVIL [*while he makes the Sign of the Cross over her*].
  In the name of the Father, and of the Son, and of the Holy
    Ghost,
  Queen Mary! Have you looked into your heart,
  And do you promise to confess the truth,
  Solemnly swearing to eternal God?   290

MARY. My heart lies open both to you and Him.

MELVIL. What are the sins your conscience would confess,
  Committed since you last made peace with heaven?

MARY. My heart has been a storm of hate and envy,
  And it has harboured visions of revenge.
  I, a poor sinner, hoped for God's forgiveness,
  But I could not forgive my enemy.

MELVIL. Do you repent, and is it your intention
  To die entirely reconciled?

MARY.   It is.
  As I may hope for mercy so I swear.   300

MELVIL. What further sin would you confess to me?

MARY. Oh I have dragged down virtue from on high,
  Not just with hatred but with sinful love.
  Vanity drew me to an empty man,
  Whose faithlessness has sent me to my death.

MELVIL. Do you regret that fault, and has your heart
  Turned from its idol to the God of life?

MARY. That was the hardest battle of them all,
  But I prevailed against my heart at last,
  And cut my last remaining tie to life.   310

MELVIL. What further sin would you confess to me?

MARY. Blood guilt returns with terror at the end,
  Long since confessed but now renewed in power,
  Like a black cloud before the gates of heaven,
  The last account. I had the King my husband
  Murdered, and gave my hand to my seducer.

Oh, I atoned with every kind of penance,
But in my soul the worm would not lie still.

MELVIL. But are there no more unconfessed transgressions
Which you repent, in your accusing conscience?   320

MARY. Now you know all that ever wept in there.

MELVIL. Speak to the heart of the omniscient!
Picture the endless horror that the Church
Reserves for those who temper their confession.
This is the sin for which eternal death
Hungers—the sin against the Holy Spirit.*

MARY. So, for my triumph in the final struggle,
Reward me with your everlasting blessing,
For I have kept back nothing I remember.

MELVIL. What! You imagine that your soul can hide   330
From God the sin for which the world condemns you?
You have said nothing of your understanding
With Babington and Parry in their treason.
You will die once on earth for that—confess,
Or stretch that death into the infinite.

MARY. Before the patient minute hand has ended
Its present revolution, I will stand
Before my God, and so I say again,
I have confessed the sins that I remember,
And I am fitted for eternity.   340

MELVIL. The heart can be a traitor to the mind,
Consider well—perhaps you have avoided
Self-blaming words by subtlety of tongue,
While in your heart you rallied to the crime.
But veiling charm, as you must understand,
Cannot deflect God's eyes of searching fire!

MARY. I set this quest for every Christian king—
To save me from my prison. But I never,
In thought or deed, aimed at my enemy.

MELVIL. Your secretaries gave false witness then?   350

MARY. What I have said is true. What they have said,
Heaven will weigh.

MELVIL.   So you ascend the scaffold,
Innocent in your mind.

MARY.   By this injustice,
God in his grace permits me to complete
My penance for an early deed of blood.

MELVIL [*blesses her*]. So change disgrace to peace by penitence!
Like an oblation on an altar stone,
A gift without stain, lay your pure head down.
Blood offered thus will answer blood betrayed.
Feminine weakness made your body sin,   360
But mortal failings cannot reach the soul
After transfiguration.
Therefore by the power invested in me, to loose and to
   bind, I pronounce over you remission of all your sins.
As you believe, so may your soul find life.

                              [*He hands her the host*
The body of Christ, that was given for you.
       [*He takes the goblet, which has been standing on
       the table, consecrates it with a silent prayer, and
       then hands it to her. She hesitates to accept it,
       and then refuses it with her hand*
The blood of Christ, that was shed for you.*
Take it! The Pope has granted you this favour,
The sacred right reserved to priests and kings*
Is yours in death.

                              [*She takes the goblet*
                  As here by mystery
God is united with your earthly body,   370
So, in the Kingdom of rejoicing light,
Where there are neither tears nor guilt, transfigured
Into the form of truth among His angels,
You will reflect the godhead everlasting.
       [*He puts the goblet down. A sound is heard, and
       he covers his head and goes to the door.* MARY
       stays on her knees in quiet worship

MELVIL [*coming back*]. A bitter fight remains. Are you
    prepared
Against returning hate and bitterness?

MARY. I fear no looking back. My love and hate
Have lifted as a cloud of praise to God.

MELVIL. Then steel your spirit to receive the Lords
Leicester and Burleigh. They are coming now.   380

SCENE VIII

[*As before.* BURLEIGH, LEICESTER, *and* PAULET.
LEICESTER *remains standing in the background,
without looking up.* BURLEIGH, *who is watching*
LEICESTER's *demeanour, steps between him and the*
QUEEN.]

BURLEIGH. I come for your last wishes, Lady Stuart.

MARY. Thank you, my Lord!

BURLEIGH.   It is the Queen's desire
That we deny you nothing that is just.

MARY. My will makes plain my wishes. It is given
Into Sir Paulet's hands. My one request
Is that it should be followed honestly.

PAULET. Depend upon it.

MARY.   Further, I petition
That as they wish, to Scotland or to France,
My retinue shall be released unharmed.*

BURLEIGH. So it shall be.

MARY.   As it has been conceded   390
That consecrated earth shall cover this,*
So let my servant take my heart to France—
Would it had never left!—and to my people.

BURLEIGH. It is permitted. Are there any further—

MARY. Convey a sister's greeting to the Queen,
Say that my soul forgives her for my death,
That I regret my rage of yesterday.
May God preserve her and exalt her reign!*

BURLEIGH. But have you not relented to good counsel?
Do you still scorn the comfort of the deacon?   400

MARY. My soul is reconciled with God. Sir Paulet,
I have bereft your age of its support,
Unwittingly, and caused you suffering.
Oh let me hope that you will think of me
Not blackly!

PAULET [gives her his hand]. Go in peace! May God be with
you!

SCENE IX

[As before. HANNA KENNEDY and the QUEEN's other
ladies rush in with gestures of horror. They are
followed by the SHERIFF, a white staff in his hand.
Behind him through the open door armed men
are visible.]

MARY. What is it, Hanna? Well, the time has come.
The man is here to lead us to our death.
So we must part. Farewell!
                         [Her ladies cling to her in great sorrow
                         You, worthy sir,
And Hanna, you, shall keep me company   410
On my last walk. My Lord, this could be granted!

BURLEIGH. It is beyond my power.

MARY.   You deny me
Such a small comfort? But respect my sex!
Who is to be my servant at the last?

You think my sister wishes that in me
Our sex should suffer at these men's rough hands!

BURLEIGH. No wench may climb the scaffold by your side,
To weep and scream—

MARY.   My Hanna will not cry,
She has a soldier's soul, I vouch for her.
Be generous my Lord, and do not rend me   420
In dying from the nurse who suckled me!
It was her arms that drew me to the light,
And they shall pass me tenderly to death.

PAULET [*to* BURLEIGH]. Allow it.

BURLEIGH.   It shall be.

MARY.   Now there is nothing.
            [*She takes the crucifix and kisses it*
My saviour! My redeemer! Spread your arms
As once in death, so to receive me dying.
            [*She turns to leave, but in this instant she catches*
            LORD LEICESTER's *eye, who had looked up*
            involuntarily at her imminent departure. At this
            sight MARY *trembles, her knees give way, she is*
            about to fall, when LORD LEICESTER *seizes her*
            and holds her in his arms. She looks at him for
            a while, serious and silent. He cannot meet her
            gaze; finally she speaks
You are an honest man, my Lord. You promised
To lead me from this dungeon on your arm,
And you extend it in fulfilment now.
            [*He stands there as if destroyed. She continues in*
            a soft voice
And Leicester, once the promise of your hand   430
Was more than freedom to me. Once I hoped
The gift of it would sweeten my escape,
And love make freedom something to be loved.
Now that I wander to another world,
Where I will be disburdened of desire,
I may confess without a blush what was.

Farewell, and if it should be possible,
Find happiness! Two Queens believed in you,
And you forsook the tender for the proud.
Kneel and receive Elizabeth's reward,   440
And may it be your punishment! Farewell,
I leave behind me nothing that is mine.

> [*Exit, the* SHERIFF *preceding her,* MELVIL *and*
> HANNA *at her side,* BURLEIGH *and* PAULET
> *behind. The others watch her, sobbing, until*
> *she has disappeared, then they withdraw*
> *through two different doors*

SCENE X

LEICESTER [*remaining on stage alone*]. Am I alive? How can
    my body live?
How can the ceiling stretch above my head,
Not crashing on me? Why does no abyss
Open to swallow this reproach to nature!
What heaven have I cast into the sea,
What unexampled pearl exchanged for chaos!
She goes from me, before my very eyes
Changing into an angel, leaving me   450
To inescapable damnation's howls!
Where are the gold and silver resolutions
With which I came, to drown my heart's weak crying?
To see her head fall with a stone expression?
Has seeing her rewakened my dead shame?
Can she inspire immortal love by dying?
Ah faithless man! It is for you no longer
To turn to tender rain. The road you follow
Leads far from love. Defend your mind with mortar,
With a smooth face, unscaleable as ice.   460
You must hold fast to evil to the end—
Or see the prize of your misdeed pass by.
Compassion, turn your gaze upon a gorgon
Within, and be a stone. I will stand near
And witness this without distress.

[*He goes towards the door through which* MARY
went, with a determined stride, but stops
half-way there

I cannot.
I cannot! Cannot move towards that horror.
My feet will not obey me into hell,
My eyes refuse the sight. What was that noise?
Oh they are moving under me already,
Downstairs, the deed is being set in motion.   470
They speak. Quick, quick, away, away from here,
Out of this place of stately, measured death!

[*He tries to flee through another door,*
but finds it locked and starts back

What? Has some god bewitched me to this ground?
Must hearing bring me what my eyes deny?
The deacon speaks—in a berating tone—
She cuts across it; in a firm, loud voice,
She prays. Now all is silent once again.
Utterly silent! Only women sobbing
And weeping hard. They are undressing her.
Oh God! The stool is moved—it scrapes the floor—   480
She kneels upon the stole, lays her head down—

[*After he has uttered the last words in an*
increasingly fearful voice and has
remained silent for a while, he is seen
to start suddenly and then fall
unconscious on the floor. At the same
time a muffled rumble of voices is
heard from below, which lasts a long
time

SCENE XI

[*The second room of Act Four.*]

ELIZABETH [*enters through a side door. Her gait and gestures*
express the greatest disquiet].
Still no one comes with news! Oh is the sun

Stuck fast in heaven? When will twilight fall?
The rack of expectation stretches me
With every minute, and the minutes mount.
I dare not question, dreading either answer.
Neither Lord Leicester nor Lord Burleigh comes,
Whom I ordained as champions of this act.
If they left London, then the deed is done,
The arrow rests no longer in the bow,   490
It flies towards, it hits, has hit the target.
Oh, if my reign depended on my patience,
I would fall now—so I surrender—you there!

SCENE XII

[ELIZABETH, *a* PAGE.]

ELIZABETH. You have returned alone. Where are the lords?

PAGE. My Lord of Leicester and the Chancellor—

ELIZABETH [*in the greatest suspense*].
Are where?

PAGE.   Are not in London.

ELIZABETH.   Is it so?
Where are they then?

PAGE.   I cannot learn for certain.
It seems both lords before the break of dawn
Secretly rode with all haste from the city.

ELIZABETH [*lively exclamation*]. Behold the Queen of England!
          [*Walks up and down in great agitation*
                    Bring me now—
Call—no, remain—she is among the shades,   501
And now at last the day and night are mine.
Why do I tremble, why a touch of fear?
My dread is in a grave, and who may say
I put it there? And I shall not keep back
Tears for that fallen woman from my eyes!
                    [*To the* PAGE

Do you still stand there? Bring my secretary,
Sir Davison, to me immediately.
Send for the Earl of Shrewsbury as well.
Ah, here he marches of his own accord.   510

SCENE XIII

[ELIZABETH, *the* EARL OF SHREWSBURY.]

ELIZABETH. Noble Lord, welcome. What important news
Hurries you to us at so late an hour?

SHREWSBURY. Great Queen, tormented by unresting doubt,
My heart, the angel guard of your good name,
Drove me today towards the Tower, where
The Stuart's secretaries, Kurl and Nau,
Are to be found in chains—for I desired
Once more to test the truth of their confessions.
Embarrassed, the Lieutenant of the Tower
Refused to show them to me—but by threats   520
I forced him. God! What sight awaited me!
The Scotsman Kurl lay on his bed, his hair
Torn by the tempest of his hands—his eyes,
As if a demon danced around the room,
Darted in terror—me, half-recognized,
He pleads with, crouching on the floor and howling,
Clutching my knees and writhing like a worm,
Begging to know what fate has seized his Queen,
Because a rumour of her death sentence
Has seeped into the dungeons of the Tower.   530
When I confirmed this and assured him further
That it was his confession that condemned her,
He leapt up, shaking and insane with fury,
And flung his fellow captive to the floor,
To tear his throat out. Only just in time
We pulled him free; at which the Scotsman raged,
Striking his chest in fury, calling devils.
He said that he had made a false confession,

And that the letters sent to Babington,
Which he had sworn were real, were forgeries,   540
That what he wrote the Queen did not dictate,
That wretched Nau had tempted him to this.
And then he ran and with a demon's power
Tore loose the window, and proclaimed so loud
That crowds assembled in the alleyways,
That he was Mary's cursed secretary,
The blackguard who accused her with no cause,
For which false witness he was surely damned!*

ELIZABETH. But you yourself denote him as insane.
Lunacy is a worthless testimony.   550

SHREWSBURY. But that he is insane proves everything.
Oh Queen! Do not be deaf to my beseeching,
Order a fresh investigation, hinder
The undesired conclusion of the last one.

ELIZABETH. I will—because it is your wish, my Lord,
And not because the peers, in my belief,
Have acted hastily in this affair.
For your tranquillity of mind, I order
A fresh investigation. Praised be heaven
That there is still time to dispel all stains   560
From the perfection of our royal honour.

SCENE XIV

[DAVISON *joins the others*.]

ELIZABETH. Where is the warrant that I gave you, sir?

DAVISON [*highly surprised*]. The order?

ELIZABETH.   That I gave into your keeping.

DAVISON. Into my keeping?

ELIZABETH.   When the people shouted,
Forced by their cries I acted as they ordered,
But gave the writ I signed into your hands,

To gain me time—you know because I told you—
Now, give it to me.

SHREWSBURY.   Worthy sir, this matter
Has shifted balance—the investigation
Must be begun again. Give her the order.   570

DAVISON. Begun again? Oh God have mercy on me!

ELIZABETH. Why do you waste our time? Where is the paper?

DAVISON [*in despair*]. I am a dead man. I am lost for ever.

ELIZABETH [*interrupting hastily*]. I hope sir, that—

DAVISON.   I have obeyed damnation.
I do not have the order any more.

ELIZABETH. What? How is that?

SHREWSBURY.   Oh God! God!

DAVISON.   Yesterday
I gave it to Lord Burleigh.

ELIZABETH.   Wretched man!
Is this how you obey my clearest orders?
Did I not tell you to preserve the paper?

DAVISON. That you did not command.

ELIZABETH.   Despicable!   580
Do you blame me, your Queen? Horrific liar!
When did I say to give the writ to Burleigh?

DAVISON. Never precisely in those terms; however—

ELIZABETH. Thief! Beggar! Do you dare to strain my words,
To load them with your meaning and your blame!
Woe be to you! For this initiative,
If misery ensues, your life will answer!
Lord Shrewsbury, my name is used against me.

SHREWSBURY. It is. Oh God—

ELIZABETH.   What do you say to this?

SHREWSBURY. If it emerges that the knight has acted   590
Beyond your will, and made his own decision,

Then he must stand before the judgement seat
Of the High Court, because he has exposed
Your name to horror and disgust forever.

SCENE XV

[As before. BURLEIGH, *finally* KENT.]

BURLEIGH [*bends a knee before the* QUEEN]. Live long, great
    Lady, may the end of all
Who hate you, be as Mary Stuart's was.
        [SHREWSBURY *covers his face.* DAVISON *wrings his
        hands in despair*

ELIZABETH. Tell me, my Lord, did you receive the order
    To do this bloody deed, from me?

BURLEIGH.   No, mistress,
    Davison gave it to me.

ELIZABETH.   Davison.
    And did he give it to you in my name?   600

BURLEIGH. That he did not.

ELIZABETH.   Yet it was carried out,
    Rashly, before my final wish was known.
    The world cannot accuse me of injustice,
    This sentence was well merited. However,
    Is it your calling to pre-empt the mildness
    My heart desired? Be banished from my sight!*
    [*To* DAVISON] A sterner court than my contempt awaits
    Your stepping over of authority,
    And your betrayal of a sacred trust.
    He is an outlaw, take him to the Tower,   610
    And let the law proceed against his life.*
    It is my will. There shall be no delay.
    My noble Talbot, you alone are just,
    Of all my counsellors; and from now on
    You, only you will be my friend and guide.

SHREWSBURY. Do not condemn or banish your good friends,
Who served you and are silent for your sake.
Allow me though, to give you back, great Queen,
This seal, my badge of service for twelve years.*

ELIZABETH [*awkwardly*]. Shrewsbury! You will not forsake
me now.   620

SHREWSBURY. Forgive me, I am old, and cannot bend
This stiffened hand to your newfangled toil.

ELIZABETH. The man who saved my life deserts my ranks?

SHREWSBURY. I could not save the better part of you.
The enemy is dead. Live happily,
Rule well, from now on nothing in the world
Can fill your heart with terror or respect.

                                                  [*Exit*

ELIZABETH [*to the* EARL OF KENT, *who enters*]. Summon Lord
Leicester!

KENT.   He is on a ship
To France, and sends you his apologies.*
                    [*She forces herself to stand in calm composure.*
                    The curtain falls

EXPLANATORY NOTES

DON CARLOS

Act One

1 S.D. *Aranjuez*: the spring residence built by Philip II, not far from Madrid.

S.D. *Domingo*: the figure of Domingo, the corrupt confessor to the King, is Schiller's invention. Schiller named him after the order of the Dominicans, founded in 1215 to convert heretics to the Christian faith. Pope Gregory IX entrusted the Inquisition to the Dominicans in 1231, though it only reached its full measure of terror under the Spanish monarchs Ferdinand and Isabella, Philip II's predecessors, who were appointed by Pope Sixtus IV to order a full-scale Inquisition, which led to the expulsion of all the Spanish Moors. The Inquisition became synonymous with political corruption and the intertwining of political and religious prerogative. The ultimate personification of this evil system of persecution comes in the final scenes of the play, with the appearance of the ancient Grand Inquisitor himself.

12 *received the homage of his lords*: in 1560 the Spanish nobility paid tribute to the successor to the throne, the Infante Don Carlos, at Toledo, the capital of Castile before Madrid.

15 *Six kingdoms*: the six kingdoms referred to were, according to Brantôme: Spain, the Indies, Jerusalem, Majorca, Minorca, Sardinia, and Sicily.

25 *your mother*: Domingo is referring here to Philip's wife, Elizabeth of Valois, originally intended for Don Carlos (according to Schiller).

30 *my mother*: Maria of Portugal, Don Carlos's mother, died in childbirth.

36 *I was his only child*: the Spanish succession at the time of this play rested on Don Carlos as Philip II's only son. Elizabeth bore him two daughters, but it was actually his son by Anne of Austria who became Philip III in 1598.

49 *Saragossa*: Saragossa is the capital of Aragon, province of Spain and independent kingdom before Ferdinand of Aragon and Isabella of Castile unified Spain in 1479.

73 *purple*: purple is the traditional colour for a cardinal's robe. Philip would have the power to suggest a candidate to the Pope for appointment to cardinal.

94 *St Peter's chair*: St Peter's chair is the papal throne in Rome. See the Gospel according to St Matthew 16: 18: 'And I say unto thee, That thou art Peter, and upon this rock I will build my church.'

100 *a hundred eyes are hired*: the historical Don Carlos was indeed under his father's surveillance, though this was due to his violent temperament.

108 *Madrid*: in 1561 Philip II declared Madrid to be the capital of Spain and in 1563 built his residence some 30 miles out of Madrid at the Escorial. Although Madrid lies on the banks of a river, the Manzanares, the site for establishing the city had been chosen for its location at the geographic centre of Spain, in an attempt to facilitate the unification process begun in the previous century.

128 *Brussels*: the capital of the Spanish Netherlands since the reign of Charles V, Philip II's father. It was also the site of the Protestant uprising in 1567.

147 *Flanders*: part of the Spanish Netherlands.

150 *Alba*: the Duke of Alba (1508–82) was Philip II's highest general. He became infamous for his bloody suppression of the rebellion in the Netherlands in 1567.

154 *Charles the Emperor*: Charles V (1500–58) was the last emperor to be crowned by a pope. His empire stretched over most of Europe. On his death in 1558 the imperial title passed to his brother Ferdinand I.

193 *sailor suits*: worn by young children in Schiller's time.

217 *My Aunt, the Queen of Bohemia*: the Queen of Bohemia was Philip's sister. Later she was married to Emperor Maximilian II and Philip II married her daughter as his fourth wife in 1569.

259 *Rome's decrees*: this is a reference to the laws of the Catholic Church. Of course, Elizabeth of Valois is not Don Carlos's natural mother, and so Carlos's offence is not incest. However, by coveting another man's wife he is also not honouring his father, thereby committing two sins, and he is threatening to commit a third, namely adultery. For the Ten Commandments see Exodus 20: 12–17.

283 *Furies*: the Furies were the Roman spirits of revenge.

346 *Henry's court*: Henry II of France, Elizabeth's father.

359 S.D. *Queen [to the Marquise]*: Elizabeth of Valois was Henry II of France's eldest daughter. She was betrothed to Philip II in 1558 at the age of 14 but did not come to Spain until 1560.

Mondecar: Schiller's Mondecar must have been derived from the name Mondejar, which appears in the sources.

378   s.d. *Olivarez*: an old aristocratic Spanish family. Olivarez occupies the position of being Elizabeth's most senior lady-in-waiting.

380   *the Pardo*: a hunting lodge north of Madrid.

386   *Plaza Mayor*: a large square in the centre of old Madrid which was used for *autos-da-fé* during the Inquisition.

388   *Autos da Fe*: an *auto-da-fé* was the public burning of heretics—a popular spectacle.

403   *Gomez*: Schiller is liberal with historical chronology here: Gomez is referred to here as Eboli's suitor: in fact he married her in 1559.

429   *my daughter*: Elizabeth's elder daughter, Clara Eudoxia.

437   *the Regent's mother*: after the death of Henry II (Elizabeth's father), his young son Francis became King of France, together with his consort Mary, Queen of Scots. As he was still a minor he was assisted in the rule of France by his mother, Catherine de' Medici, mainly to ward off the warring factions of the Guises and the Bourbons fighting for influence over the French throne. When Francis II died in 1560 his younger brother Charles IV became King of France and his mother's regency became even more crucial.

452   *the tournament at Reims*: the tournament at Reims to which Elizabeth refers here was held by her father in honour of her marriage to the King of Spain. Tragically, he died during it.

513   *I am a friend of stories too*: this line echoes lines 1207 ff. during Act V of Lessing's Nathan der Weise: 'I have always been a friend of stories told well.'

514   *Mirandola*: a small town in northern Italy. Posa proceeds to tell a parable of the love of Don Carlos and Elizabeth. The parable gives the reader the background to Don Carlos's grievance.

516   *Guelfs and Ghibellines*: warring factions during the Middle Ages—the former supporting the pope, the latter supporting the emperor.

610   *That you and I were found alone together*: Carlos's intrusion poses a grave danger for Elizabeth, should she be discovered in his company without a chaperone. This is not so much because of their supposed love affair but would apply to any man visiting the Queen without supervision. Elizabeth's fear portrays very succinctly Schiller's preoccupation with an atmosphere of ubiquitous surveillance, which he associated so clearly with the idea of tyranny.

662 *If an old man's consideration*: Schiller gives us the impression that Philip is an old man; in II. x Domingo says Philip is 60. The historical Philip was only some 18 years older than his son.

691 *Escorial*: at the Escorial Philip II built not only a palace but a monastery, a church, and a college. He was to be buried there.

810 *In my domain the sun does not go down*: Philip II inherited the largest empire the world had ever seen. With the seizure of the Philippines in 1564 it could be said that the sun never set on his realm, which stretched from Europe to America and Manila.

815 *And in her only can he suffer loss*: Philip here distinguishes between the good fortune which is his because of his position as king and that which is his because of his position as an individual.

832 S.D. *Lerma*: Count Lerma (1550–1625) was a long-serving courtier and became seneschal to Philip's heir Philip III.

847 *the oath . . . blood*: the king during his coronation had to swear an oath to protect the faith. Philip had also sworn to protect the Inquisition—something that Charles V had insisted on from his deathbed.

Act Two

145 *Brabant*: the largest state in the Spanish Netherlands and part of the Habsburg empire since 1477 and the marriage of Mary of Burgundy to Emperor Maximilian. Brussels is the capital of Brabant.

253 *St Quentin*: the battle of St Quentin in France took place in 1557 and involved English, Spanish, and French armies. The French were defeated. The following year they suffered defeat once more at the hands of the Spanish under the leadership of Egmont at Gravelines in the Netherlands.

255 *Duke Henarez*: Henarez is not a recognized aristocratic Spanish name but, rather, Schiller has borrowed the name of a river.

352 *Germany*: Alba was known in Germany since he commanded the armies of Charles V at the battle of Schmalkalden in 1547.

358 *You never fail to vindicate our faith*: Carlos is referring to Madrid's faith in Alba, not to religion.

372 *the Portuguese*: Maria of Portugal, Philip's first wife, who died giving birth to Carlos.

703 *The famous merchant of the South prevails*: Carlos, by referring to his father as the merchant of the South, is borrowing two images.

'Merchant' refers to the practice of arranged marriages for political gain. 'Demon of the South' was an epithet used throughout the sixteenth century to describe Philip II, based on Psalm 91: 5–6: 'Thou shalt not be afraid for the terror by night; nor for the arrow that flieth by day; nor for the pestilence that walketh in darkness; nor for the destruction that wasteth at noonday.' As the Bible commonly in circulation in the sixteenth century and until recently was based on the Vulgate, a fourth-century Latin translation, some inaccuracies made their way into common usage. One such inaccuracy was to translate '. . . et daemonio meridiano' as 'the demon of the south'—compare the French word *midi*, meaning both 'midday' and 'south'.

720–3 *Much like the merchant . . . beneath its worth*: Schiller found this anecdote in the notes to the last scene of the German translation by Eschenburg of Shakespeare's *Othello*.

798 *Oh horrible! Oh God, what have I done?*: this long scene between Carlos and Eboli has been frequently criticized for being too long and involved and for detracting from the main plot. For the sake of clarity a brief summary of the events is given here: Eboli is in love with Carlos and does not want to marry Gomez: she has ambitions of marrying the King's son. Meanwhile, however, the King himself has designs on her and she believes in part that if Carlos will declare his love for her openly, this threat will be removed. She has sent a page from the Queen's entourage (of which she herself is a part) to take a key and a letter to Carlos with a secret rendezvous. Carlos mistakes the letter as being from the Queen herself and is distraught at his mistake. Eboli, however, simply thinks he is shy and evasive, believing that she has ample evidence of his love for her. When Carlos realizes that Eboli is confessing her love for him and that the letter came from her, not the Queen, he tries to extricate himself from an embarrassing situation, but only offends the mortally embarrassed Eboli more. Eboli, however, shows him a letter from the King, making advances towards her. While Eboli gives it to him to suggest he should prevent the King's advances, Carlos now realizes that the letter also proves that the King is not necessarily faithful to Elizabeth. This revelation comes as a triumph to him, as he believes the King's indiscretion gives him a moral licence to love the Queen. He leaves with the letter and Eboli remains to puzzle over her misinterpretation of the situation. Soon she realizes that all the previous flirtations she presumed were directed at her were in fact directed at the Queen. As she feels slighted and offended at Carlos's rejection

and as she is horrified that she confessed love to someone who did not return it when she thought he would, she decides to seek revenge on the Queen, whose moral integrity she has long admired, but who now seems to have usurped Carlos's love. Eboli does not believe Carlos's passion could survive if it were not reciprocal and so she decides to destroy the Queen's happiness by undermining her position at court with the suggestion of adultery, while at the same time seducing her husband. If Eboli cannot be betrothed to the King's son, she wants to establish her position of power as the King's mistress. Carlos is therefore very wrong in assuming that Eboli is of the highest moral integrity: she is as politically motivated as Posa later suggests.

890–1   *A strange discovery . . . for interpretation*: Domingo and the Duke of Alba have their own machinations to maintain. Even though Carlos is the King's only son and heir he does not enjoy his favour. Alba is the King's right-hand man and throughout the play Domingo and Alba are at pains to ensure that the balance of power at the court remains in their favour. This means that they must ensure that Carlos remains marginalized. For this reason Carlos's private audience with the King was initially cause for concern, and yet it remained fruitless. Nevertheless, Alba feels his favourable position with the King is no longer unquestioned, though his later encounter with Carlos lets him suspect evidence of Carlos's love for the Queen—information which can naturally be used to Alba and Domingo's greatest advantage in undermining the Prince.

953   *Toledo*: the Duke of Alba's full title was Ferdinand Alvarez de Toledo, Duke of Alba.

1007   *Valois lilies*: the fleur-de-lis was the French royal arms—and so Elizabeth's arms.

1133   *And so the King may hope?*: by showing Domingo's involvement in the King's advances to Eboli, Schiller gives us a glimpse into the full measure of his corruption. In this scene we see how Eboli's vendetta and the power intrigues of Alba and Domingo dovetail into a common purpose.

1176   *This sanctuary is for everyone*: traditionally, a church or monastery was a sanctuary to which criminals and others could flee from persecution.

1332   *How little I have understood your feelings*: Carlos believes that the King's infidelity nullifies his marriage to Elizabeth, thereby enabling him to ignore those marriage vows too. Posa tries to persuade

Carlos that this is not a valid argument, and that furthermore, showing the King's letter to Elizabeth will merely hurt her.

1341 *the provinces*: the provinces referred to are the Netherlands.

Act Three

42 *They pour forth molten gold*: the King's isolation is made clear here, as he feels he can never be given an honest answer by those around him who are too conscious of his power and are too anxious to please and flatter. Later, in his meeting with Posa, the King comes to the realization himself that he is alone, and Posa's lack of ingratiating flattery is his main appeal. The image of striking stones for water is borrowed from Exodus 17: 6: '. . . and thou shall strike the rock, and there shall come water out of it.'

65 *must have cost her more . . . than she has to spend*: this exchange vividly portrays the King's suspicion and paranoia of those around him—and of his wife.

155 *Sin rose when I received her from your hands*: it was the Duke of Alba who was sent to Paris in 1558 as Philip II's proxy in the marriage to Elizabeth, who was not brought back to Spain until 1560 because she was still so young.

205 *They are a gift of the confessional*: Eboli did not impart this information to Domingo in the confessional. Domingo is using this excuse to shield his information from the King's inquisitiveness, as confessions are supposed to be confidential.

363 *I have lost a fleet*: this reference is a contraction of actual historical events. Alonso Perez de Guzmán, the Duke of Medina Sidonia (1550–1615), a Spanish admiral, has come to announce the loss of the Armada, which did not actually set sail until twenty-one years later. The Armada was a huge fleet of 130 galleons and 30 smaller warships, manned by over 8,000 sailors and carrying nearly 20,000 soldiers and armed with 2,500 cannon. It was dispatched in 1588 to invade England, partly in revenge for Elizabeth I's execution of Mary Stuart, the Catholic Queen of Scotland, but also as part of the ongoing battle for power between the Protestant English kingdom and the Catholic alliance led by Philip II.

369 *Nephew, your mother asks*: the Prince of Parma's mother was Margaret of Parma, Charles V's illegitimate daughter and therefore Philip II's half-sister.

375 *Calatrava*: the Order of Calatrava was a Spanish order of knights founded in 1158 to protect the town of Calatrava against

the Moors. Later appointment to the order became a matter of honour conferred by the King on members of the nobility.

405 *Suleiman*: Suleiman II el Kanani (1496–1566) besieged the island of Malta for four months in 1565.

408 *Valetta*: Jean Parisot de Lavalette (1494–1568) was the Grand Master of the Knights of St John (Knights of Malta). He gave his name to a place La Valette. The castle of St Elmo is nearby.

412 *Hassem, Piali, and Ulluciali*: Mustafa, Hassem, Piali, and Ulluciali were all Turkish military leaders.

422 *plot in Catalonia*: this plot is Schiller's invention.

450 *An opportunity as rare as this*: Horace, *Odes* I. xi. 8: 'Carpe diem', 'enjoy today'.

577 *This side of me?*: this is the beginning of Posa's duplicity, in that of course Carlos has already seen this side of him.

638 *And what you do is necessary*: the King must support this policy if he supports the Inquisition. That he *does* support the Inquisition horrifies Posa.

660 *universal spring*: the universal spring refers to the contemporary reformation of religion, which gained its biggest momentum under Martin Luther (1483–1546) in Germany.

671 *Elizabeth receives your refugees*: Elizabeth I (1533–1603) of England, champion of the Protestant cause.

687 *Nero*: Claudius Caesar Nero (AD 37–68) was a Roman emperor infamous for his cruelty.

688 *Busiris*: a legendary Egyptian despot.

Act Four

261 *When I lay near to death in Alcala*: Carlos has several letters from Elizabeth, so he ought to have recognized her handwriting on the letter that in fact came from Eboli.

S.D. *Scene vii. The King's office*: Grillparzer later borrowed this scene for his story *Das Kloster bei Sendomir*.

334 *St Germain*: Saint-Germain-en-Laye, near Paris, was one of the French royal residences.

370 *Castile*: Castile here stands for the whole of Spain.

478 *Tacitus*: Cornelius Tacitus (AD 55–115) was a Roman historian.

800 *The Queen has ordered . . . into my keeping*: ladies-in-waiting carried crosses and keys as a sign of their office.

811 *You know now*: at this point the reader is as anxious as the Queen to receive an explanation of Posa's doings. He used the King's confidence in him to gain access to the Queen, to enlist her support to persuade Carlos to leave the court and go to the Netherlands and fight for their freedom—with the Queen he discusses a rebellion to be led by Carlos. He takes Carlos's letters from him for his own protection and shows some of them to the King, who has told him to get to know his son. The crucial letter he shows to the King is that written by Eboli to Carlos, inviting him to the secret rendezvous. In the meantime the King has received letters from Carlos to the Queen stolen from her casket by Eboli with the King's knowledge, in order to provide evidence of an affair between Carlos and the Queen. It was Eboli who first sowed the seed of doubt in the King's mind and he now sees himself the victim of a plot, which has sought to alienate him from his wife, whom he has just humiliated and allowed to faint. Posa asks the King to assign custody of the Prince to Posa alone, to which the King agrees. He even gives him an arrest warrant. Posa soon makes use of this, which causes outrage at court, but Posa does this to stop Carlos asking Eboli for her help in obtaining an audience with the Queen. He realizes, however, that it is too late and that Eboli will destroy the Prince with what she knows. Therefore Posa changes his plan to put the blame on himself. He writes a letter suggesting that he himself is in love with the Queen and sends it to the Netherlands, knowing that it will be intercepted. He hopes that this will buy time to allow Carlos to escape to the Netherlands and pursue the cause there.

908 *I have surrendered two short evening hours*: the two short evening hours refer both to Posa's own life and to the rest of Philip's reign, which Posa hopes to end with a rebellion led by Carlos from the Netherlands. Carlos's reign is referred to as a summer's day.

1030 *We were in Saragossa*: the princes of Parma and Feria were in the King's audience the day before. They cannot therefore have just arrived from Saragossa, some 150 miles away.

1037 *the Cortes*: the Cortes is the highest court of law, and the only body that can pass judgment over members of the royal family.

1066 *Te Deum*: the Te Deum is a prayer of praise, in use since the fifth
century. Alba sees his position of power restored once more with
Posa's fall from grace.

Act Five

69 s.d. *Alba [approaches the Prince . . . throughout the scene]*: Posa
has been revealed as a traitor, as he had planned. Alba therefore
shows him no respect, despite his recent position of power as the
King's favourite confidante. Alba is himself restored to his position of power at Philip's court, as is symbolized by his assignment
to release Carlos from custody. Carlos, however, refuses to be
released by Alba, but insists instead on receiving the explanation
from his father himself. Only then will his position at court be
fully restored and not tainted with disgrace, even though he was
innocent.

258 *Since mothers first bore children*: Carlos is referring to Jesus Christ.

431 *Cadiz*: a harbour town in the south of Spain, and the main port
for the American silver trade of the sixteenth century.

432 *Vlissingen*: a seaport in the northern province of Zeeland in the
Netherlands. One of the centres of the rebellion against Spain.

436 *Rhodes*: the property of the Knights of St John from 1310, but was
captured in 1522 by Suleiman. During these years the Turks were
a constant naval threat to Philip II. They were finally defeated at
the sea battle of Lepanto in 1571.

484 *Indies*: the West Indies, brought under Spanish control by
Columbus in 1492, whence Spain derived great income.

587 *Santa Casa*: Santa Casa was the court of the Inquisition.

657 *Our order tired you with its exigency*: the order of the Dominicans,
appointed by Pope Gregory IX to conduct the Inquisition.

666 *Samuel*: compare this with 1 Samuel 28: 17 f.: 'And the Lord hath
done to him, as he spake by me: for the Lord hath rent the kingdom
out of thine hand, and given it to thy neighbour, even to David:
Because thou obeyedst not the voice of the Lord, nor executedst
his fierce wrath upon Amalek, therefore hath the Lord done this
thing unto thee this day.'

667 *I set two kings upon the throne of Spain*: the two kings were
Charles V and Philip II.

684 *Amenable to this interpretation?*: Schiller took this interpretation of Philip's action from St Réal, who reported that the Inquisition compared Philip to God, for sacrificing his only son.

763 *Ghent*: the capital of eastern Flanders, part of the Netherlands.

MARY STUART

Act One

s.d. *Fotheringhay Castle*: a castle in Northamptonshire. Mary Stuart was transferred there in 1586. Nothing now remains of the castle.

s.d. *Hanna Kennedy*: Jean Kennedy was one of Mary Stuart's most trusted ladies-in-waiting.

s.d. *Paulet*: an English Protestant, who served among other things as Governor of the Channel Islands and as ambassador to France. He was entrusted with guarding Mary Stuart from 1585 until her death.

18 *Fleur de Lys*: the fleur-de-lis has been the royal coat of arms of France since 1179. It consists of three golden lilies on a blue background.

Drury: Drudgeon Drury was assigned to Sir Amias Paulet as a second guardsman over Mary Stuart in 1586.

30 *Where is the sky / That ought to blaze into my lady's rooms?*: Schiller's line in the original, 'Wo ist die Himmeldecke über ihrem Sitz?', is a play on words. As Mary is, in Schiller's play, incarcerated and denied the sight of the outdoors—see her ecstasy in Act Three— that Hanna should here lament the absence of the sky is apt enough. In fact, however, the Himmeldecke also refers to a small baldachin or canopy over Mary's chair, which was removed in 1586, thereby denying her her royal status. In its place she hung a crucifix on the bare wall, much to the annoyance of her warder Paulet.

36 *with her husband . . . with her lover*: the husband referred to here is Lord Darnley, the lover is Bothwell. The pewter plates signal the somewhat straitened financial resources of the Scottish royal family at this time.

45 *the court of the Medici*: this is a reference to the court of Henry II of France and his consort Catherine de' Medici, which was renowned for its interest in, and patronage of, the arts.

46 *Who was a Queen when she was in her cradle*: Mary Stuart was born four days before her father died, leaving her to be an infant Queen of Scotland.

60 *where the disgrace was done*: an aspect of Mary Stuart's dispute with England was whether or not she was subject to the laws of England as a foreign sovereign.

64 *the torch of civil war*: throughout the play Mary is associated with images of fire. For an interpretation of the play which goes into considerable detail about this imagery, see Ilse Graham, *Schiller's Drama: Talent and Integrity* (London, 1974).

70 *Babington and Parry*: Anthony Babington was the leader of a group of young Catholics conspiring to murder Elizabeth and to release Mary and place her on the English throne. William Parry was an agent of the English secret service, who conspired to murder Elizabeth, though his motives are unclear.

71 *noble Norfolk's heart*: the Duke of Norfolk, the highest noble-man of England, was found guilty of treason for his involvement in a plot to free Mary and marry her, and then to place her on the English throne. He was beheaded at the Tower of London in 1572.

81 *this Helen*: Helen of Troy, daughter of Zeus and Leda, the wife of the Greek king Menelaus, was a symbol of female beauty. She was abducted by the Trojan prince Paris and thus precipitated the Trojan war and the eventual downfall of Troy.

84 *kindred*: Mary and Elizabeth were related via their shared descent from Henry VII.

97 *bloody Mary's times*: Mary Tudor, daughter of Henry VIII and Catherine of Aragon, came to be known as 'Bloody Mary' because of her ruthless efforts to re-establish Catholicism in England during her brief reign (1553–8).

100 *the treaty / Of Edinburgh*: the Treaty of Edinburgh was signed by representatives of Scotland, England, and France in 1560 and provided for the withdrawal of French troops and administrators from Scotland, as well as demanding that Francis I of France and Mary, Queen of Scots, remove the English ensign from their coat of arms, thus relinquishing their claim to the English throne. Mary refused to ratify this treaty.

137 *bridal treasure*: the jewels are those from her first marriage, to the Dauphin of France.

154 *an audience*: in real life Mary Stuart and Elizabeth I never met, though plans for such a meeting were laid and nearly came to fruition. Above all, Mary wanted to defuse the animosity between them and to persuade Elizabeth to set aside her father, Henry VIII's will, which banned foreigners from the English succession, and to nominate her as her successor.

195 *A painful month*: Schiller has contracted the time since the hearing, which was in fact not one, but four months.

198 *Deprived of any counsel*: contrary to accepted practice in treason trials the historical Mary was not allowed to have access to counsel.

224 *Hatton*: Sir Christopher Hatton was appointed by Elizabeth as Lord Chancellor and Keeper of the Seal in 1587.

Westminster: the seat of the English parliament, and also the highest court in the land.

230 s.D. *Mortimer*: Schiller's invention. He is based in part on known conspirators such as Babington. He personifies the enthusiasm of a whole generation of young men, who had forgotten the crime of Darnley's murder at Kirk o' Field and who romanticized their cause in the figure of Mary Stuart.

255 *it is this date*: in fact, Darnley was murdered on 9 February 1567 and Mary Stuart was executed on 8 February 1587. This is therefore not quite the anniversary of Darnley's murder, but the near coincidence of these two dates must have caught Schiller's imagination.

290 *Rizzio*: an Italian singer, who became Mary's court favourite. He was brutally murdered in front of her on her husband's orders.

301 *hellish arts*: James Hepburn, Earl of Bothwell, was the leader of the anti-English faction of Scottish aristocracy. In the aftermath of Mary Stuart's unseemly alliance with Bothwell her supporters spread rumours that Bothwell practised witchcraft and that, with these powers, he had cast a spell over their queen. Bothwell himself escaped to Norway, where he was held captive until his death. Compare these lines from Shakespeare's Othello, I. ii:

> Judge me the world, if 'tis not gross in sense
> That thou hast practis'd on her with foul charms,
> Abus'd her delicate youth with drugs or minerals

315 *the royal sword of Scotland*: on the way to the last Marian Parliament Bothwell carried not the Scottish sword of honour but the sceptre. As he was governor of the southern provinces, this was in

itself not unusual. However, this parliament took place two days after his acquittal.

319 *in a farce of justice*: Bothwell was clearly guilty of Darnley's murder.

350 *The Cardinal of Lotharingia*: the Cardinal of Lorraine and Archbishop of Reims was Mary of Guise's brother and therefore Mary Stuart's uncle. However, in reality he died in 1574 and his involvement at this stage in Mary Stuart's fate is Schiller's invention.

386 *Oh Queen, my feelings then!*: note, throughout the following passage, that, by contrast, Schiller himself was a Protestant, once destined by his family to be a Protestant preacher.

436 *the rock the Church relies on*: see Matthew 16: 18: 'upon this rock I will build my church.'

450 *blessed Preacher on the Mount*: see ibid. 5–7: the Sermon on the Mount.

454 *Society of Jesus*: in 1568 the English College was founded in Douai for the education of Catholic refugees from England and Scotland and for the Jesuit training of missionaries to try to reintroduce Catholicism into the British Isles.

456 *the noble Scotsman Morgan*: Thomas Morgan, a Welshman, and Bishop John Leslie of Ross were active supporters of Mary Stuart in France.

477 *house of Tudor*: Mary Stuart's claim to the English throne rested on her descent from Henry VII through his daughter Margaret Tudor, who had married James IV of Scotland, Mary's grandfather. Henry VII's son Henry VIII of England had three children, Edward VI, who died in 1553, Mary Tudor, who died in 1558, and Elizabeth, his daughter by Anne Boleyn, who was considered illegitimate by English Catholics, because they did not recognize Henry VIII's divorce from his previous wife, Catherine of Aragon. Some English Protestants, who watched Henry VIII and his Parliament first declare her illegitimate and then revoke that declaration with the Act of Succession of 1544, also did not believe Elizabeth's claim to the throne was particularly conclusive. Mary Stuart herself never wanted to usurp Elizabeth's position whilst she held the English throne—her demand was simply to have herself recognized as Elizabeth's successor, until such time as Elizabeth herself bore children, who would be more direct heirs.

509 *the British nation*: Schiller uses the term 'British' somewhat loosely. Scotland and England were only united, with Ireland, as Great Britain in 1801.

558 *the Duke d'Anjou*: for the purposes of dramatic impact Schiller has much simplified what was a long negotiation for a marriage to the French royal family for Elizabeth.

567 *Catherine Howard also, Lady Grey*: both Anne Boleyn and Catherine Howard were beheaded for adultery. Lady Jane Grey was also beheaded after her brief spell as Queen of England.

590 *Babington and Tichburn*: both were conspirators wanting to assassinate Elizabeth and free Mary Stuart in order to place her upon the English throne.

612 *the Earl of Leicester*: Robert Dudley, Earl of Leicester, was for years Elizabeth's favourite. He was, however, also suggested by Elizabeth as a suitable match for Mary Stuart, before she married Darnley. Elizabeth had even raised him to the nobility to facilitate this match.

626 *Lord Burleigh*: Sir William Cecil, Lord Burleigh, was Elizabeth's principal Secretary of State and served her from the beginning of her reign until his death. From 1572 he acted as her Lord High Treasurer.

669 *If the impartial blade that Themis wields*: Themis is the Greek goddess of Justice, symbolized by a blindfolded female statue, with a set of scales in one hand and a sword in the other.

685 *the brave Howard, Lord High Admiral*: John Whitgift, Archbishop of Canterbury, George Talbot, Earl of Shrewsbury, whom Schiller makes the Keeper of the Seals, and the Lord Admiral, Charles Howard of Effingham, were all appointed to be part of the commission to assess Mary's guilt on charges of conspiracy against Elizabeth.

716 *Four times in four reigns tacking to the wind*: Mary is referring to the reigns of Henry VIII, his son Edward VI, his daughter Mary Tudor, and his other daughter Elizabeth, each of whom had different views on religion and legality.

756 *And shall a Stuart unify the Kingdoms?*: Mary Stuart's son, James VI of Scotland, became James I of England, thus uniting the two kingdoms under a Stuart sovereign in 1603.

765 *Two roses to untangle bloodstained armies*: this is a reference to the English Wars of the Roses, between the House of York, whose coat of arms contained a white rose, and the House of Lancaster, whose coat of arms contained a red rose.

776 *The Act of last year*: the Bond of Association or Act for the Queen's Surety of 1585 provided that the beneficiary of any plot

against the Queen would be held as guilty as the conspirators themselves. The Act was clearly passed with Mary Stuart in mind and was soon put to its intended use.

804 *Kurl and Nau*: Mary's secretaries, Gilbert Curle and Claude Nau, testified against her before the court.

845 *Mendoza*: Don Bernardino de Mendoza, Spanish Ambassador to Elizabeth from 1578, was asked to leave in 1584, owing to his part in a conspiracy.

959 *Or hope that you—*: the suggestion that Paulet should do away with Mary clandestinely is based on historical fact, as is his vehement refusal to comply.

975 *household gods*: the idea of household gods to protect the home comes from antiquity.

Act Two

S.D. *The Palace at Westminster*: note the juxtaposition of the sombre opening scene of Act One with these royal festivities at Elizabeth's court. A tournament did actually take place to honour the French delegates in England to negotiate for Elizabeth I's hand.

S.D. *Davison*: William Davison had recently been appointed as Second Secretary of State at the time of Mary Stuart's trial. After her execution he was imprisoned in the Tower and fined heavily. He never regained political favour.

10 *the Seneschal*: a seneschal is the steward or major-domo of a medieval great house.

40 S.D. *Bellievre*: Bellièvre was sent by France specifically to intercede on Mary's behalf during her trial. The French ambassador in England at the time was Guillaume de l'Aubespine, baron de Chateauneuf. His appearance in this scene is another example of Schiller contracting several separate historical events into one.

43 *the splendour / Of St Germain*: the court of Catherine de' Medici and Henry II of France was not only known for its patronage of the arts but also for its extravagance.

52 *in Catherine's unfading garden*: Catherine de' Medici.

79 *'Here lies the virgin Queen'*: despite all the pressure put on Elizabeth I to marry and provide England with a direct heir she died according to her own wish with the epitaph, 'the virgin Queen'.

95 *Thankfully all those houses have returned / To serving Nature*: under Henry VIII the Church's power and wealth were attacked in the dissolution of the monasteries.

134 *'Honi soit qui mal y pense'*: this is the motto of the Order of the Garter, the highest order in the Kingdom of England.

177 *the Guises*: the Guises, Mary Stuart's French relatives, formed a powerful Catholic pressure group to campaign for her release.

193 *Ate*: initially a Greek concept of folly bearing no moral reproach, which later came to be interpreted as an infatuation which led men to their own destruction. More specifically Ate came to be the personification of conflict and war.

204 *They have persuaded . . . title of the Queen of England*: Henry II of France claimed the use of the English arms for Mary, then his daughter-in-law to be, when Mary Tudor died in 1558. Henceforth Mary Stuart included the English insignia in her own coat of arms, which ultimately led to her downfall.

232 *this land is not the world*: in 1586 Mary addressed herself to her judges and said: 'Remember that the theatre of the world is wider than the realm of England.'

289 *In Woodstock*: While Mary Tudor was queen she imprisoned Elizabeth in the Tower briefly and then kept her under supervision at Woodstock Manor for a year.

327 *Henry's will*: Henry VIII's will, in addressing the succession, specifically barred passing the English crown to a foreigner. Mary Stuart was thereby ineligible, though historical evidence suggests that Elizabeth was prepared to set this will aside in negotiations with Mary regarding her claim to be acknowledged as Elizabeth's successor.

385 *Walsingham*: Sir Francis Walsingham, a strict Protestant, was Secretary of State from 1573 and organized the English secret service. He was passionately convinced that only the removal of Mary Stuart from the political scene would ensure lasting peace for England.

386 *Pope Sixtus*: Pope Pius V excommunicated Elizabeth in 1570 and declared her deposed. In 1588, just before the Spanish Armada set sail in direct retaliation for the execution of Mary Stuart, Pope Sixtus V reissued this bull.

424 *the oldest throne in Christendom*: Clodwig, the Frankish prince, converted to Christianity in AD 496 and on him rests the claim that the French throne is the oldest throne in Christendom.

425 *she would have worn three crowns*: the three crowns referred to are those of France, Scotland, and England.

642 *ten lost years*: the ten years referred to here are another example of Schiller's liberties with the actual chronology of historical events and the contraction of time for the sake of dramatic unity: in fact Leicester was Elizabeth's favourite for nearly thirty years.

656 *Argus*: in Greek mythology Argus was a hundred-eyed giant, whom Zeus commanded to watch over Io, a priestess loved by Zeus, and turned into a heifer by him.

778 *The houses / Of Howard and of Percy*: the Duke of Norfolk, Thomas Howard, and Thomas Percy, Duke of Northumberland, were both executed at the Tower of London for treason in 1572.

865 *She is the younger woman*: in a letter written to the director of the Berlin Theatre in June 1800 Schiller states that Mary should be '25 at the most' and that Elizabeth should be '30 at the most'. In reality Mary was 45 and Elizabeth was 53 in 1587.

904 *To see my cousin fallen so profoundly*: when Mary Stuart was first taken captive in England she was maintained in considerable splendour, receiving both her previous allowance from France as Francis's widow and a grant from the English government. She continued to display her cloth of state and to have a lively correspondence with the outside world. Only after her implication in conspiracies were her circumstances straitened and her correspondence monitored.

Act Three

112 *Gorgon hair*: the three Gorgons sat at the western end of the world, according to Greek mythology. Medusa, with her snake hair, is the most famous image of these horrors.

243 *Death's poison fangs*: this image of laying a snake to one's breast, only to be bitten later, comes from Aesop's fable about the farmer and the snake.

263 *St Bartholomew*: the Guises and Catherine de' Medici were behind the St Bartholomew's Day massacre of French Huguenots (Protestants) in 1572.

283 *Another Armida*: Armida was a beautiful pagan princess who misled and beguiled Christian crusaders.

342 *Went to the scaffold*: Anne Boleyn was executed on charges of adultery and incest.

350 *basilisk*: the basilisk is a fantastical creature from medieval imagery, with a cock's head and a snake's tail, whose 'looks could kill'.

444 *Tyburn*: the old execution ground in London, not far from present-day Marble Arch.

487 S.D. *He presses her forcefully against himself*: this is the scene that members of the first audience found obscene.

520 *Sauvage*: John Savage was a member of the Babington plot.

529–31 *The Toulon Barnabit . . . the Queen's anathema*: Schiller portrays Savage as a member of the order of the Barnabites in Milan. It is not clear why Schiller chose to do so. An anathema is an excommunication decree. Here it refers to the papal bull excommunicating Elizabeth.

Act Four

69 *an Atlas of importance*: Atlas was a Titan in Greek mythology, son of a god. His punishment for his part in a rebellion against the gods was to hold up the sky on his shoulders.

484 *By the rage of God*: this outburst by Burleigh was cut from the first performance.

491 *Shall legates sent from Rome uncrown our kings*: during the reign of Mary Tudor the Houses of Parliament knelt before the Papal legate, thereby finalizing England's renewed submission to the Church of Rome.

520 *Spanish Mary*: Mary Tudor, Elizabeth's half sister, whose mother was Catherine of Aragon, was known as 'Spanish Mary,' in part due to her strong Catholic belief.

528 *The Continent is reaching at my throat*: Elizabeth saw herself constantly threatened by a Continental Catholic alliance against her.

531 *While Spain caulks, victuals, and fits out attack*: Spain was making its preparations for an attack on England in order to save Mary Stuart—this attack was later made in revenge with the dispatch of the Armada.

Act Five

S.D. *Melvil*: Mary Stuart had been denied the services of her steward Andrew Melvil until the preparations for her execution.

70 S.D. *Margaret Kurl*: Margaret Curle is Schiller's blend of several of Mary's ladies-in-waiting.

118 S.D. *Mary enters dressed in white*: this was traditionally the colour of mourning in France at the time and was also a colour that

Mary favoured for her wardrobe, as it showed off her complexion most advantageously. She is carrying several Catholic symbolic items: a rosary and an *agnus dei*, a medallion of wax showing the Lamb of God, which has been blessed by the Pope.

229 *Form is the body, faith its heart and spirit*: this echoes 1 Corinthians 4: 20: 'For the Kingdom of God is not in word, but in power' and 2 Corinthians 3: 6: 'for the letter killeth, but the spirit giveth life.'

247 *transubstantiation*: the Catholic belief in the conversion of the Eucharistic bread and wine into the body and blood of Jesus Christ.

261 *'Where two or three are gathered in my name, / There am I also.'*: this entire scene caused considerable controversy for the first performances and was in fact cut by Schiller to avoid offence to the audience. The printed copy, however, does not incorporate these cuts.

269 *This is no church, there is no host, you say*: the 'host' is the term used to describe the bread consecrated in the Eucharist.

272 *I am a priest*: the historical Melvil was a Protestant.

274 *the seven consecrations*: there is a hierarchy of orders in the Catholic Church, not officially determined to be seven, but usually stated as such. Only the highest one, the order of priest, can celebrate mass.

276 *Blessed by himself*: Mary Stuart did in fact receive the host blessed by the Pope.

280 *Led the apostle from a broken dungeon*: compare these lines with Acts 5: 18–19: 'And laid their hands on the apostles, and put them in the common prison. But the angel of the Lord by night opened the prison doors, and brought them forth . . .'

326 *the sin against the Holy Spirit*: compare with Matthew 12: 31: 'Wherefore I say unto you, All manner of sin and blasphemy shall be forgiven unto men: but the blasphemy against the Holy Ghost shall not be forgiven unto men.'

366 *The blood of Christ, that was shed for you*: this portrayal of the communion rite follows Protestant rather than Catholic lines. In a Catholic communion the words 'Corpus Domini nostri Jesu Christi custodiat animam tuam in vitam aeternam' in Latin or in the vernacular would be used. There are other liturgical inconsistencies in this scene.

368 *The sacred right reserved to priests and kings*: the kings of France were allowed to receive both the wine and the bread at their coronation, a privilege normally reserved for the priest alone.

389 *My retinue shall be released unharmed*: Mary's retinue was kept at Fotheringhay for many months before it was finally released.

391 *consecrated earth shall cover this*: Mary Stuart was first buried in Peterborough Cathedral and later, during the reign of her son, moved to Westminster Abbey in London, where Elizabeth I is also buried.

398 *May God preserve her and exalt her reign*: this line is a direct quotation of what Mary Stuart really said, as reported by Brantôme, Mary Stuart's personal friend, as well as by the eighteenth-century historians William Robertson and Friedrich Gentz, all of whose accounts of Mary Stuart's life Schiller used as source material.

548 *For which false witness he was surely damned*: there is still controversy surrounding the evidence given by Mary's two secretaries of state, though most historians agree that the so-called Casket Letters were in fact a forgery. Schiller has us believe for the purposes of his play that his Mary Stuart is innocent of the Babington plot; however, it is inconclusive whether Mary Stuart really had knowledge of yet another plot to free her and assassinate the Queen of England.

606 *Be banished from my sight*: Elizabeth banished Lord Burleigh from court for a while.

611 *And let the law proceed against his life*: Davison was incarcerated in the Tower for a year and a half and fined heavily.

619 *This seal, my badge of service for twelve years*: the historical Shrewsbury never held the Seal.

629 *He is on a ship / To France*: Leicester did not in fact run away to France but helped to defend the country against the Spanish Armada in 1588.

The Oxford World's Classics Website

www.worldsclassics.co.uk

- Information about new titles
- Explore the full range of Oxford World's Classics
- Links to other literary sites and the main OUP webpage
- Imaginative competitions, with bookish prizes
- Peruse the Oxford World's Classics Magazine
- Articles by editors
- Extracts from Introductions
- A forum for discussion and feedback on the series
- Special information for teachers and lecturers

www.worldsclassics.co.uk